Hitting Secrets from Baseball's Graveyard

A Diehard Student of History Reconstructs Batsmanship of the Late Deadball Era

John R. Harris, Ph.D.

Aliena vitia in oculis habemus, a tergo nostra sunt.
"The faults of others we keep before our eyes; to our own we turn our backs."
Seneca

This book donated to
SUNRISE OF RICHMOND
by resident
TOMMY GILMAN
from his personal collection.

June 1, 2024

Coach Gilman was head baseball coach
at the University of Richmond, 1977 - 1984

Hitting Secrets from Baseball's Graveyard

John R. Harris

Copyright 2017 John R. Harris

Cover photos courtesy of the National Baseball Hall of Fame Library in Cooperstown, New York; also drawn from author's personal collection.

Acknowledgments

I wish to extend my thanks to the National Baseball Hall of Fame Library, and especially to John W. Horne of the Photo Archives Department, for the use of nine extremely helpful photos reproduced in this volume (and for scores of others through which I was allowed to browse). Likewise and equally, I thank the online journal *Stripes* (published by the United States Department of Defense) and, for his special service and guidance, David Gardiner for permitting me to reproduce a splendid photo of a living samurai in action.

Naturally, I offer my warmest apologetic thanks to my son for being a guinea pig *malgré lui* in all of my early inquiries into the manly art of hitting; and I am grateful, as well, to the many fine ballplayers of the University of Texas at Tyler who have humored my rambling conversations about the game over the years. God bless you all!

My sincerest thanks, finally, to Professor Roy Kerr, author, scholar, and gentleman, who proofread the manuscript of a complete stranger, offered valuable suggestions, and—most important of all—gave priceless encouragement. Few of his ilk remain in these times.

Contents

Part One: Swinging at a Ghost-Ball 9

Chapter One   10
The Myth of Progress: How Intellectual Arrogance Has Locked the Doors of the Past

Chapter Two   15
My Credentials: The Gap Between Doing and Researching

Chapter Three   20
The Slicing Saber: How a Poetic Image Can Overpower Good Detective Work

Chapter Four   25
Fouled Lines: How Imparting Effective Backspin Differs From Undercutting

Part Two: The Way of the Samurai 31

Chapter Five   32
The Hammer and the Axe: How the Major Chasm in Hitting Styles Began with a Tiny Crack

Chapter Six   38
Hit by a Mack Truck: How the Swing's Dynamics Radiate from the Maximal Acceleration Point

Chapter Seven   43
Peddling the Metal: How the High-Tech Bat Transformed Hitting

Chapter Eight   47
The Hammer's Engine: How the Top Hand Drives into the Ball's Center

Chapter Nine   55
Identity Crisis: What the Bottom Hand Did NOT Do in 1900

Chapter Ten   60
Spread Hands: How to Drive a Whirlybird's Blade

Chapter Eleven   70
A Shot in the Dark: How Lower-Body Movement May Have Assisted the Downward Stroke (Part One)

Chapter Twelve   79
A Second Shot at Footwork: Lower-Body Movement and "Striding to the Pitch" (Part Two)

Chapter Thirteen   87
Hopscotch in the Box: Lower-Body Movement and the Mobile Rear Foot (Part Three)

Chapter Fourteen   95
Samurai Training: How the DBE Hitter Achieved and Retained His Balance

Part Three: Between the Lines   105

Chapter Fifteen   106
The Golden Age: Memories of a Perfection That Never Existed

Chapter Sixteen   113
Fashionably Late: How the DBE Hitter Would Handle the Fastball

Chapter Seventeen   121
Hanging Back to Stay On Time: Handling the Fastball (Part Two)

Chapter Eighteen   127
Adaptability in a Pinch: How the DBE Hitter Handled Pitches Other Than Fastballs

Chapter Nineteen   135
The Phantom Clue: How "Place Hitting" Hides Major Evidence in Plain Sight

Part Four: Turn It Over to the Bull Pen   145

Chapter Twenty   146
The Usable Past: Elements of the Deadball Style That Deserve Revival

Chapter Twenty-One   154

"He Could Have Played With Us": How the Old School Has Lingered in Certain Recent Swings

Chapter Twenty-Two   161
Snapshot Album: Brief Profiles of Deadball Era Swings

Chapter Twenty-Three   172
A Postscript on Validation: One Last Look at Our Proposals From a Historical Perspective

Notes 181

Contact the Author   193

List of Illustrations

A boy and his bat   30
Frank Frisch, high follow-through   54
Ty Cobb, set-up position with spread hands   68
Author, set-up typical of 19th-century promo shots   69
Honus Wagner, set-up deep in box   77
Honus Wagner, one-handed follow-through   77
Honus Wagner, two-handed follow-through   78
Author, alternative sequences of DBE swing   85-86
Samurai swordsman, spread-handed load   103
Sam Crawford, bail-out follow-through   104
Mickey Mantle, hands loaded tight into body; Roger Maris, hands more tight and rear   112
Tris Speaker, high follow-through   133
Tris Speaker, load with spread hands   134
Ty Cobb, straight drive into pitch   144

Part One

Swinging at a Ghost-Ball

A justification for researching the game's past in ways that have never been undertaken systematically; the researcher's methods and credentials, and his personal motivation for pursuing this research; some initial propositions exploded, creating space for others to crystallize.

Chapter One

The Myth of Progress: How Intellectual Arrogance Has Locked the Doors of the Past

After Ted [Williams] got through with the photographer and the writer of this magazine article, he came down to the dugout. I can still see him and hear him.
"Bobby [Doerr], get up here," he growled. "Goddammit, one time you've got the bat up here, another time you've got the bat down here. Open stance, closed stance, feet apart, feet together, what the hell's the matter with you?"
This went on for two or three minutes, and Bobby hadn't opened his mouth.
Finally, Ted said, "Get a good stance and give it a try."
Bobby looked him right in the eye and said, "But Ted, I'm not you."   Johnny Pesky [1]

A decade and a half before the year of my birth (which I will not volunteer), a coelacanth appeared in the net of a fisherman trawling the deep channel between Madagascar and the African mainland. The catch made quite a stir, for this heavily armored, trap-jawed warrior was supposed to have gone extinct along with the dinosaurs. The scientists were sure of it—yet the scientists were wrong. Since that glorious year, about a dozen more of the species have been drawn squirming into the light of day. Divers have also lately filmed one in the twilight of its submarine habitat.

I don't know if such a thing as a Sasquatch or a Yeti exists; but as an academic, I know only too well what sort of derision a researcher like Dr. Jeffrey Meldrum (of Idaho State University) must absorb simply to go through the clinical work of analyzing suspicious footprints. Though mildly agnostic about "Bigfoot," Meldrum exposes himself to professional censure merely by daring to investigate the possibility of such a creature's eking out a life somewhere on the planet. Science can enforce orthodoxy in ways almost as rigorous as the Spanish Inquisition's. Despite the "party line" in such matters, however, the discovery of strange hominid remains not two decades ago in Indonesia strongly implies that we have much yet to learn even about species similar to our own. The dwarf-sized *Homo floresiensis* (lovingly dubbed "the hobbit" by researchers) exited the scene only a few thousand years ago—and may, as far as that goes, not have completed its exit. Hundreds of locals (and a few Western investigators) insist that they have seen the diminutive Orang Pendek (or "short man") in the remote rainforests of Sumatra.

I raise the subject of "crypto-zoology" here because the common response to it reveals much about human nature. People are vain, ignorant, and attracted to crowds in some of their less-than-stellar moments. They—we—tend to receive anything smacking of the oddball with a superior mockery that advertises us as brighter and better informed than the target of our wit. The controversial figures are "conspiracy theorists" and "flat-earth wackos"; we, in contrast, have "science" on our side. In fact, few of us generally have any exceptional knowledge of any given issue; but the smart money seems to back the view that we've embraced, and so we pretend that objective evidence has drawn us to our position rather than the fear of risking humiliation in a desperate cause. For good measure, we join the scoffers and fling a stone or two, just to show our solidarity with the "right" side.

I discern this kind of reaction even in such relatively trivial matters as how ordinary baseball fans estimate yesteryear's great hitters. Know-it-all-coaches as well as players, older men as well as kids, are all very comfortable in the notion that right here, right now, is the ideal spot from which to determine the truths of the cosmos. If Ty Cobb or Tris Speaker or Wahoo Sam Crawford had really possessed any hitting secrets worth passing along, we would have found them out, whether or not they were ever intentionally transmitted. Our state-of-the-art video analyses would have captured those secrets in contemporary swings, or else our Space Age technicians would have restored grainy footage that revealed new minutiae about ancient swings. Our physicists can figure out the optimum weight, length, and taper for an accelerated stick whose mission is explosive contact, and our kinesiologists can calculate the positioning of hands, feet, hips, head, and knees most likely to achieve maximum impact of barrel upon ball. We're too smart to learn anything from the past. If those old-timers were so bright, why did so many ruin their careers with alcohol and never figure out the importance of nutrition and strength conditioning?

Some of the details that tend to embellish this rather arrogant protest strike me as self-contradictory. I hear that today's hitters are so much better than yesterday's because (as was just referenced) they eat healthily, don't get pasted after every game, and lift weights to build appropriate muscle groups. Yet how, exactly, do these quite plausible sources of physical superiority explain why the old guys occasionally struck out just two dozen times in 600 at-bats while hitting .400? If their diet and their practice were performance-impeding instead of performance-enhancing, then… then the logical conclusion should be that they would have hit a hundred points higher if they had known about and embraced today's methods, or that their averages back then ought to have been a hundred points lower. Their technique must have been immensely better than the modern paradigm to overcome so much bad living!

No, comes the response—because pitchers are also in much better shape today. Furthermore, the old campaigners might see the same pitcher four or five times in one afternoon. That never happens now. The hitter may face the starter twice, rarely three times; then he has to deal with a "relief specialist" in each of his remaining trips to the plate.

That's a better argument, yet not as much so as it seems at first. Pitchers of the so-called Deadball Era didn't show the hitter their whole arsenal the first or second time they faced him. They would create expectations early on, and then exploit those expectations later. They "knew how to pitch." Those were also times when decking a hitter was common; and, of course, hitters didn't wear helmets or body armor, nor did they usually charge the mound after a dusting off (which would have been viewed as showing the hurler that he had succeeded in frightening them). And I could continue.... The mound was also higher; the ball, brutally scuffed up after an inning or two, might well stay in play for the whole game; the spitball was still legal, along with a half-dozen other ingenious preparations and mutilations of the tortured sphere; and the hitting background quite often featured a sea of white shirts glaring in the sunlight, a mass of advertisements plastered over the center-field wall, or—prior to the game's being called due to darkness—intense late-evening shadows. For good measure, one might add that all kinds of Bugs Bunny twists and whirls might be tossed into a delivery just to throw off the hitter's timing. The hesitation pitch wasn't ruled illegal until Satchel Paige began having too much success with it.

What makes hitting a challenge is less true velocity than perceived velocity. Pitchers of yesteryear were master illusionists and tricksters. Yet Tris Speaker struck out 14 times in 653 plate appearances during the 1915 campaign, when spitballs were still kosher.

A friend who patiently heard out my case promoting the great hitters of yore digested my argument for a few days and then cam back with the observation that, a century ago and even more recently, baseball wasn't selecting pitchers from a very large pool. The best arms of the Negro Leagues and of Latin America were denied admittance to the Major Leagues' exclusive club. No wonder so many batsmen were topping .400 before World War I: the pitchers of their generation who might have carved dozens of points off their average weren't allowed to suit up!

I thought for a few days myself. First of all, Latin American players were not universally denied participation in big-league ball a hundred years ago: fair-skinned hurlers like Lefty Gomez, and even American Indians, were amply represented. But the most sensible rebuttal is simply to reply that the sword cuts both ways: some of the pre-war generation's best hitters, too, were banished from the game's highest level right along with their brethren on the mound. There were no Oscar Charlestons tearing up Major League pitching at the time... and yet, strikeouts still tallied up to paltry numbers and batting champs still flirted with two-for-five.

No one can dispute that players are better today in several ways. They eat more responsibly, most of them have forsaken excessive boozing while religiously keeping themselves hydrated, tobacco is finally beginning to vanish from the game, and sunscreen use is universal. Sophisticated weight-lifting is part of the regimen both during and after the season, stretching before each game is lengthy and focused, and more players all the time are discovering the benefits of yoga. Sports psychologists coach athletes in how to "be in the moment" and achieve laser-like concentration. Muscular tweaks and twinges are instantly and seriously addressed rather than hidden from the manager or packed in chili peppers by some quack sawbones. Miraculous surgeries have become routine, and rehabilitation is a fine art presided over by career professionals. Did you know, by the way, that yesteryear's heroes were ashamed to wear eyeglasses, though several suffered from acute vision impairment?

Again, to what interpretation does all of this lead except to the presence of better technique a century ago? Or to flip the coin over, does it not imply a de-emphasis or deterioration of technique today? Precisely because they're such Olympian physical specimens, our hitters now appear better able than ever to get away with mechanical flaws. Who cares that they strike out once in every three at-bats if they belt a home run once in every twelve? We have accepted the accomplishments of almost superhuman physique in lieu of the master-craftsman's study and rehearsal. What definition of "progress," though, would require giving up on the latter and exclusively promoting the former?

All of the striking out, by the way—excused as the inevitable result of having equally superhuman dynamos on the mound—has come at the same time as the strike zone has shrunk. A century ago, strikes were called almost at the shoulders. To be sure, the zone has grown to include an inch or two more around the knees than it used to; but low pitches are actually the ones that require waiting on, so the lowering of the zone should somewhat have compensated for the much-rumored (and surely genuine) acceleration of contemporary fastballs. Modern hitters routinely set up very deep the batter's box, as well: the back chalk line is invariably gone by the bottom of the first inning. A hundred years ago, batsmen would not infrequently place their back foot about even with the rear of the plate in order to get at breaking balls sooner. They would thus be further speeding up the much-maligned fastball of yore (if you're keeping score in this exchange of forensic volleys).

Some baseball historians note quite correctly that old-fashioned gloves had much shorter fingers and virtually no pocket compared to today's models—and that the resulting inequity in the number of grounders allowed to sneak through to the outfield could account for several points on a yearly batting average. Maybe. The difference in reach was bound to have been more consequential, though, in first-baseman's mitts than in fielder's gloves. A ground ball is generally handled in the palm rather than snagged in the pocket. A backhand stab at third or deep short might be the exception; but that big butterfly net at first base didn't exist a century ago, and it's there that hitters might have caught their biggest break when an off-balance, one-hop throw wasn't easily scooped. ("Scooping" hadn't been invented yet, either: first-sackers used two hands until Vic Power's "hot dog" style caught on in the Fifties.)[2] Still, ballplayers of those days didn't on average get down the line as fast as do today's versions, or so one must suppose; they certainly weren't allowed half a month to recuperate after pulling a muscle. If we're talking about which era had the greater advantage on ground balls in play, the contemporary player's healthy burst of speed from home to first probably produces about as many scratch hits as a hopper scooting under a small pocket ever did.

Whatever the truth of that matter, the percentage of grounders turned into outs sheds no light on the stark inability of the present day's typical slugger simply to make contact. The claim that ballparks of a century ago had far less foul ground than today's, likewise, is scarcely a put-away point for the lab-coated advocates of our Sports Science Era. In a way, diminished foul ground should lead one to expect *more* strikeouts, not fewer: the pitchers would presumably get to two strikes more often. Besides, a hitter has to pop the ball up, to begin with, before massive amounts of spare real estate can threaten his at-bat. Maybe what we see in our contemporary slugger's misfortune is a swing that sends pitches up the chute rather than terrain that spreads lots of green grass beneath the chute. Then, too, the parks of Seventies vintage with all the foul space have largely disappeared now—but anemic averages and whopping strikeout totals have not. Carew, Brett, Raines, and Gwynn seemed to fare well in the structures of the Seventies and Eighties. Architecture probably wasn't Adam Dunn's essential problem.

Our argumentative tennis match could continue all day long—and I am confident that the points on my side of the ledger would keep pace with the other side's. There simply isn't any sound explanation for why hitters could often have flirted with .400 a century ago while struggling now just to finish a hundred points lower; or, I should say, there's no good explanation if one begins in the premise that the fine art of hitting is finer than ever today. The physique of the hitters, yes; the technique of the hitters... where is the evidence for that?

It is highly ironic that Ted Williams, who couldn't understand Bobby Doerr's frustration in Johnny Pesky's story above, would dub his thin little instructional manual *The Science of Hitting*. Williams wanted to believe that his success was based upon strict analysis applied with rigorous precision; yet what he started with and perhaps never really worked beyond was the mystery of his own extraordinary gifts, much though he longed to give his brilliant career an intellectual pedigree. In this book, I shall take another shot at empirical method, at least insofar as it relates to the great hitters of the game's distant past. I intend to collect and analyze hard evidence in the hope of assembling coherent, somewhat testable theories. My research is not meant to explain the successes of superstars in the Golden Age of the Fifties, or indeed those of any great batsman belonging to the era of the livelier ball. Just because the Deadball Era cannot transmit to us the most direct sort of testimony, however, doesn't mean that some of its secrets might not have survived as an undercurrent in later times; and just because the general habits of 1900 seem to us more reminiscent of a coelacanth's design than a satellite's doesn't mean that an aspiring hitter today may not learn anything from Ty Cobb.

Furthermore, considering me—yours truly—as an author, we don't encounter the Ted Williams problem: a peerless performer's possibly being a little blinded by his own luminosity. My personal achievement in this area is more on the order of Black Body Radiation—something that no instrument known to man has ever actually detected. What I write must therefore have the authority of common sense if it is to have any authority at all.

Chapter Two

My Credentials: The Gap Between Doing and Researching

Why should anyone listen to what Walt Hriniak has to say about hitting when he obviously wasn't a great hitter himself? Let me answer by saying that over the years the best managers and coaches in the game generally have been those to whom the game didn't come all that easily.   Walt Hriniak[1]

It would be useless for any player to attempt to explain successful batting.   Tris Speaker[2]

When the soul of the Roman poet Virgil meets Dante at the opening of Hell's vortex and announces that they two are destined to make the descent together, the terrified poet protests, "I am not Aeneas! I am not Saint Paul!" Ordinary people are not supposed to trespass where angels fear to tread. To tiptoe across the interface that separates common knowledge from mystical wisdom, shouldn't one have heroic credentials?

To extend the point with which the last chapter concluded... like Dante (and Walt Hriniak), I have no heroic credentials. But then, Dante was being betrayed by the false humility of cowardice in pulling back from his sacred mission. If my own undertaking is far less metaphysical, I still need a lot of nerve to attempt it. Here is where I find my courage: the truth is the truth, no matter how humble its delivery system. Facts do not change just because they are communicated by Jimmy Olsen rather than Superman. Intelligent, fair-minded people will hear anybody out if they sincerely seek the truth, and will make a decision based on how well the offered testimony matches the evidence rather than on what kind of suit the witness wears. Only dull or corrupt judges arbitrate cases based on the residential zip codes of the parties involved.

In the spirit of full disclosure, then, I must confess that my face appears on no baseball card. Nobody ever paid a dime to see me pick up a bat. Furthermore, I am not the best friend or brother-in-law or nephew of any big-league hitting star. I am not even a professional sports journalist. No aging clean-up hitter ever said, "What'd you think of my hit today?" as I wandered through the locker room after flashing a pass. I've corresponded with an All Star or two, and I enjoyed exchanging several letters with Hall of Famer George Kell before he passed away... but, no, I am not George Kell, nor even George's official biographer. Editors do not accept my manuscript submissions as soon as they see my name on the envelope. My greeting has never been heard by the curator of the Baseball Hall of Fame—for I live far from Cooperstown, I hold a full-time job, and I have no budget to travel and do research. I'm probably like just about everyone else in the crowd....

Or perhaps not. Immediately prior to revising this manuscript for the fifth time, I was dusting off another for the umpteenth time. Its objective is to fit beneath one mythic umbrella three medieval Celtic romances that I translated from Irish, Welsh, and Norman French. I offer this morsel of seemingly random information for two reasons: 1) to show that I am trained in doing research, and 2) to suggest that I have plenty of experience in the detective work of connecting dots after the passage of time has worn most of them away.

For I revere the past: that's another of what might be called my special credentials. I must surely have betrayed in the opening remarks of this book my suspicion that yesterday's story was much more intricate than it appears today, and that today's "experts" also show a tendency to oversimplify the past in the process of reducing it to a tidy narrative. It is a principle of mine that we humans have not really changed much from our progenitors who lived two or three millennia ago. Anthropologists frame that assertion as physical fact, and push back the plateau of genetic stasis tens of thousands of years; but what I have in mind is more of a moral assertion. I'm suggesting that we are not better people just because we have more technology, and even that our hopes and fears and miseries and joys are about the same now—under a veneer of circumstantial difference—as they were when the first sandal was made.

It seems to me that an investigator who is striving to uncover the truth about a practice largely forgotten for over a century should have a basic respect for earlier generations. How will you truly understand the habits of 1900 if you begin in the assumption that people of that era were pitiable, inept rubes and clods?

Finally—and at considerable risk of sounding horribly arrogant—I will venture to say that I'm in better physical shape than most sports journalists digging into distant events. Not many sexagenarians have experimented with various "submarine" pitching deliveries and managed to throw their age in miles per hour. That attribute is an asset in my present undertaking because much of my research has forced me into experimentation—trial-and-error inference, that is: formation of theory followed by practical enactment followed by review of results and revision of theory. Necessity has dictated that I must be my own test-pilot. Let me explain why.

It's brutally logical, really. If you want to see how a certain swing works, you have to repeat it so much that it becomes second nature to you. Total immersion is required. Now, a young man interested in baseball and capable of handling an adult bat will obviously have had some modest successes at the plate; otherwise, he would have given up so demanding a sport. If he's had success, he will not be at all interested in jettisoning completely the routine that he has worked hard to develop and master—and with no guarantee, either, that the alternate method will bring him anywhere close to his current level of happy results.

Using an active young player as a test case, then, is out of the question. Yet a subject who doesn't care for the game and has no familiarity with its tools will not understand the simplest instructions when asked to adjust his swing this way or that way. His young joints and unspoiled eyesight are a distinct benefit to the experimenter, but not nearly sufficient to compensate for his lack of basic skills.

So the experimenter is stuck with… himself. And why is this so terribly bad? A foot-long balsa wood plane in a wind tunnel isn't a sleek aluminum jet prototype shooting through a gale, but the former can give the draftsman important clues about how to design the latter. If a subject with reactions slowed by age can hit a baseball better by swinging one way than by swinging another, and if the "contact threshold" for this wizened subject is 70 miles per hour, why would the lessons of the experiment not have carry-over to a young hitter who can connect with a pitch at 90 m.p.h.?

Such is my reasoning.

Now, I naturally began my work in the analysis of old photographs and newsreels. For the first decade or two of the twentieth century, such sources are both rare and of poor quality… but they're a starting point. I also devoured every page I could find written by or about every great batsman of bygone days who showed any interest in sharing a secret or two. I dug back far beyond Charley Lau and Ted Williams to the likes of Stan Musial, Johnny Mize, George Sisler, and Ty Cobb. Such literary evidence was surprisingly unhelpful in most cases, however. Hitters even today are notorious for not really knowing what they do in the box against live pitching; when the video replay, with slow-motion and freeze functions, is still decades in the future, one is apt to find some really impressive examples of self-unawareness. Then, too, the thing you *don't* say because you assume that every contemporary reader takes it for granted is often the most interesting thing you might have said for historians peering back from a century in the future. I frequently suffered through the frustration of watching my sources work neatly around the very topic that I wished to see addressed.

From such beginnings, at any rate, I hatched theories and devised tests using tees, thousands upon thousands of "shadow ball" swings in my workout room— and then, at last, pitching machines and live pitching. I employed various lengths and tapers of bat in these exercises, trying to replicate the dimensions of yesteryear's club as nearly as possible. Finding a suitable bat turns out to be a major impediment; I shall explain fully the significance of changing generations of bat in a later chapter. The comfort of today's young men with one kind of stick is yet another reason, by the way, why enlisting any of them in my experiments would have been a great challenge.

I do not hasten to add (for it doesn't do much for anyone's résumé who wants to establish himself as an authority on hitting) that I was a volunteer coach for years. Doctors take the Hippocratic Oath before they practice medicine: "First do no harm." I tried to honor the same vow. Often I would say little or nothing to boys who were receiving earfuls of advice from other adults— probably the single greatest reason, that advice, for why youngsters drop baseball and never look back. A swing with which a boy feels comfortable but which has a lot of holes is still better than one that's "perfect" on the drawing board but just doesn't quite fit the human guinea pig's body type. I tried not to be that coach— the one who gives so much good advice that he permanently ruins his pupil's hitting technique. Thus much, perhaps, I will add to the résumé: that I know hitting to be a very tough skill to master, and that I know the guys with a patented formula for the skill to be pretty dangerous characters.

Maybe what rare tips I did impart were too many. Already in those days, I was fascinated by the so-called Deadball Era: the period before about 1920, when somebody seemed to flirt with .400 every year and when dozens of hitters each season struck out under five percent of the time. (The ball was considered dead, or at least unlively, because it was hardly ever removed from play and acquired the resilience of a wet sock. Only after the fatal beaning of Ray Chapman—who probably never saw Carl Mays's soiled projectile closing on his temple in the evening shadows—were balls replaced more regularly. The first use of cork in the baseball's core is also posed as a boundary for the "dead ball": i.e., the year 1910. Yet after three or four innings of play, even these balls grew pretty ragged.)[3] As various hitting theories ancient and modern swirled in my head, I sometimes proposed to struggling youngsters an adjustment here or there that might have worked with a different bat—but which had little chance of prospering with a toothpick-handled, brick-barreled, ultra-short metal-alloy model. Again, I will discuss later how shifts in bat design have had a major impact on hitting technique. In the minds of some of us, the results haven't improved the game over the last thirty years.

The worst coaching errors I made were with my own son. I suppose the doctor has the same problem when his Hippocratic Oath is on one side and his child on the other. It must never be easy to watch a child waste away… but if it's someone else's, you can still go home and sleep in the knowledge that you are honoring the Oath. If it's your own, you have to try, no matter how desperate and experimental the procedure. Not that my son was a terminal case, as a hitter. In fact, he often led whatever team's uniform he wore in batting average. He had very quick hands, which can cover up a lot of technical flaws and make accurate diagnosis almost impossible. Besides, what I was telling him essentially fit right in with Hitting Coach Orthodoxy. I thought that Ty Cobb and his generation were taking a level slice at the ball with their bottom hand, more or less as one might backhand a melon with a saber. I didn't assign much importance to the top hand. This dogma played right into the Charley Lau/Walt Hriniak paradigm, which produced immortals like Tim Raines, Bill Buckner, and Dwight Evans. (Or it appeared to produce them: it didn't derail their careers, at any rate.)

The method didn't generate much in the way of power, however (with all due respect to Lau's potent poster-child, George Brett). By the time my son reached high school, the professional coaches who now held sway over him wanted more pop. They ruined him, sure enough, and I blamed them for it as the years went by… until, that is, I realized that they had simply extended the theory upon which all my own "wisdom" was built. The line from Tim Raines to Frank Thomas to Alex Rodriguez is pretty straight, and all three of that lot have finally made it to Cooperstown. For some hitters, the theory obviously works. But it didn't work so well for my son—and it most definitely, absolutely, unequivocally, and indisputably was not what Ty Cobb did.

In my defense, I might add that misreading something with as many moving parts, as much intricate connectivity, and as much eye-deceiving rapidity as a baseball swing is easy to do. As I noted just above, ballplayers have been known to be stunningly clueless about their own swing. Mickey Mantle joked that Ted Williams once asked him at an All Star game if he gripped the bat tighter with his top or his bottom hand. Mick fell to thinking so deeply about the question that he slumped for a month thereafter (rather like the old man with the long beard who couldn't sleep after someone asked if he put it above or beneath the blanket).[4] Teddy Ballgame himself remarked in *The Science of Hitting* that he didn't like to spread his hands in the manner of many old-timers—but at least one widely circulated photograph (owned by Getty Images) shows him doing precisely that.[5] Stan Musial counsels (in a priceless LP record that my father brought home one day) not to let your stride exceed about ten inches, and the foldout in the album shows him stepping with the recommended modesty.[6] Perhaps The Man had never seen action footage of himself recoiling, in Babe Ruth fashion, almost to a front-cleats-on-rear-toes position before lunging nearly the length of the box. Curt Flood wrote of approaching Musial in the batting cage and asking for tips. Stan thought hard for a moment, and then delivered those great words worthy of the Delphic Oracle: "I see the ball, and I hit it."[7]

As a mater of fact, great hitters typically make dismal hitting instructors. Their gift is often a natural one. Even though they may spend countless hours refining their technique, they don't necessarily know what they're refining. They may realize that results improve if they hold the elbow in or close up their stance a bit; but as for having an overall theory, they can't really risk the kind of poking around that would lead to such abstract heights. Effective theorizing requires that you be open to all possibilities. When one thing works, you often have to reverse it while keeping the other variables just the same in order to be sure that you are attributing success to the proper source. A professional ballplayer would be insane to fool around in this manner with the technique that has made him a millionaire. Maybe that's why Tris Speaker remarked that a player shouldn't attempt to explain his successes at the plate: maybe "player" should be emphasized, since the man actively pursuing a career must apply himself to performing rather than understanding. The people who do that kind of messing about are the ones who have nothing to lose—the has-beens and also-rans.

Says the proverbial wisdom, "Those who can, do; those who can't, teach." In the best of worlds (which is not remotely the one we live in now, at least in the Ivory Tower), those who teach, experiment. If you put all that together, you emerge with the syllogism, "Those who do, don't experiment." Q.E.D.

Chapter Three

The Slicing Saber: How a Poetic Image Can Overpower Good Detective Work

The top hand mainly provides support. It adds stability, and cushions the impact when the bat hits the ball. That's why all the best hitters know to keep the top hand underneath at the point of contact, not over as I was taught. When the bat hits the ball, the top hand should be underneath the bat. This may contradict what seems logical and natural to a lot of hitters. Most righties bat right-handed, so they expect their right hand, which is the top hand when they hold the bat, to be the dominant one. But this just isn't the case. The bottom hand is the power hand and the top hand is just along for the ride.   Walt Hriniak[1]

    It's almost impossible for me to find a proper starting point in my technical discussion of hitting. On the one hand, I know that anything I write will be subject to modification as soon as I wake up tomorrow. The research I have done in this area convinces me that every door I open leads into a room with at least two more doors on the far side. Divertissements on the theme of old-school hitting—or on any style of hitting—are virtually infinite. Indeed, I have lately concluded that no such thing as a single generalized "old school" prototype exists. Techniques of hitting were, if anything, far more diverse a century ago than they are today; though they do combine in expressing a few significant tendencies, one tiny modification here or there can send ripples through the whole arrangement. For the detail-minded detective working this unsolved (and stone-cold) case, the Spanish proverb is apt: *la paz empieza nunca*—"peace never comes."

    From another direction, my initial framing of the question must carry me, not into tomorrow, but almost as far back in my yesterdays as I can remember. I lived to play baseball from a very early age, even though many of my "games" were one-boy affairs consisting of my tossing the ball up and trying to stroke it with stances copied from various players or entirely made up. I soon acquired an affinity for hitting left-handed, despite my dextra-dominance in all other affairs, because Mickey Mantle was a switch-hitter; and, like every other kid of my generation, I wanted to be like Mick. (Once the Saturday *Game of the Week* started to broadcast only Yankee contests, due to financial considerations—and much to the irritation of Dizzy Dean, who seems to have gotten himself fired over the issue—all of us lads down South and out West got to know Mickey, Yogi, Whitey, Roger, and the Moose very well.) More often than not, when a righty starts working on a left-handed stroke, devoting a grossly unequal amount of practice time to it due to the position's novelty, he ends up forgetting how to hit right-handed. That's what happened to me.

    This turns out to be a small clue in my investigation, because most of the hitters I have highlighted for closer study—Fred Clarke, Joe Jackson, Speaker, Collins, Cobb, and Cobb's protégé Charlie Gehringer, to name a few—were right-throwing lefty hitters. (Yes, Speaker threw left—but only because a childhood accident disabled his naturally dominant right arm during his formative years; and Edd Roush actually began his baseball life throwing right because he could find no left-handed gloves![2]) We should recall, too, that true left-handers of the era would have been distinctly more rightward-tending than they are today, since the education system demanded (with rather brutal reinforcement sometimes) that they learn to write from the starboard side. Stan Musial, in fact, signed his highly publicized $100,000 deal in 1958 with his right hand. Ruth, Gehrig, and Sisler did their scribbling in like manner.

This was the origin, perhaps, of my "intuition" that smooth, level swings were entirely bottom-hand dominant, like the motion of a saber halving a melon (if I may recycle an odd metaphor: it seems to nail both the act and the frame of mind). Hitting left just felt so "right" to me. I've never been able to produce the same fluidity from my right side, though I could sometimes find more power there—more ability to slam down on the pitch with a strong top hand and shoot it up in the air. From soaring heights, saying hello to passing swallows, the white orb might eventually cross a fence amid distant cheers… or it might be caught by the catcher. Such was the stroke of the Steroid Era, when baseball became a really boring (to my mind) game of pop-ups, strikeouts, and home runs. A tall, rangy kid like Juan Gonzales, Alex Rodriguez, or Mark Maguire (Mark was really quite lean as a rookie) would undercut the ball as it crossed the plate, release the top hand entirely once it had "thrown down" on the target, and hope that the big fly would carry. I hate that style to this day, though it worked for many and continues to work for some, even now that upper bodies are not artificially enhanced. My loathing is somewhat irrational, and probably roots deep in my childhood, where most of our tastes begin to grow. I simply find it wanting in finesse, in artistry.

Not that, as a boy, I couldn't get my left-handed hits to carry. On the playground, where we always used softballs (a hardball would eventually break our one bat, for all bats were wooden back then), I would pump a deep hitch, take a ridiculously long stride, and crush the ball over the right-fielder's head. On a line. The other outfielders would all move to right the next time—and I would still send them running tardily for the treeline. After all these years, I continue to recall clearly how much fun that was. Possibly the most fun I ever had in my life.

A lot of things happened to interrupt my brilliant career. The Reserve Clause was still in effect during my childhood, so my parents were more inclined to see baseball as a frivolous pastime than as a career opportunity. Vietnam was heating up; most of us boys assumed without uttering any embarrassing comment that we would die long before we could embark upon either baseball or any other profession in our adult years. (I don't think anyone has ever adequately calculated the impact on my generation's adolescents of seeing—every evening as the TV flickered to life—mutilated soldiers wrapped up in bloody towels and writhing on stretchers.) In my native state of Texas, as well, there was little tolerance of baseball in underfunded high school athletic programs that absolutely had to field winning football teams. Baseball was amusement: football was religion. Even now, I haven't forgiven that robotic game of brutally regimented downs, yards, time-outs, and quarters for cheating me of so many swings.

One-minute sermon to all youngsters with a high opinion of their baseball skills: you're not the best. You never will be. Alfred Hitchcock was once asked if there had ever been a perfect crime—to which he answered, "Yes." Naturally, the interviewer wanted details, and pursued, "So... what was it?" Hitch replied in his unique deadpan manner, "We don't know." Same with baseball. The best base-reacher, the best base-stealer, the best long-ball hitter, and the best hard-thrower all bear names that you will never hear, unless on a higher reality's Field of Dreams. No matter how good you are, you've also met with a lot of luck merely in being able to play your beloved sport unimpeded. Better men than you have been cut off from it for reasons utterly beyond their control. Pete Reiser, Herb Score, Tony Conigliaro, and Bo Jackson are just a few of the more widely recognized names associated with cautionary tales... names we actually know!

But back to swings. So the better-hand-on-bottom approach was Exhibit A. As a boy, I could simply feel how much smoother my swing was from that side. The analogy of the saber is also powerful. It would occur to me much later and stay in my head as I read Charley Lau. In my defense, it really is hard to connect Tim Raines's stroke with Arod's if you view them superficially. One features a smooth glide in the stride and a smooth tennis-like backhand, the other a dramatic leg kick and a slam-down from a steeply descending top hand. I further reasoned that the Raines approach, being obviously more level, had a better chance of putting the ball in play even if contact were early or late. When my son came along, this became the clenching argument, for I knew that my boy was unlikely ever to be one of the taller kids on the diamond. A good objective for him would be to lead his league in hitting, not in home runs.

And I connected my case, for good measure, to whatever I could find out about the Deadball Era's great .400 hitters. I was aware that most of them routinely followed through with top hand firmly on bat, and not in the Lau/Hriniak fashion. That bothered me a bit... but I figured Charley and Walt had just gotten that part wrong, while being bang-on with the rest of it. I was also aware (or thought I was, at the time) that Cobb, Speaker, and Co. lifted their forward leg stiffly rather than taking a smooth backward coil and then flipping the knee. That bothered me, too... but I figured the old-timers must have been copying the fashion of the day, and that we could now safely discard one or two such items of gingerbread trim.

(Another quick aside: I am trying to reconstruct a former state of mind, not represent what I now believe to be true. And the truth, at least in terms of the Deadball greats whom I highlight later, is that the top hand's early release was an irrelevancy. They did and did not release early, depending on whether or not they were a bit ahead of the pitch. They lacked our obsession with reproducing the same swing in all circumstances; instead, they seem very much to have prized adaptability and versatility. Even the "load" with the front leg could vary.)

In my historical cherry-picking, I was mixing my methods shamelessly, without even suspecting it. I was only using my intelligence at this point to rationalize my way off the hook of enlightenment and to swim into more confusion. I had good company down there in the murky pool of delusion. In this chapter's banner-citation, Walt Hriniak (whom Wade Boggs credited with making him a successful hitter) also seems to have forsaken partly-cloudy depths for the opaque abyss. A young Walt had been hounded by his coaches with the order, "Top hand over!"—but not blessed by them with any remotely adequate explanation of just what the order meant.[3] I'd bet that most of the coaches didn't know themselves. They didn't realize that the formula they had ingested in their own childhood was supposed to encapsulate the complex action of the top hand's bent wrist straightening itself into a slightly downward punch through the ball. Much more on that later... but the older Hriniak, having been given a fragment of useful information without context, misassembled it into his stroke, struggled as a hitter, and finally—as a coach retired from active duty—decided to discard any and every notion of the top hand's supplying primary power. I understand. I was reaching similarly wrong conclusions from the reverse direction.

One thing I felt pretty secure about: the propriety of hitting off the front foot. As a kid, with my deep hitch and my long stride, I had always ended up heavily on my forward side—especially when I batted left. Photos of the great old-timers almost always show them doing the same. Henry Aaron certainly did so, as well, along with many of the sluggers who came through the Negro Leagues as he did, including Ernie Banks and Jackie Robinson himself. (If you can find the video of Clemente hitting his homer in the 1971 All Star Game, you'll notice his back shoe several inches off the ground as he makes contact.) Now, front-foot hitting was considered a cardinal sin even while all the superstars above were doing it. One of the few black players in the Fifties who struggled to hit .200 yet found big-league clubs extending second chances to him was Willie Kirkland; and Willie seems to have subscribed fully to the then-sacrosanct doctrine of pivoting hard over the back foot and upper-cutting the pitch.[4] The same mantra was still being recited when Charley Lau was trying to make it in the Bigs (and not doing so well): "Fifteen years ago all you ever heard was, 'You've got to hit off your back leg,'" recalls Charley. "I tried to work it out, but I couldn't see any way to do it."[5] I have to smile nowadays when I observe how an elite few of the coaching community have finally decided that the shift of weight forward should be one hundred percent, Lau's revision of the old formula having fallen on deaf ears a generation earlier.[6] Blundering amateur though I was, I had deduced as much in my early days of returning to the study of baseball as a new father; and, as regards front-foot hitting, I may add that I'm still a fan of Charley's.

But if I believed that driving into the pitch from the rear with a strong weight shift was so important, and if I didn't like having the top hand slide off during the swing, then why did I continue to think that the front arm packed most of the upper body's power? Why would the top hand need to stay on board if it was just along for the ride? I was as inconsistent as the gurus I sometimes scoffed at. I had become infatuated with the image of the slashing saber, and I allowed its poetry to forestall any further analysis.

Chapter Four

Fouled Lines: How Imparting Effective Backspin Differs From Undercutting

To produce a level swing, you also have to get on top of the ball by swinging down at it. That may sound strange, but it's really another case of aiming at an extreme in order to reach an ideal middle point. Even with a proper weight shift, many hitters still have a tendency toward a slight uppercut, which, as long as it remains slight, isn't all that bad. In fact, it's possible that in the perfect swing you do have a slight uppercut. The problem occurs when the uppercut is an extreme loop. That's what you want to stay away from, and getting on top of the ball by swinging down is a good way to counteract this tendency.   Charley Lau[1]

    To make matters worse for me in my early days as a hitting theorist, I was registering a lot of antagonistic resistance to coach-speak about backspin. (A "gut reaction" can be productive when it yields an inspiration; in the form of aversion, however, it gets in the way of impartiality and makes everything worse.) All I seemed to read and hear was backspin, backspin, backspin. The word couldn't have been more popular if it had been introduced in a Super Bowl commercial. The adherents of the "backspin gospel" routinely had recourse to aerodynamic palaver, as if they were rocket scientists. They would explain that the backward-spinning ball would create lift, just like an aircraft's wing, and thus carry much farther before the eventual landing. Topspin, by the same token, would cause the ball to dive. Backspin, good: topspin, bad.
    I interpreted this chatter, somewhat over-aggressively, as a direct assault on my evolving theory about the level swing. The saber-stroke guided by a firm bottom hand would plainly not impart as much backspin to the ball as the heavy top-hand, lower-the-boom stroke with early release. (And most of the hitters with pronounced early releases at the time were, in fact, the "steep throw-down" bludgeoners of the Juan Gonzalez/Ryan Howard stamp: Walt Hriniak had extolled Mays and Clemente for their one-handed finishes, but we had entered a new millennium, and those fiercely long strides were distant memories.) The heavy hitters just might be able to backspin their pop-ups over the chain-link fence... but the little guys like my son would surely be condemned to producing a series of unproductive cans of corn. It was a conspiracy, I felt (in my moodier moments), and it was aimed at shorter-than-average boys. As if the tall guys hadn't already tilted the world's cultural axis enough in their favor, now they wanted to ban short fellows from the game of baseball entirely so that they, the elite giants, could continue to dumb a great sport down into a degenerate species of home-run derby!
    My fighting blood was stirred. I didn't want to hear anything more from the

Backspin Conspiracy. I wanted my kid to nail the ball smoothly in the middle; and if he imparted any spin to it at all… well, I'd settle for topspin. A hot grounder speeding through the infield is turned into an out much less often than a weak pop-up.

Just recently, I discovered a celebrated hitting instructor online who employs much the same rebellious terms as I was using well over a decade ago in my capacity of frustrated father. He speaks of "the myth of backspin in hitting," and writes about a specific video analysis of a home run that he has published, "you can tell… [that], rather than coming off the bat with backspin like a fastball, the ball is coming off the bat with little to no spin like a knuckleball."[2] Coaches, it seems, are even driving other coaches to pull their hair out; and this gentleman, like Charley Lau—and me, and my son—had earlier in his playing days been undermined by the poorly explained but religiously preserved systems of his "mentors."

In a cooler moment such as the present one, I will charitably concede that ballplayers and coaches often don't express themselves with great eloquence. They mean well, but they can't get from A to B verbally. (In my less charitable moments, I might say that eloquence is wasted on them; Cicero and Bossuet would leave them drowning in tobacco juice.) You can't just end your spiel after praising backspin, O Golden Fraternity of Coaches! To many of us, you make it sound as though you're recommending an undercut swing; and since the examples you point to most admiringly—Arod, Ryan Howard, Carlos Beltrán—are indeed pop-up machines as well as home-run kings, you leave the impression that you don't really understand the distinction yourselves.

Backspin is not good *per se*. I have only lately realized, after surmounting years of blind prejudice and ill will, that, yes, backspin is an essential part of creating most well-struck line drives. After all, the arms have to come at the ball from the shoulders, where Mother Nature has attached them to the body—and the shoulders are above the strike zone. The swing must descend. The aerodynamic argument, too, is sound. Yet a plane whose joystick is pulled fully back on take-off will soon come right down again, and so will a backspun ball that's undercut. Spin must be integrated effectively with forward thrust. Forward thrust is maximal when a ball is struck squarely in the center.

My one-time patron saint, Charley Lau (may God rest his gentle soul!), trots out a scintillant sample of Batting-Cage Mandarin in this chapter's opening quotation. Coaches have long spoken of an "uppercut swing" as if the bat's head could possibly rise without first descending—or as if the hitters in question wanted to contact the pitch on the ascending rather than the descending curve of the swing's hyperbola. Actually, they did, at one time (see Chapter Fifteen). That time was already waning in Charley's day; and even when the uppercut technique was enjoying a golden noon, it required that hitters look for inside pitches and pull them—not exactly the Lau gospel. Charley himself, I must add, precedes the opening citation above by warning, "uppercutting can cause an awful lot of harm."[3] He alerts us to the dreaded pop-up and other ruinous results; yet he appears to be making my own mistake of identifying simplistically a dipping swing with backspin. The smooth stroke of a Ted Williams could impact the ball from beneath even as the swing began to climb from its original dive, avoiding topspin, because the hyperbola's dip was exceptionally broad and level: i.e., its ascent was quite mild. To achieve such an entry into the pitch, however, hands had to set up below the rear shoulder, as the more seasoned among us will recall from the posture of great Fifties sluggers like Williams, Mays, and Mantle (and Billy "Sweet William" Williams, too). Lau's exemplar George Brett poised his stick a little higher: maybe he represented the seam of an era, and maybe that accounts for the faint hedging in Charley's comments.

The two photos in *Art of Hitting .300* in which Brett caricatures the upper-cut swing, furthermore, don't resemble anything known to terrestrial man.[4] They cloud the issue by creating the impression that, yes, one might actually swing a bat along an upward plane all the way from the rear shoulder. Yet I cannot picture how this would realistically happen, and I've never seen any hitter at any level attempt it. As I was first reading Lau's comments, more than a decade after their original publication, Mark McGwire's stroke was all the rage, and it was against that backdrop that I was trying to process the notion of uppercutting. No one had been emulating the Williams or the Mantle stroke for a long time.

Today's heavy-artillery guys, to be clear, all start with hands above rear shoulder and back elbow cocked, generating a narrow, severe dip in the swing. Uppercutting backspin on the steep upward curve is impossible in them (as opposed to in the much milder ascent of a Williams/Mantle swing). As if to accommodate their tendencies, the strike zone has crept lower and lower; backspin, therefore, has more than ever become a matter of undercutting along the barrel's downward curve. Why, then, may some contemporary hitting gurus who chant "backspin" still be heard praising the uppercut swing when quoting their sacred texts or volunteering their own commentary on television? Up, down, back, top... the head begins to spin faster than the seams of a pop-up to the catcher.

In one of my banner-citations later on, I present Dusty Baker replicating Charley's rather feverish rush to scuff up boundaries that he suspects haven't been correctly drawn. Maybe... actually... you know, the perfect swing might just have a bit of an uppercut... but still... you can easily get too much of this good thing, so... so pretend that you're swinging down on the ball... which you really won't be, so don't worry about beating it into the ground....

Woe to the young person who tries to profit from reading or hearing such instruction (or to the father who's attempting self-education)! Fact: good contact does descend because it *must* to impart backspin. Even the classic uppercutters of the Golden Age (Williams, Mantle, McCovey, Killebrew) struck their home-runs with the barrel slicing somewhat down into a high pitch relative to that pitch's descending transit. But the barrel doesn't cut *under* the ball, because that would just spin the orb straight up. We need a lot more daylight in this thicket.

In a commendable effort to provide that illumination, coaches will sometimes talk about "hitting the top half of the ball" or "hitting through the ball." But alas, once again... this almost makes it worse. Hitting the top half of the ball only produces backspin if it comes from a deeply descending stroke (of the sort admittedly common—but not universal—today), and if contact is very late. More level cuts will instead deliver topspin by following such advice: the result depends upon the particular hitter. And as for hitting through the ball... what exactly is that supposed to tell us? Hitting "through" as opposed to what? To dropping the bat from both hands upon contact as if bunting? Is an adolescent really intended to decipher these cryptic batting-cage idioms if a word like "through" is delivered with a raised voice?

Just to add one more strong dash of obscurity to a muddy brew, the official hitting-manual catechism (as I implied in the previous chapter) also usually connects backspin hitting with "letting the ball get deep": in plain English, hitting the pitch as it passes over the plate. Depending on whether the ball is boring outside or diving inside, this can be excellent or disastrous advice. Cobb and Speaker would have understood implicitly the importance of varying the point of impact with the pitch's location. The notion of trying to backspin everything served to you after waiting for it to reach the heart of the plate is preposterous; or it's a recipe, to be precise, for a tournament that nets the hitter one home run, two bloop singles, four unproductive pop-ups, and five strikeouts. Come to think of it... I believe I've just painted a portrait of the Contemporary Slugger!

Hitting is hard, to be sure, and describing the successful swing may be even harder. I've already admitted that I have reached plenty of mistaken judgments about the swing in my lifetime... and I confess that I continue to do so. If I'm peeved at the level of incoherence in these "tips," perhaps it's because I have seen so many young people get terribly frustrated in trying to execute them—to the point that they give up the game after an experience of bitter failure that stays with them for years.

One also hears a lot about "going straight to the ball" or being "short to the ball." To me, this again begs the question, "As opposed to what?" Is this just the old "don't hitch" warning that I constantly received as a kid (as if hitches were part of the actual swing instead of a preparatory load)? Every hitter naturally wants to get right at the pitch. In arcane coach-speak, "short to the ball" means coming right at the pitch from where the hands load instead of forcing those hands to lift over or circle around the rear shoulder. Good advice; yet even after translation, it seems more descriptive of an efficient swing than instructive in how to achieve such a swing. If hitting were as simple as setting the hands up in the proper place, anybody could do it.

At least we seem to be converging here, however, on the idea of not undercutting the ball. An undercut can scarcely be described as going straight to its target. From a similar interpretive vantage, maybe "hitting the top half of the ball" is meant as a corrective to undercutters (as the Lau citation implies), rather in the way that a catcher may set up far outside for a pitcher whose corner pitches are consistently working their way back over the middle. Maybe, in the undercutter's tortured mind, "top half" gives a mark to shoot at that pulls his swing up toward the ball's mid-section. Hitting "through" the ball, likewise, could only be of use in describing contact that does not hit "around" the ball: i.e., neither undercutting nor topping.

Why not just say, "Aim for the bull's eye"? If the bat's barrel is descending into the pitch, as it must be in an "on time" swing unless the hitter chases one above the letters, then central contact will produce both backspin and powerful forward thrust. The only explanation I can imagine for why the hitter's task is seldom framed so simply by his coaches depends, once again, on the assumption that young batsmen are being told these days to wait for every pitch to reach the plate. They're supposed to "let it get deep." If you hit the top half of a pitch at your knees as it reaches the plate, *and* if that pitch is on the outer half of the plate, you will indeed likely send it far aloft. The vector of the descending barrel will be cutting the orb's back half from a high angle rather than driving it straight into the ground: at least, that's the likely result using today's steep slugger-stroke. Yet even in the event of success, your stick's downward angle may be so severe that the pitch ends up over the backstop; or if the ball should cut a little to the inside part of the plate as you aim for its top half... well, you may soon discover the advantages of investing in a shin guard.

Honestly, I don't really know how to reconcile all the coaching advice I've heard over the years. No matter which way I add up all the figures, I can't get the right sum. Let us finish this chapter on the following apparent point of universal agreement: backspin creates line-drives that carry, but only when it is applied in a mildly downward stroke whose vector is a) much more decisively forward than downward, and b) whose direction at contact is indeed the vector's straight cut rather than the looping section of a circle's curve. At the instant of impact, the barrel should be driving along a slightly inclined plane that bisects the ball's sphere almost perfectly.

Now... how do you get there? That calls not just for another chapter, but for another section, since the Deadball artists whose work we have been approaching very circuitously were particularly good at achieving such contact. So the evidence suggests, at any rate.

A boy and his bat

No doubt about it: my son was using his bottom hand altogether too much when he was ten years old, courtesy of Charley Lau and Dad. He would sometimes get into trouble with the umpire for throwing the bat after a hit—an infraction he could scarcely avoid, since I had taught him to "saber" the ball. Yet there's a lot here that looks very good to me, even now. The hands are well positioned to deal a level swing with a high probability of contact. Professional coaching would later take care of that. "Don't straighten that bottom arm! Get those hands higher!" The memories are truly painful.

Part Two

The Way of the Samurai

Reverse-engineering the component parts of the Deadball Era swing by seeking a convergence in available items of evidence; review of information drawn from still photographs, rare moving picture sequences, first-hand accounts, sports reporting, and personal experimentation in a controlled setting.

Chapter Five

The Hammer and the Axe: How the Major Chasm in Hitting Styles Began with a Tiny Crack

Your arm should be like a continuation of the bat. In golf this is called swinging through, and is all-important. There is an important difference, however. In baseball you should chop at the ball. You should take a short, sharp swing and still keep your arms in the position I have described. The long swings may knock a ball out of the lot occasionally, but you get much better results by meeting it squarely with a short chop.   Ty Cobb[1]

Of course, I hit very different from the way they hit today. I used a 48-ounce bat, heaviest anyone ever used. It was a shorter bat, with a big handle, and I tried to hit to all fields. Didn't swing my head off, just snapped at the ball. Until 1921, you know, they had a dead ball. Well, the only way you could get a home run was if the outfielder tripped and fell down. The ball wasn't wrapped tight and lots of times it'd get mashed on one side. Come bouncing out there like a jumping bean. They wouldn't throw it out of the game, though. Only used three or four balls in a whole game.   Edd Roush[2]

    Please keep the geometrical blueprint from the previous chapter's end (slightly sloping line entering the sphere's center) in mind. Cobb did. One of the very few motion-films I have ever seen of the Georgia Peach shows him fidgeting with his bat before the camera... but was he fidgeting, really? The revelation suddenly overtook me, as I was still digesting the complex truths of backspin, that Cobb was rehearsing a cleaver-like chop down into the ball. Every time he picked up a bat, I would wager—even for photographers to waste a few seconds of his precious time—he was creating muscle-memory. "Just like this, straight down on the ball...." Over and over and over, perhaps hundreds (or thousands) of times a day, he must have repeated that motion. It was the key to his success, the butter on his bread. Like Archilochus the mercenary leaning on his spear to grab a spot of lunch, Ty Cobb throttling his bat's handle in that back-and-forth motion was the craftsman's caress of the tool which had made him prized.
    And you find a very similar pose, though frozen in a still shot, if you thumb through photographs of celebrated batsmen of the late nineteenth century (e.g., Dan Brouthers, Buck Ewing, and King Kelly).[3] There rarely seems to be much dynamism in their lower body, or much coil in their shoulders. They have all the poise, rather, of a big-game hunter resting his boot on the beast's head as he awaits the flash of the photographer's plate, rifle cradled in arm. But is the position of the hands merely this sort of cradling? We tend to think so today. The hands are not drawn back toward the armpit to strike: the bat isn't even lifted to rest on the shoulder. The loose fingers, aligned almost along the uniform's buttons and perhaps held out a bit from the body, imply anything but a lock-and-

load readiness… to us.

But what if, nevertheless, they were loaded, or in rest but strategically positioned for a short, quick load? What kind of attack could be launched from such a position? How do you sting a ball with your top hand projected in waiting from your collarbone, or even a little lower than that?

Above, I called Cobb's fidget the chop of a meat cleaver. (I apologize if my analogies are proving a distraction. They're how I think; and sometimes, as with the saber, their vividness gets me into trouble.) A hammer might be an even better image: a sledgehammer, say, that requires two hands to hold. Picture a contestant standing before one of those five-cent challenges at an old-fashioned carnival where you try to hit the plank so hard that it launches the ball upward to ding a bell. How would you take your swing? Obviously, one hand would be above the other: you couldn't get a good grip on the sledge's handle if you interlaced your fingers. You would likely rear back without moving your feet and drive straight down on your target. Yet if you really wanted some extra acceleration in your blow, and if the hammer weren't so heavy as to throw you over on your back, you might also lift a leg up and then bring it sharply down to catalyze the descent of your hands. Imagine that complex movement carefully. The lifted leg would need to be stiff and straight, its knee probably locked, or nearly so. If the knee veered inward even slightly, it would cock the hip and create subsequent dip in your stroke as the hip opened back up; and that minute curve could inhibit the hammer from striking its target bang-on. You want to bring the heavy head into impact as close to the dead-straight as possible.

I think I may just have described the essential stroke of several Deadball Era batting champions: probably Jesse Burkett, Ginger Beaumont, and George Stone, at least. (Edd Roush is also a candidate; but Tris Speaker was already adding more powder to the charge, and Cobb himself was looking for rocket fuel to propel his hand attack. As for Wagner and Lajoie, they were entirely another matter, as we shall see.) To be sure, a bat's barrel is descending along a very moderate slope, not perpendicularly onto some fairground fulcrum; that cannot be emphasized enough, for most of what once made me very suspicious of backspin has to do with *excessively downward* swinging. Yet even a moderate descent must be straight to strike hardest, and everything in this stroke is committed to the linear.

That's what I most admire about the approach implicit in Cobb's obsessively repeated chop, quite apart from any practical results it may have achieved: its rigid adherence to the discipline of "straight line driving down through ball's center." All else is limbering up or crescendo-building—and there could indeed be considerable stylistic difference in where feet were placed or whether the torso was bent. I will try to sort through such minutiae later. It all starts, however, in the "Cobb fidget": the straight, slightly downward drive into the ball. The descent of the hammer.

Of course, once that implement comes out of the toolbox, we all start thinking of Hammerin' Hank. To my mind, the fundamental uniqueness of Henry Aaron's swing—and the source of its stunning success—is indeed this straight descent into the ball. The Hammer was able to produce the combination of backspin and forward thrust that made pitches jump off his barrel as low line drives: not as towering "big flies," that is, but as gappers that would have become triples in earlier ballparks and—happily—scooted over the nearer fences of later ones. Reggie Jackson put it in much the same terms: "Aaron swung down on the ball. He'd get backspin on it and hit line drives that would start off close to the ground and just keep going unless the fence got in the way."[4] In the trailing sweep of Henry's back foot as he came up on his forward one to make contact, in the high finish over the shoulder with top hand still riding the handle… in several of his movements, we see how the .400 hitters of yesteryear attacked the ball. Personally, I wish Aaron had gone for the .400 mark and 4,000 hits instead of Ruth's record (which, of course, has since been mauled by the "human hybrid" ethic of the Nineties). I understand the financial and cultural reasons that riveted him upon Homer Number 715; but as a baseball purist, I would rather have seen him be a career "two for five" hitter.

He could have done it. He could probably have done it hitting cross-wristed; for, as an adolescent, this is precisely how Hank did his hammering. Only when advised by big-league scout Dewey Griggs that he would never be taken seriously if he didn't uncross his wrists did he begin to hit the "correct" way—"except," confides Hank, "for now and then when a tough pitcher had two strikes on me."[5] A chap by the name of Dan Bancroft (he's in the Hall of Fame) collected over 2,000 hits with his left hand on top while batting right-handed. How, I would ask, could Bancroft and a young Aaron possibly have stroked the ball so well from such an impossible set-up—how, unless they were driving down and through the ball's center in the fashion I have described? Cross-wristed hitting actually works quite well with that approach. Imagine trying to ding the carnival's bell by raising a foot on the same side as the hand atop the sledge's handle. You would likely get a really straight descent, with no hint of "pulling out." This manner of swing with a bat, likewise, would produce a remarkably linear attack and very little dipping.

Now, if swinging hips are what you're after, then you had better uncross those wrists—and also look for another carnival game. As I have already suggested, even a slight swing of the hips would introduce a curve into the hammer's linear descent. My intention is to address feet, hips, and the rest of the lower body in later chapters; but I have to mention them here so as to account for the epochal shift in hitting style that launched us upon our present course. In his videos and his unforgettable hitting manual, Ted Williams puts the rotation of the hips front and center, where it has remained (with some modest degree of de-emphasis) to this day; but the Splendid Splinter was far from being the first to practice this gospel, if he was the first to preach it. I think hip rotation must have been the essential difference between Ty Cobb's swing and that of his protégé and harbinger of the Thirties, Harry Hooper. Hoop's fiercely long stride, not really much different from Cobb's, ended in a backward tilt and a sweeping one-handed finish almost never observable in Ty's follow-throughs. Hooper somewhat exaggerates the Williams stroke's notable characteristics without exceeding them: he belongs in the later batting champ's category, it seems to me, more than in the earlier one's. During a career that almost perfectly overlapped Hooper's (both debuted in 1909), Zack Wheat displayed an even longer stride, it appears, and powered all the way through with a top hand that wrapped the forward shoulder in Williams fashion. "Unlike most Deadball Era hitters," testifies one researcher, "he held his hands down by the knob, choking up only a little. 'There is no chop-hitting with Wheat, but a smashing swipe which, if it connects, means work for the outfielders,' wrote one reporter."[6]

The more horizontal, rotational swing, then, was in the tea leaves early on. Perhaps surprisingly (to those who would associate vigorous rotation with raw power), Babe Ruth does not yet exhibit many of its essential characteristics. (Gehrig comes much closer.) The Babe's hands dipped to let the barrel fall away from his body, his leg came so far back that the forward heel practically touched the rear toes, his front knee remained nearly locked throughout the entire stroke, he fell heavily on said forward leg in executing a swing that finished high with top hand firmly on board... all of this is typical of the twentieth century's first years. The hands pressed down tightly one on the other at the stick's end are perhaps the single obvious departure from hitting dogma during the Teens.

The throwing open of the hip generates a motion more amenable to swinging an axe than a sledgehammer—and the analogy this time comes courtesy of Ted Williams, for whom the axe's hacking into a tree trunk holds the secret to effective hitting.[7] The "hammer" approach brings the front foot down hard and late: the foot's fall maps out the line of the hammer's descent and initializes that straight, mildly descending attack. The "axe" approach, in contrast, lets the forward foot plant with relative gentleness and then, after a delay that maximizes the strain between forward leg and the backward-drawn hands (often compared to a stretched rubber band),[8] draws the two extremes together by action of the hips. Ruth, by the way, claimed that his style was copied from Joe Jackson. He might have been alluding to numerous similarities, such as the set-up with both feet touching or the fondness of both hitters for gripping the bat toward the knob and for swinging all-out, regardless of the count.[9] Yet Jackson appears to have been the more rotational hitter of the two. "He stood in the box with his feet together, then took a long step into the pitch..." does not quite sound like the style that brought the Bambino up heavily over his front foot.[10] From an admittedly fragmentary photographic record, it appears that Jackson more often finished leaning back somewhat, with his front toes pointing distinctly up and out. Through Joe—more than through the Babe—the rudiments of the "axe" stroke can be dated all the way back to the dawn of the twentieth century.

Shoeless Joe, Lou Gehrig, Teddy Ballgame... those are some pretty heavy hitters. It would be difficult to argue that their method was putting inferior backspin on the ball, if backspin is what makes hits carry. The first two were no doubt still at an intermediate point between these technical polarities in some respects, or else they wouldn't have been able to sling such heavy lumber. (For while the bat's weight can accelerate it in a succinctly descending stroke, as in

Ruth's case, weight becomes a real obstacle in a more lateral stroke—not to mention a potential threat to muscle and joint.) In Williams' day, however, we find some of the most aggressive hip action in the game's history. Musial, Mays, Mantle, Matthews, and McCovey—just to name a few M's—all featured long strides with the bat wrapping in a level circle around mid-torso to finish. (Ex-Negro Leaguers like Dobie, Irvin, and Hank Thompson may have been "persuaded" to swing this way. Many of their brethren were not allowed to advance unless they displayed what the Big League brain trust considered a power stroke; and the Negro Leagues, as I hinted earlier, were really the last bastion of Deadball techniques.) How did the Age of the Axe so prosper if its recipe for power were flawed?

Such, of course, is not my argument. What I would say, rather, is as follows: the "hammer" approach concentrated so intensely on the movement of barrel sloping straight through ball, minimizing everything else as much as possible, that it produced crisp hits from all parts of the strike zone which shot to every field. Edd Roush confides (in the second quotation at this chapter's beginning) that he had mastered just such an attack with a bat that weighed half again as much as today's favorite models. He certainly didn't bat over .300 for eleven straight years and win two batting titles by swinging from the hips with a three-pound hunk of kindling. He had to be generating most of his force with his hands—or with a massive barrel's weight working *through* his hands.

Think of it this way (yes, another analogy looms). All swings are somewhat circular because all hands are attached to a body, and hence must orbit that axis. You're trying to hit something traveling in a line with a motion that's fixed on hinges. The pernicious effects of the swing's curve, however—notably, undercutting and pulling off—can be diminished to the degree that the circle can be turned on its edge to approach a plane perpendicular to the ground. (The bat head could either drive forward-and-down from this circle's "ten o'clock" point, cutting straight under noon, to three or four; or it could drive backward-and-down from the extreme-rear ten o'clock, cutting above six, to four or five. That is, the hitter could attack either a very high pitch or a very low one. This is a first glimpse at the ancient swing's extraordinary versatility.) Any error in timing is now mitigated because the barrel, as viewed from directly overhead, wheels out of the ball's flight path less quickly, even though it may be above or below that path much of the way when viewed from the side. (Shifting to the front foot minimizes the risk by flattening the descent: more on that later, too.) In more publicized and current words, this hitter is being "short to the ball."

On the other hand, if the swing's wheel turns more or less parallel to the ground, then its window for potent impact with the ball becomes tiny. It's "long to the ball." A level swing may indeed stay in the ball's plane of flight for a long time: this was my own reasoning when I once believed in Charley Lau's gospel. The problem is that the bat's sweet spot is transiting in and out of the actual *line* of flight within the plane—especially on outside pitches—very quickly, leaving "bad wood" in its place as it passes. Coaches have barked at kids since the days of Williams (and before, I'm sure) not to "pull off" the pitch: i.e., to keep the bat head in the zone. This typifies the unhelpful genre of coach-speak, for emphatic lateral hip action requires you to pull off the pitch quickly whether you like it or not (and whether Coach likes it or not). The problem is one of timing, since the margin of error is so small—and keeping your head down and your front shoulder closed won't solve a timing problem. That didn't stop Walt Hriniak from having his disciples do endless drills where they stared down into the plate long after their bat had sailed over the front shoulder.

The axe brigade probably wins in power because its stalwart soldiers are throwing everything they have, from the toes up, into their attack. But the hammer brigade wins in good contact throughout the strike zone because its sharpshooters can so quickly execute a "barrel smackdown" with so few movements. I'll take the sharpshooters… but, really, my preference or yours isn't the issue for the moment. We're trying to reconstruct the swing of an era dominated by choking up and landing on an erect front leg. Crisp contact was definitely the objective of this attack.

Chapter Six

Hit by a Mack Truck: How the Swing's Dynamics Radiate from the Maximal Acceleration Point

Because I was strong, I could hit the ball out of the park without pulling it and also without lifting it. A lot of home-run hitters will uppercut at the ball, but the best hitters don't do that. It was a lesson I learned from Dick Allen. We had long conversations about hitting. I wasn't able to duplicate his style, though, because he could keep his hands low and go to the ball from that position. My method was to build up force with my rotation. So I held the bat higher. But I still dropped the bat head on the ball, essentially swinging down, like Allen did. Dick's power was based on natural explosiveness. Mine was based on strength and natural mechanics, which combined to make me explosive.   Reggie Jackson[1]

If a pitch is thrown at 90 MPH, each of the boxes [imagined in the strike zone] the pitch could enter will have a different reaction time—some slightly different and some radically different. Each pitch has only one perfect time and place to be hit at 100% on-time contact and with 100% efficient swing mechanics.   Perry Husband[2]

   Ty Cobb, in repeating his "fidget," never breaks his wrists. Coaches and other master-mechanics of the game used to swear that powerful contact occurs only as the top hand comes driving over the bottom one—that an explosive "snap of the wrists" was responsible for the superhuman deeds of Ted Williams and Henry Aaron. This mythology perhaps flits about the edges of Reggie Jackson's utterance above, where we find the notion again expressed that certain sluggers could "uppercut" the ball out of the park. Charley Lau was talking the same language a couple of chapters ago, and I was at pains to stress that a barrel just embarked upon the swing-hyperbola's upward curve must still drive downward relative to the pitch's incoming vector. I don't think Reggie really disagrees. His remark never implies that the wrists are rolling over as the most desirable contact is made, for a fiercely rotational hitter like him could still be leading the barrel with the handle even as his bat started upward. As for Charley... I'm not so sure. He does claim, after all, that letting the top hand slip off the handle allows the barrel to make contact with maximum force. That's just where the wrists would indeed be rolling over if the top hand stayed put.[3]
 Once again, we encounter a worn-out theory so vague in conception that morphs of it keep clinging to life. Who knows if Cobb would have held a detailed rebuttal of the "wrist-snapping" doctrine in his hip pocket? Whether through careful thought or murky intuition, however, he knew that the moment of greatest impact happens *before* the wrists roll over. Our sledgehammer hero at the carnival isn't snapping his wrists as he brings the mallet down and rings the bell. Our axe-wielding lumberjack isn't snapping his wrists, either, as he rains

blows into a tree trunk. Dick Allen had a hammer (as did Hammerin' Hank); Reggie wielded the Williams axe. Yet, as Jackson shrewdly observes, he was driving down into the ball just as was the mighty-handed Allen.

Fact: the bat head is maximally accelerated as the top wrist is still tautly driving down through the ball and the top arm's elbow not yet—not quite—fully extended (see n. 3). If the swing is taken even a tiny millisecond beyond that point, we find the bat entering into rapid deceleration. I have a hunch, personally, that Ty Cobb was keenly aware of this. That's why his practice maneuver didn't go beyond the straight-wristed stage into the wrist-breaking stage. (By the way, I've sometimes observed Buster Posey practicing the same little maneuver between pitches, a century later.) What Cobb was anchoring in every muscle of his body that would store memory was the Big Bang, the contact point that gave the best results.

For convenience, I shall call this the Mac Point (short for "maximal acceleration"). Now, the Mac Point as I have just described it is one of hitting's "inflexibles." It isn't what Charley Lau would call an absolute, because those can be variously calibrated and nuanced. (Any individual's position of best balance, for instance, is somewhat open to interpretation.) Charley's objective in naming his honor role of technical components as he did was to emphasize that they weren't just stylistic add-ons, but he also didn't insist that each fell from a single cookie-cutter. The Mac Point differs in that it allows no degree of individuation according to a given hitter's body type: it doesn't come a little before the top wrist straightens in some and a little after the wrist roll in others. If you've hit a low liner that carries like a missile into the gap, it's because you caught the ball at the peak of your bat's acceleration, which can occur at only one place—and with all due deference to Charley, that place is not right as or right after the top hand comes off the bat. There's simply no engine to drive acceleration at that stage.

Every hitter who makes such ideal contact always does so just before the wrists break, whether he knows it or not, practices it or not, or accurately portrays it or not in some publicized theory. The Mac Point is a physical fact, and a logical necessity. It's not a paving stone laid on the road to success: it's the sun that comes up every morning. A human body cannot strike a laterally moving object with a stick as solidly in any alternative position. A lot of hitters, apparently (to judge from the number of coaches giving them bad advice all along), were reaching this position subconsciously. They were merely answering the call of the wild.

And then we have those hitters, sometimes considered quite successful in the game's lower echelons, who have never hit the ball very solidly, or certainly not up to their potential for doing so. Within this hapless group reside a few Division I sluggers, and probably even a few high draft picks that mysteriously couldn't make the transition to wooden bats. The next chapter will explain the mystery in most specific cases. The zone of maximal acceleration (to drop a clue) is very difficult, if not impossible, to enter in these cases, for Mother Nature's expert coaching has been compromised by man's artifice.

What Cobb, Speaker, and Co. did, in contrast, was to place the Mac Point explicitly and deliberately at the center of all their training. Everything preceding it was designed to get to it; everything following it was a natural, free-flowing exit from it. (The game of "pepper," I very strongly suspect, was originally intended not to limber up infielders, but to rehearse batters on catching the ball just at that magical point before the wrists start to roll. Now a pepper drill during warm-ups is a thing of the distant past.) As I stressed in the preceding chapter, the magnetic core of the Deadball batsman's planet was that small, critical space where the bat head drives forward and slightly down into the ball's center. Additions to or subtractions from the swing occur insofar as they assist or impede proper entry into that fragment of space/motion.

I would add here the important detail that explosion into the hitting zone's climax requires the wrists to be closely aligned, such that they form less than a forty-five degree angle. This means, further, that the bat must have been gripped somewhat loosely in the fingers just before the swing so as to allow the slippage (before severe tightening) of at least one hand. In other words, the set-up grip should facilitate the alignment of the "knocker knuckles" that Cal Ripken, Jr., and others have long advocated in print and at training camps; and this means, further, that the thumbs cannot be clamped tightly around the handle, locking it hard and fast into the palm of either hand.[4]

Loose hands, knuckle alignment, top hand driving through with palm up... now I am echoing the standard hitting manual from the mid-to-late twentieth century. But those manuals are far from disagreeing with the Old School about everything. Charley Lau was surely correct to say that all successful hitting observes certain fundamental rules, though the great hitters of yesteryear don't validate every item on his list. What must appall anyone who has watched baseball astutely for the last half-century is how many young hitters—at tournaments, and even on national television—violate the most basic of basics. (For instance, check out the number of thumbs locked tight around handles the next time you watch a Major League game.) In this book, we can scarcely review DBE (Deadball Era) hitting without remarking some of the contemporary departures from the golden road; and while commenting upon the divergence may draw us away from a strictly historical focus, surely it will also help us bring the past into focus by creating a clear contrast with it. Whether or not today's players wish to embrace some of the past's discarded methods must depend on individual readers; my study's primary objective is not to advocate some kind of restoration. Yet I am also convinced that the past can whisper valuable lessons to us if we listen—and it is not my objective, either, to muffle those whispers.

Intellectuals of the game like Brian Kenny who brood over the alarming increase in strikeouts argue that a return to earlier methods might more than compensate for the decrease in power that they would probably usher in. Kenny often speaks in his television appearances of using a bigger bat that stays in the zone longer, almost as if one were to visualize a batsman of bowler-hat days simply thrusting a thick tree limb over the plate and holding it there. I would take issue with that representation to this extent. The old-school stroke organized around the Mac Point was not necessarily weak. The quality of the contact-making blow itself, measured over a minute distance, was indeed maximal (hence my acronym). Yes, Rabbit Maranville managed to wedge an extra-base knock in among his 2,605 hits less than ten percent of the time. The Rabbit's photos often show him gripping a bat fully midway up; one cannot imagine him, indeed, swinging his stick two-handed without receiving a punch in the solar plexus from its knob. That is, one can't imagine it if one can picture only the lateral, hip-throwing swing of post-World War II baseball: the downward, hammering stroke would not prove so punishing to the hitter's gut. Maranville appears to have had little more in his attack than this linear segment of the stroke: virtually no use of legs or hips, no harnessing of gravity or thrust. He merely reached out and lowered the hammer. Yet he piled up a good chunk of the divine 3,000 hit total. That should tell you that balls were departing his bat pretty fast and straight, even though his energy source was all hands.

The same cannot be said of our poster-children for this swing, Cobb and Speaker. They fly high among the all-time leaders in extra-base hits to this day. Ty ranks fifth, as of the present writing (2017), in total bases, and Tris comes in at Number Sixteen. The Grey Eagle also logged 792 career doubles, a tally never remotely approached by anyone else (with Pete Rose a distant second). We will see in subsequent chapters how these two, and probably many other worthies, took advantage of lower-body strength and a dynamic grip of the handle.

In concluding this chapter's case for the potency of a proper contact point, I should like to make two observations of a physical nature. While I am not a physicist (nor even the survivor of an upper-division college physics class), common sense should suffice to justify my assertions. First, "maximal acceleration" is a polysyllabic way of stressing that the old-timers' bat heads were really moving when they struck the ball. If you can figure out a way to make the barrel streak over a very short space (as the batsmen in question obviously did), then it needn't be a particularly big barrel for the rate of contact to increase. Armed with a lightning punch, you can wait a long time before offering at the pitch; and then, in some cases, you can hit it almost out of the catcher's mitt. You shouldn't require a lot of extra wood to boost your percentage of contact per at-bat, *pace* Mr. Kenny (and the weighty-weaponed Edd Roush notwithstanding). In fact, the barrels of old bats were comparatively thin by today's standards, even if the overall stick was longer. In short, contact rises with effective, well-directed speed, not with diameter of bludgeon. An even balance and amenability to hand operations are likely much more relevant in the stick than its maximum diameter.

A final observation—and one which will be developed much more thoroughly later—is that the Mac Point must necessarily vary with respect to the pitch's location. (Coach Perry Husband describes these shifting power-points with multiple charts in an intense little book developed for pitchers.) I spoke of Rabbit Maranville's reaching out to hammer the ball. He and other old-school hitters with a spectacular degree of choke-up (Wee Willie Keeler's was even more alarming) could never have wanted to hit a pitch as it passed over the plate while standing square—not unless they were wearing large protective belt-buckles. Yet I also wrote just above that a hitter of yesteryear might want to stroke the pitch right out of the catcher's mitt in some instances. The point of maximal acceleration differs throughout the strike zone, being sometimes far in front of the plate and sometimes actually behind it. You can make a kind of three-dimensional graph in thin air of these shifting Mac Points by gripping a bat as you would hold it at that instant (i.e., with wrists close together and "knocking knuckles" more or less aligned) and extending the top arm until its elbow is not quite locked. Carry that hand position all throughout the strike zone, never allowing the top elbow to extend fully. You find that ideal contact is made deeper in the zone as the pitch rides farther outside; and you find, as well, that the Mac Point moves farther back for lower pitches, since your hands must reach down to get them. The high-inside pitch is the one that—theoretically—you could catch farthest in front of the plate. (Since fastballs are most likely to prowl through this location in practice, meeting them out front may become problematic.) The low-away pitch is the one where you may almost part the catcher from his beloved mitt if he reaches too soon.

    We shall see later that Speaker, Roush, and others deliberately shuffled their feet as the ball was being delivered so as to hasten contact on inside pitches and delay it on outside pitches—a bit of lower-body magic observable in no contemporary player, and already a distant memory when I was a child. (A mobile back foot that doesn't dig itself a hole as the hitter steps into the box may be the most forgotten and time-obscured element of all the techniques I shall explore.) For now, let us hold in healthy skepticism one golden rule of our contemporary hitter—or of his coach, I should say. The modern hitting guru's insistence that his pupils "hit the ball as it passes over the plate" is what makes pitchers who memorize Perry Husband's chart effective, since certain points of direct pass-over are unhittable in today's context. If we understand why this is so, then we will further understand why the great "stickers" (as Cobb calls them) of yesteryear were a lot less "dug in."

Chapter Seven

Peddling the Metal: How the High-Tech Bat Transformed Hitting

The spate of home runs since 1995 has not been caused only by the lively ball and the other usual suspects--the smaller ballparks, diluted pitching that has come from expansion, added muscles on batters, and their unwillingness to cut down on their strokes when they have two strikes. No one talks about the newer bats. They should, because they might be the biggest factor of all.   Ralph Kiner[1]

There is a special sensation in getting good wood on the ball and driving a double down the left-field line as the crowd in the ballpark rises to its feet and cheers. But I also remember how much fun I had as a skinny barefoot kid hitting a tennis ball with a broomstick on a quiet, dusty street in Panama.   Rod Carew[2]

Aluminum bats became big in the Seventies, if memory serves, and especially within college programs. Money was the prime mover. These programs often didn't have much of a budget, and wooden bats regularly snapped, cracked, or split, necessitating complete replacement. I owned one of the earliest metal bats for a long time (before it was stolen off the practice field— a single item among a thousand dollars' worth of gear claimed by the same destiny over the years). I recall how very like a wooden bat it was in all visible dimensions. And it had about the same weight, as well.

That would soon change. As aluminum yielded to various metal-alloy concoctions, manufacturers grew cleverer in ways to distribute mass while lightening the overall load. The later-generation bats sported broomstick-thin handles and wine-bottle-fat barrels connected by incredibly abrupt flares with twenty degrees or more of taper. The name of the game was now to bring that big fat paddle down on the pitch. And because weight had been concentrated in the barrel, players were left with little handle to caress in those intricate, often unique ways that great hitters do. In fact, contact with the metal bat could really sting down at the end, so young hitters developed a relationship with their handle that less resembled Casanova embracing his lady than Marlon Perkins bagging a wild raccoon. Gloves were worn; they became standard equipment. The toothpick handles were also insulated in a rubbery coating or (later) wrapped in thick tape; and, still chicken-neck thin, they were pressed back into the fleshy part of the hand, thumbs locking around them. There the sting was dulled.

This grip, adopted by both hands, was reminiscent of a mountain-climber's upon two spikes as he tries to claw his way up an almost sheer ice face. Reduction of sting was only part of the motivation, and maybe not the most significant part... but the whole story will take me some little while to explain fully. Picture the metal-alloy bat again, with its weight intentionally packed into eight or ten inches toward the end. It has been shortened both to lighten it up and to free more weight for loading into the barrel. The diminution of length renders it virtually useless as the kind of balancing pole that DBE artists could employ when raising their forward leg. Feet can no longer move much; or if they do so, they must do so very quickly, forsaking poise. Only a Japanese hitter, reared in a culture where training in intricate body control is routine, might hearken back in certain respects to American styles before the world wars. For our guys, the coach's expert advice urges, "If you have to move that front foot, get it back down early."

Meanwhile, what's going on with the hands? They are virtually forced to rise far over the rear shoulder if the hitter is to use his lower body at all; for with such a short length of bat left to balance any motion of the forward leg, the arms have to supply the deficit. Japanese home run king Sadaharu Oh, poised on one leg like a crane watching for a fish with his hands straight up over his head, would be the extreme example of such adjustment. American boys opted for a cocked rear elbow that would shift enough body weight to the rear for a quick forward leg kick. And then… and then, down hard with those hands! As hard as possible—as hard as ever you can, straight down on the ball as it passes over the plate.

There really aren't any other options. High hands can neither reach a ball very far in front of the plate nor sideswipe it productively as it passes behind the plate. Their descent is too steep: the curve of the descending stroke has no room to flatten out. A pitch struck in front of the plate will be weakly topspun as the bat begins the steep ascent inevitable after its sharp dive; a pitch struck behind the plate may end up rattling off the unfortunate catcher's mask, but certainly won't fall in play. The only happy outcome within this uncomfortable set of new parameters is that the severe backspin imparted to a ball just as it passes over the plate may bloop it up high in the stratosphere; and there, with a little timely help from the wind god Aeolus, it may land on the other side of the scoreboard.

But to achieve this "happy" result (which, to the purist, can appear ugly even at its happiest), the infusion of backspin must indeed be formidable. This means, first of all, that tall boys have a better shot at hitting success than short boys, since their longer reach translates into more velocity along the bat's sweet spot. I tried to be forthright about the kneejerk antipathy to the "gospel of backspin" that I registered as the father of a not-so-tall son; and I surely cannot be alone, even though my response was marred by subjectivity: I continue to feel that the state-of-the-art hitting style is rigging the game against boys of lesser stature. By the way, allow me to observe, as well, that the steep downward stroke's emphasis on upper-body strength created an incentive for young men to beef up some of their frame's naturally weaker muscle groups through performance-enhancing drugs. With success at the plate now invested almost exclusively in the ability to drive the ball way up in the air, it seemed that no batter could inject too much height into his hits. Anything that would accelerate the massive barrel's descent even further was to be desired. Jimmie Foxx, Mickey Mantle, Willie McCovey, Reggie Jackson… they all hit long, long home runs that followed the trajectory of bullets fired from a rifle. Juan Gonzales, Mark McGwire, Sammy Sosa, Alex Rodriguez... their howitzer-shots didn't travel so far but were a danger to low-flying aircraft.

I will not write that such infamous sluggers as the latter did not feature the classic Mac Point in their swing that I described earlier. I haven't made a close study of them, but it appears improbable that their rate of success did not reflect excellent basic mechanics as well as whatever help they may have drawn from a syringe. I know, however, that many young men whom I observed during my son's high school and college career did not and could not drive straight through the ball's center at a mild downward angle. If backspin is a good thing—and, in a glorious day of triumph over prejudice, I finally recognized that it was, in moderate doses—then their quasi-golfing stroke was too much of a good thing. Invariably, they were tall. That's why they were still playing baseball: because they had built up impressive power numbers using the terrible mechanics that the metal bat inspires. Their hits were of three types. One sailed over the fence, of course. Another was the lofty blooper that fell just in front of two or three converging fielders, the outfield naturally playing very deep. These safeties were the blemished fruit of hitting the ball as it passed over the plate: they rolled off the bat's very end if the pitches were low-away, and they fluttered like a dying quail if the pitches were high-in. Then, finally, there were the weak ground balls: the result of the steep swing's starting too early and catching the pitch in front of the plate during a rising, reverse-steep follow-through. Strikeouts were also liberally featured—very liberally... but strikeouts are not a variety of contact.

So here we return to hand position, and I may now attempt to put everything together. The metal-bat power stroke consists of cutting down on pitches, steeply and fiercely, as they pass over the plate. The power has two essential sources: the speed of the bat's descent and the bat's hard metal surface (aided, in recent years, by a pliant alloy in the upper handle that allows the barrel to whiplash). Of course, this latter source dries up in professional ball, and it has also receded (with very telling results) in the college game as the alloy has been required to approximate wooden qualities more closely. That leaves the former: speed of descent. From a "load" position well above the rear shoulder, most boys can never close their wrists to anything within a forty-five degree angle as they attack the ball. (Sadaharu Oh, like so many Japanese sluggers, hit off his front foot, usually making contact well in front of the plate; so the curvature of his stroke actually leveled off as it entered the strike zone, and his wrists would have closed. Consider, too, Albert Pujols' signature outward thrusting of his high-held hands in order to force the handle into his fingers and narrow his wrist angle. Few of his generation understand the advantages of this.)

The imprecise flail of most college sluggers must use the only sources of acceleration at its disposal. Our New Age boys of summer, with the small handle jammed into their thumbs and the heavy weight at the end of a short stick encouraging them to beat on the ball rather than punch through it, do what now comes natural, in a set of very artificial circumstances: they yank their bottom hand down on the pitch and accelerate that hand by driving on it with the top one.

As soon as the rear elbow locks, the top hand flies completely off the bat; and the bottom hand, still gripped above the knob as the mountaineer grips his spike, carries the costly metal miracle into a high finish. Not surprisingly, many hitters who practice that wild finish end up with lower back problems: Gonzalez, McGwire, and Rodriguez all did. Dean Palmer destroyed his front elbow with it.[3]

In an effort to flatten the swing out a little, I'm told that young ballplayers are often counseled now to snap their elevated rear elbow down immediately so that the top hand descends at a milder angle. Outstanding sluggers in whom this strategy is observable include Bryce Harper, Daniel Murphy, Joey Votto, and rising star Michael Conforto. Each of them gets back under the handle with his top hand so effectively that both mitts remain attached during the follow-through. Yet the barrel's descent probably describes a more circular motion in approaching the pitch this way than it would if simply driven down by a top hand that releases. The liabilities of swinging the twenty-first century bat, in short, don't appear to be evaporating.

I will address in future chapters how the stride of a Cobb or a Speaker differed from that of a Musial or a Williams… but I really have nothing more to say about the "leg kick, get your foot down early, keep your balance, hit the ball over the plate" approach. It belongs to the metal-bat era; and the metal-bat era, by restricting severely a lithe body's ability to direct sharp, focused contact on the sweet spot, has produced a new period of waiting all afternoon for a pitch to stray into the small box where attack will prove successful. The game has slowed. Hitters take pitches endlessly, it seems: many third strikes are call strikes. The more lateral "lumberjack" hitter whom Ted Williams evoked was also a great taker of pitches (if he did his job as the Master recommended); but the mobility built into the coil-and-stride action of his lower body allowed for more split-second adjustment. The boy brought up on metal bats, in contrast, doesn't wield his tool like a Bo staff (in Kung Fu) to be fondled, balanced, and then precisely flipped. It's essentially a stone on a string—a mace, to sustain the martial-arts analogy.

Has it occurred to anyone that so many great young hitters may be reaching us from Latin America because kids there are too poor to pay half a grand for the latest Raptor Predator XK Thunderball, but instead learn to hit (like Rod Carew) with the shaft of an old mop or broom?

If those of us with strong prejudices on one side or the other of this "ancients versus moderns" dispute can momentarily suspend our judgment, we will all remain in agreement on one point: today's game at the plate has changed radically from what it was even fifty years ago, and traveling a century into the past would bring us to an alien world.

Chapter Eight

The Hammer's Engine: How the Top Hand Drives into the Ball's Center

Be relaxed and don't wave the bat, don't clench it. Be ready to hit down with the barrel of the bat. Just swing it and let the weight drive the ball.   Paul Waner[1]

"Hit 'em where they ain't," he [Willie Keeler] used to say. And could he ever! He choked up on the bat so far [that] he only used about half of it, and then he'd just peck at the ball. Just a little snap swing, and he'd punch the ball over the infield. You couldn't strike him out. He'd always hit the ball somewhere.   Sam Crawford[2]

    I have explained my gut reaction against the cult of the God Backspin, whose votaries came to his altar with precious metal alloys, contorted themselves into strange dances that sent balls into the clouds, and sacrificed short people by the thousand at try-out camps. I have also openly confessed to my loathing of some of their barbarous practices—not without occasional shame; for Backspin, as it turns out—considered as a friendly woodland spirit rather than a sky god—isn't all that bad. I was so averse to his rituals in my earlier blindness, however, that I paid little respect to the top hand. I joined the followers of Charley Lau in a worship of the bottom hand, whose smooth sweep I assumed would produce level cuts and drive lots of base hits through the infield. The top hand was a kind of freeloader, a parasite. He was just along for the ride.
    I couldn't have been more wrong, if I was trying to reconstruct the attack of great DBE hitters like Cobb and Speaker (Speaker even more than Cobb, as I shall explain later). No doubt, the misleading fact that these two—as well as Fred Clarke, Eddie Collins, and other superstars of yesteryear—were born right-hand dominant yet batted left further persuaded me of the top hand's relative unimportance. I still haven't figured out what key connection might be latent there, frankly; that is, why so many of these immortals batted with their better hand on the bottom if the top was so vital to success. The answer they themselves typically offered was that they wanted a step or two of head-start to first base; but the alternative answer I shall offer tentatively in ensuing chapters is that both hands did indeed make significant contributions. The bottom hand's job, while less involved with power, probably required more intricacy—more "touch." That may explain why right-handed switch-hitters, even when using techniques very different from the ancient approach highlighted here, usually show more power from the right side but a better average from the left. In short, it may well be easier for the weaker hand to supply modest power than to become terribly clever.
    For the explosive impact at the Mac Point comes mostly—though not quite

entirely—from the top hand: that much grows very clear upon brief examination and a little experimentation. How does one generate drive without a lot of coiling and kicking from the body's lower half? Let us consider the fine art of pugilism. Students of the martial arts know that you don't achieve much impact if you throw a punch in a circling motion around the target with your elbow up. That's a natural approach in untrained brawlers, but it mostly produces swollen ears, bruised knuckles, and sprained wrists. The really devastating punch comes straight from the shoulder. The palm turns down just before the knuckles reach their mark, and the shot drives straight through the bull's eye.

The top hand working explosively on a bat varies from this model only in that the palm turns up as the straight line drives through the ball. If I were an anatomist, I could probably explain why such a motion makes best use of joints, muscles, and tendons. (The only person to whom young players might listen more closely than a Hall of Famer nowadays is the therapist who can name every bone in the human skeleton.) All I know is what I have seen working and what I have found to work in experiments. It doesn't hurt, either, to have a celebrated coach on one's side. Joe Brockhoff, once the head coach at Tulane for over two decades, teaches his Super-Eight Hitting System through materials marketed very widely over the Internet. His approach is most certainly not the DBE method in very many respects; but his emphasis of the top hand in a powerful, compact, well-aimed attack upon the ball carries conviction and is convincingly explained. I will defer to his vast experience.

I would say that the entry to the Mac Point has another important resemblance to a potent punch, as well: the last-instant flexing of the top wrist from a limberly bent to a tautly straight-out position. This final straightening accounts for the palm's turning down (in a punch) or up (in a swing). Could you achieve the same degree of acceleration if your wrist were taut all the way through impact? I don't see how. Again, I haven't the education to ramble off the names of relevant tendons and ligaments... but it seems reasonable that smaller, more finely articulated joints would be capable of quicker, more explosive movements. Johnny Mize had reached the same conclusion when, after over 6,000 Major League at-bats, he wrote with blunt common sense, "If you grip the bat too tightly, you will lose coordination when swinging at the ball, for you will be too tense."[3] Or allow me to append another of my analogies in the form of a teaser: would a uniformly fat whip produce the same loud crack from its tail as a more conventional whip with its slimly tapered tail? The answer is clearly negative. Surely something of the whip-effect resides in that wave of force which travels from shoulder through elbow and into wrist.

Slugger Zack Wheat might have preferred the boxing analogy. In the chapter of F.C. Lane's *Batting* titled, "The Secret of Heavy Hitting," Wheat and other stars of yesteryear's game line up to express their disagreement with Babe Ruth. The bone of contention? That heavy hitting results from having a big body swinging a big stick, with lots of arm muscle to do the driving. Zack is only one of perhaps half a dozen interviewees who stress the role of quick hands in clever collaboration. His rebuttal of the Bambino, however, offers much the most detail:

> The strength to hit as I do is in my wrists and forearms. It isn't so much the swing you give the bat as the quick snap just as you meet the ball. That's what drives the ball. It's the same as in boxing. A long, roundhouse swing that comes halfway across the ring and then bumps into a man will shove him out of the way, but it won't hurt half so much as a quick, short jolt from a boxer who knows how to hit. When you snap the bat with your wrists just as you meet the ball, you give the bat tremendous speed for a few inches of its course. The speed with which the bat meets the ball is the thing that counts. You can tell when the ball is going to travel by the quick, sharp crack when the bat meets it.[4]

Manual celerity is of the essence in fighting off the attack both of a human assailant upon one's person and of a baseball upon one's strike zone. What has long intrigued me about Zack Wheat, in particular, is the photographic record's indication that he sometimes almost did the splits in the process of striding. Since his lower body appears anything but passive in these shots, an investigator could easily suppose that he represented a new trend in hitting. In fact, many (if not all) of the photos in question were taken over the period following the Deadnall Era, technically—a dividing line that cut Zack's career rather neatly in two. Of course, that epochal shift was signaled by no one player more than by Babe Ruth. Might Wheat, then, have decided to emulate the Babe in taking all-or-nothing strokes as the home run proceeded to become king? We see in the testimony above that, even if he had made such a resolution, the longer stride didn't impact his keen focus on the point of contact. The ballplayer who is speaking to Mr. Lane here has constructed everything in his stroke around the entry of the hands into the pitch's plane. It all comes to a climax with that "quick snap." Harry Heilmann, another long and level strider of the Twenties, had also extolled the power bestowed by "the quick snap you get in your wrists" just a few pages earlier in Lane's chapter.

By way of contrast, recall what happens to our Iron John of the Metal Alloy Age. The bat held high over the rear shoulder with elbow pointing steeply up into the backstop is his set-up position. No bent wrist snapping taut at the last instant for him: his top hand drives like a piston all the way down, and then releases at once. To bend the wrist from his set-up, indeed, would be almost physically impossible. As we noted earlier, it is precisely this extreme position, so characteristic of our time, that Albert Pujols is modifying when he works the handle farther into his fingers, bending his wrists in the process. I don't think Zack Wheat would have approved of the contemporary paradigm, either—and not because he was addicted to a modest Maranvillian chop that didn't wage all-out war.

We may conclude, therefore, that today's tall slugger with his exaggeratedly downward cut on the ball as it passes over the plate is not necessarily getting the most out of his top hand. At any rate, we will be forced to conclude that what he wishes that hand to achieve has changed drastically from what earlier generations were after.

We can now also qualify, if not dismiss, my original suspicion that the top hand played only a small part in yesteryear's classic stroke. If the top hand were just hitching a lift on the swing, then none of the knuckle-aligning and wrist-bending would matter. Indeed, if the bottom hand were essentially "sabering" at the pitch and the top hand just adding a small initial shove, then the top hand's palm might as well be nestled against the bottom hand's thumb, as one sees in many of today's hitters. (I shall eventually introduce proof that many great hitters of the 1890's, a decade just beyond the horizon of this book's focus, spread their hands noticeably even when they choked up.) Alternatively, the "sabering" hitter, if such a one was yesteryear's, might as well have set up with his bat trailing down his jersey's number toward the ground: a station from which his bottom hand could have sliced down on the ball with just a bit of help from the top hand to ease clearance of the shoulder. I've never encountered any evidence whatever, either photographic or narrative, of a DBE "sticker" doing this.

Ty Cobb left us a lot of tips about his approach, but not always in a form very decipherable today. In fact, many of these tips, as we typically interpret them now, have been universally denounced or derided by expert hitters as hoaxing or delusional. Certainly Cobb's recommendation that the bat be held far out from the body has not aged well. In the present context, I would speculate that one reason for promoting this position would be—like the "knocker knuckles" maxim—to ensure a bend in the top wrist. Cobb admired Speaker and Eddie Collins, specifically, for the degree of bat control they achieved by means of their relaxed, extended hands. "These two depend largely on science for their averages," he concludes one statement approvingly (after mildly castigating Lajoie and Joe Jackson for a less disciplined approach).[5] If you hold an old-school bat (a yard long, more or less) straight out from your body and no higher than the armpits, one thing that happens is that the top wrist will bend; another is that it will preserve the curl through entry into the Mac Point, especially if the barrel is allowed to droop a little in a limp, poised wait for the pitch. The image that materializes within these parameters seems more than faintly reminiscent of Rod Carew, I might add.

Pardon me if yesteryear's illustrious Three Horsemen lure me into brief digression… but I would speculate that Speaker may have had a more potent swing than Cobb. (Records vary for these remote times, but indications are that Cobb had about five more extra-base hits than the Grey Eagle after two seasons-worth of additional at-bats.) I have been nursing this suspicion only lately. Part of what draws me to it is that Cobb's technique—the strangely extended hands that rocked back and in as he strode (it turns out) and the side-by-side, bent-kneed legs that sprang into a long stride—appear awkward and improvised, not smoothly dynamic. (We have little enough film evidence for such claims to be made, yet much more than is available for others of Cobb's era before Ruth). I believe, to use my own term, that Cobb was somewhat closer than Speaker to "sabering"; and of Collins, I feel even more secure in that assertion. The few photos revealing Eddie's follow-through are yet sufficiently numerous to suggest that he had no distinctly characteristic finish. Eddie, in other words, was just getting his hands to the ball, apparently, without much thrust from below the belt, and those hands ended up wherever the instantaneous attack took them. He was likely more of a slasher than a hammerer.

To return to the top wrist's curl… picture for a moment a black-belt karate king coiling into a defensive pose as an assailant approaches him. His hands lift loosely before his face, almost as if holding an invisible globe—and his wrists, of course, bend. This is the position from which his blows will acquire maximal acceleration. The Cobb-style batsman has his wrists in a very similar position as he waits to identify the delivery. Everything going on in his poised coil—the straightly lifted front leg, the top hand no higher than the strike zone's highest reach, both hands extended from the body, the bat head allowed to dip (unless the hitter happens to be Cobb himself)—contributes to facilitating a quicker-than-the-eye burst into the Mac Point.

Even a DBE hitter of the Punch-and-Judy style popularly ascribed to the Gay Nineties would have observed most of the elements reviewed above. (And there may not have been as many lightweights back then as is commonly supposed: like Cobb and Speaker, Dan Brouthers and Buck Ewing both extended about a third of their safeties to extra bases.) The gentlemanly single-pinger's leg-lift might have been slight (more of that soon) and his enlistment of the body's muscular core therefore reduced; his top hand might have rested well below the armpit, and both hands might have projected almost straight out from his jersey's buttons rather than shifting farther back. Yet if the bat head loosely overhung the plate, as it typically did before the century's turn, then the top wrist would bend. The fundamental components of the hammer's slightly downward smack would all be primed for action.[6]

I should clarify the "hammer" analogy in this somewhat altered setting. Obviously, the contestant wielding a sledge at the carnival would not bend his wrists for a directly downward blow as much as would a hitter aiming somewhat laterally at a pitched ball. Yet neither would his wrists be strictly straight and taut as he lifted the hammer's head. You may make the simple trial yourself. The wrists want to bend as the hammer is "loaded" higher. They seem to know, with a wisdom of the blood bestowed upon them by Mother Nature, that a stiffening and straightening into the point of impact will give them their best chance to ring the bell—but that locked joints and tight muscular flexure before that instant will make them, in Johnny Mize's word, "tense."

Finally, I suppose a few comments must be devoted to the top hand's position in the follow-through, especially since this issue excited such controversy in the wake of Messrs. Lau and Hriniak. It seems a non-issue for the hitters of a century ago. Photographic evidence strongly implies that the overwhelming majority of DBE successes kept the top hand on the bat all the way through a high finish… most of the time. But the type of pitch thrown or the pitch's location must sometimes have determined how thoroughly the hands would conform to the prototype. The objective was to get barrel to ball with maximal acceleration—not to execute a suitable-for-framing flourish at the end. A famous photo of Eddie Collins shows his legs twisted around like an ice skater's coming out of a pirouette as his bat trails far behind him in his bottom hand, almost dragging the dirt. In a sense, I suspect that the faintly bizarre contortion in this shot is routine. I think strikers like Collins would have taken flight like Mad Sweeney of Irish legend if it would have won them a single. Though Collins (as suggested above) may have been the most adaptable and fluid of the lot, his compatriots were cut from the same cloth. They seem to have manifested no great worry about preserving a certain posture in the swing's execution. In fact, releasing the handle early on a stroke intended to retain it in both hands turns out to be a good split-second adjustment to a change-up or breaking ball. If you routinely release the top hand, however, then trying to keep it on the bat when a high hard one suddenly bores in on you presents much more of a challenge.

In short, the two-handed stroke was likely the default motion from which impromptu reactions could be launched effectively. Two hands can readily shift to one, but one can't very well shift to two. We see this illustrated in the photographic record of Honus Wagner, whose finishes end up in every posture but a pretzel's (perhaps more so than Collins's, because Wagner *does* have a lot of lower-body thrust driving him and never seems under full control). Napoleon Lajoie's biographer, David Fleitz, claims that the Frenchman had "perfected a one-handed swing" that gave him extraordinary range, and soon after cites New York Giants pitcher Amos Rusie to the same effect (viz., "He lets go his bat with one hand as soon as it meets the ball").[7] It would be unwise to argue with Rusie, who was an eye-witness from close quarters; but the more common truth in the case of free-swingers is that they released the top hand as needed—not that they did so invariably.

In any case, when trying to reconstruct the stroke of 1900, we must surmount our contemporary notion of the swing as a copyrighted creation reflecting the batsman's unique style the way brushwork reflects a painter's special gift. In an era when executing hit-and-run plays and spoiling pitch-outs would be considered mandatory skill sets for any hitter, one couldn't get too caught up in this or that inimitable personal flourish. Walk-up songs bristling with individuality were a long, long way down the road.

To return to the follow-through, we may safely generalize that a hand coming sharply down into a ball will have to rise with extreme abruptness through the hyperbola's counter-curve. This is because the original vector of attack into the ball carries the hands so far forward so quickly that, once they reach the anatomical "end of the line," the wrists must reverse the barrel's direction in very short order. The bat's head necessarily flies up. That so many top hands in so many old photos indeed finish up so strongly over the front shoulder must be read as evidence of their powerful linear descent an instant earlier.

Yet all the photos, testimonies, and experiments in the world remain mere indications. I see no need to move from description to prescription. If I may compare our ancient superstars to an aging circus clown, I personally have much more difficulty keeping my top hand on the handle all the way through when I attempt the "hammer" stroke from my right (or strong) side than when I do so from my left (or weak) side. I've noticed the same tendency in Honus Wagner, Napoleon Lajoie, and other artists who employed a style broadly similar to Cobb's and Speaker's—yet who batted with their stronger hand on top. When the weaker hand is on the bottom, it may not always be "smart" enough to whip the knob around so nimbly that the top hand can remain aboard.

One further thought on this subject: the reason that one-handed finishes are more common in players who throw and hit from the same side may have something to do with the lower body (which will occupy more of our discussion as we proceed). If your strong side dictates your approach to every facet of the game, the leg on that dominant side may very well launch into the pitch with such force that the weaker leg doesn't know how to catch all the thrust and allow the top hand to finish high over the front shoulder. Honus Wagner and Willie Mays had enormous, incredibly explosive strides thanks to their being almost unnaturally high-waisted; and, though their hitting styles were far from identical, neither could reel in his striding leg (I would suggest) in time for the top hand to finish routinely on the bat. Both also possessed huge hands and used massive sticks, which somewhat obviated the need for pinpoint contact to generate power. A lot of poor contact would have produced dying-quail safeties because fielders had to play these two stunning specimens so deep.

So for Nap Lajoie, who was also a big man—very big for his era. Two scholars of yesteryear's game have lately encapsulated his swing as follows:

> An expert bunter who was capable of hitting the ball to all fields, Lajoie was nonetheless completely undisciplined at the plate, regularly swinging at pitches down at his ankles or up at his eyebrows, and occasionally thwarting attempts to intentionally walk him by reaching out for those pitches, too.[8]

I shouldn't be surprised to learn that he, as well, exploded into the pitch with a backside drive capable of launching his lead leg out of the box. At some point, one must believe that thrust of this order would prove capable of disrupting basic mechanics; and it seems that Lajoie, particularly, was more susceptible to extended slumps than a Cobb or a Collins.[9] Yet to equate the one-handed finish with an all-out blitz on every pitch is entirely unjustified. Just because a flailer tends to let the bat escape his grip doesn't mean that everyone who favors a loose grip is a flailer.

Frank Frisch, high follow-through

Switch-hitter deluxe Frankie Frisch, the Fordham Flash, carried DBE techniques into the next generation. Here we see the classic finish from Frank's weaker left side: weight transferred vigorously to front leg as the back foot trails around behind and top hand high over the front shoulder after driving down-and-through. The pitch was likely a bit up and in. Had it been lower and more over the plate, the finish would have wrapped far above the front shoulder. Photo courtesy of the National Baseball Hall of Fame Library in Cooperstown, New York.

Chapter Nine

Identity Crisis: What the Bottom Hand Did NOT Do in 1900

I was a contact hitter who sprayed the ball around, hitting behind runners and stuff like that. I had always been a good hitter, but my first year in spring training [with the Detroit Tigers], 1953, I was given three or four hitting instructors, including Joe Cronin, who taught me three or four different ways to hit: one to chop down, one to swing level, one to swing up, one to swing inside out. It was confusing. I was a front-foot hitter, but they were teaching me to hit off my back foot. Harvey Kuenn was hitting line drives off his front foot. He was the best front-foot hitter I ever saw. They didn't try to change him, and he went on to be a batting champion. But they tried to change me, and I think it hurt me.   Coot Veal[1]

It now appears that we have relegated the bottom hand to the negligible role of parasite, bequeathed to it by the newly redeemed top hand. How suddenly fortunes change! For a while, as I stumbled through the dark forest of naïve misconception and bad coaching advice, the bottom hand had been my saber-wielding hero. In my revised view of yesteryear's classic swing, however, he has been demoted to a court jester, pretending to be important and hoping for a few crumbs to fall off the table.

Except that my esteem for the bottom hand's role never fell this low, even when I found myself betwixt and between theories: I always knew that it must be doing something important. The most mature wisdom of today holds that it guides bat to ball. Coach Brockhoff says so in his videos, and he adds the helpful analogy (for those of us who think in analogies) that it "shines the flashlight" of the bat's knob upon the incoming pitch. Wonderful image! Yet it scarcely helps to explain the DBE batsman's approach, for his bat was often already comparatively low as he awaited the pitch, and a very simple forward move would have flattened it. The flashlight was already pointed in the right general direction.

Furthermore, the "flashlight" explanation implies that the bottom hand has little or nothing to do with power. This may be true: we certainly have to consider that possibility in the DBE stroke after seeing how much power the top hand provides in driving the barrel straight through the ball during a short, concentrated "hammer" attack. Yet Ichiro and other Japanese hitters today manage quite well by "running" through the box, more or less, and trailing the bat behind them with their lead arm. This is also essentially the style of many successful softball players (in leagues, I mean, where the ball is pitched very fast).

Frankly, with Lau's *Art of Hitting .300* beside me and my young son's future on the far horizon, I had made my boy a stellar nickel-and-dime batsman by using an Ichiro-like approach. That is, the bottom hand kept the bat back as the stride shifted weight dramatically forward. Indeed, once the hitter was leaning decidedly upon a firm front leg, the lead arm was supposed to be completely stretched out to the rear, elbow locked. This resulted in a saber-swipe that was both formidable and level. Only when later coaches tried to integrate their backspin-calculation into my design did something unworkable emerge—something like a wheel spinning on an axle skewed to the ball's plane of flight. They and I were both responsible; neither parent nor coach achieves the total meltdown in a typical boy's batting average all alone—it's usually a collaborative effort. Mixing several styles of hitting can turn out as unhappily as mixing up the blueprints of several aircraft. A saber that moves like an arrow fired from a cockeyed carousel by means of a hammer is probably less suited to driving baseballs out of parks than to driving ballplayers out of their minds.

As noted earlier, I once heard Rudy Jaramillo (when he was the Texas Rangers' hitting instructor) talk about the "stretched rubber band" effect (might as well throw in another metaphor) of tensed front-rear separation in the swing. The batter was to produce this effect as the front foot came down, just before "pulling the trigger" on the backward-stretched hands (maybe the same metaphor there: one *can* shoot a rubber band, after all). I thought I was having my son do this very thing by jamming his bottom hand hard a-port as his lead foot went hard a-starboard. (We've definitely gone nautical now.) The results, as I have written before, were very encouraging: not many extra-base hits, but reliable contact and a slew of bounding base-knocks. To my mind, these humble singles were better than the majestic pop-ups that end many a lad's hitting career.

What none of us, man or boy, really seemed to understand in my experience was how much this variety of lower-hand hacking depended upon throwing the front hip. To get power out of such a swing, you have to stretch that rubber band until it wants to snap: hence my own lunging stride as a boy when I hit with my better hand on the bottom. Without a viciously aggressive stride to lead it, the bottom hand simply doesn't have enough energy to drive the ball hard. Other things being equal, the only way you can obtain power from a short stride such as the Lau/Hriniak method promotes (Gwynn and Boggs occasionally had no stride to speak of) is to adopt the preeminent contemporary approach: i.e., drive down on the ball severely. And then we veer into the hostile territory of tall boys hitting long flies and short boys hitting cans of corn.

Other things needn't remain equal, to be sure, if we turn the clock back a little: not nearly as far back as the Deadball Era, either. You can start allowing the top hand to drive through with reinforcing assistance if you adopt a Fifties style. Then the bottom hand, however, can no longer be quite such an effectively stretched rubber band. Instead of coming directly forward after the long stride, it has to yank upward as the top hand, punching down and then carrying around the front shoulder, describes the only geometric shape that it possibly can: a very lopsided hyperbola, starting short and steep and ending on a long, majestic curve. I'm a natural righty myself; and when I would hit right in my halcyon days, the top hand always tried to steal the show from the weaker bottom hand. I strode less far, my bat dipped more, and I mixed an annoying number of pop-ups into my long blasts. With the apologies that every pygmy owes when throwing his puny shadow on the toes of a Colossus, I can recognize those tendencies in a lot of great switch-hitters.

Such a top-handed, hip-throwing sweep creates the uppercut so characteristic of Fifties and early Sixties sluggers: Mantle, Matthews, McCovey, Snider, Colavito, Killebrew[2]... and even a big ne'er-do-well kid named Willie Kirkland. The other guys learned to control a fundamentally out-of-control approach somewhat and keep their head from pulling off the ball routinely. Kirkland ended up in Japan. I have no doubt that coaches were shouting at him constantly—at least on this side of the Pacific—"Stay back! Stay back!" That was the mantra, at the time: take the long stride but stay back so that you put a ferocious uppercut on the ball. Oh, and don't turn your head away.

More classic coaching counsel: utterly contradictory and impossible to execute. In the opening quotation of this chapter, you can see what the hitting gospel of the time did for—or to—a mild-mannered Georgia boy named Orville "Coot" Veal. Within a few weeks, four different coaches had urged Coot to hit four different ways. The only thing they could agree upon was staying back. What was it that old Seneca wrote? *Argumentum pessimi turba est*: "If you want to find the worst way to do something, take a poll and go with the majority." It seems to work for hitting instruction, anyway.

Throwing open the front hip powerfully, in the patented Ted Williams manner, actually impedes the top hand from driving straight down through the ball. It does so by forestalling forward weight transfer and making the barrel enter the ball through a dipping curve (as opposed to a straight line) as the body pivots tightly over the back foot. This is the famous (or infamous) uppercut swing. Back in the Fifties, its advocates held that contact occurred *after* the barrel had completed a short descent and as it began its long rise; and indeed, the swing would likely turn much more linear along that protracted upward slope. Problems crop up with finer analysis, however. For one thing, the ball runs considerable risk of being topspun rather than backspun whenever the barrel is ascending; and for another, I don't think effective contact can actually have happened along the rising plane very often. The ball would almost certainly be pulled foul, even if not topspun. On a relatively high and inside pitch, a limber, lanky, "wristy" kid like Ted Williams might have stayed inside the ball enough to keep it fair; but I have a strong suspicion that even the Splendid Splinter struck most of his four-baggers while the barrel was in its descending stage (and hence not uppercutting).

I shall revisit this critically misrepresented issue of "uppercut swing dynamics" in Chapter Fifteen. The notions clustering around such dogma are contradicted by the mechanics of the DBE swing (and I'm sure that the hapless Coot Veal's "swing down" hitting instructor was an old-school loyalist who just didn't understand his articles of faith or else couldn't teach them). Emphatic hip rotation is ultimately not compatible with the concise "hammer" stroke. Any such rotation has to be reduced in order for an ideally linear-downward delivery to the Mac Point to take place through a significant part of the strike zone. The lower body must work so as to allow a more decisive forward weight shift.

Obviously, I'm now talking about the lower body instead of the bottom hand; and almost as obviously, I hope, such discussion is not entirely avoidable, since the thigh bone's connected to the hip bone, etc., etc. What I would like the reader to understand at the present juncture is just that one of hitting pedagogy's most sacred cows—the rotating hips—can easily work against the top hand's straight, true drive into the ball's center *and also* against the bottom hand's straight downward slash into the ball (a point somewhat buried in the digressive remarks above, I fear). In the Williams model, the bottom hand follows the opening hips outward, jerking the handle laterally and scarcely pulling down at all: it can no more preserve the slightly downward line than can the dipping top hand. In his excellent manual for young players, Major League pitching coach Bob Cluck writes, "A hitter should drive the knob of the bat (bottom hand) down in order to obtain a level swing." Precisely! Cluck's illustrative photo is matched with another showing (in exaggerated form) the lateral bail-out of over-active hips.[3] This seems a fitting moment to emphasize for the first time (and I'll return to the point) that the "hammer drop" in fact produces an amazingly level stroke as long as the batsman's weight is properly shifted forward. Line-drive backspin is best imparted at a *slight* downward angle. Mr. Cluck has noticed this; but he, like too many other coaches and players of later days (such as Coot Veal), has been introduced only to grotesque misrepresentations of yesteryear's "swing down" catechism.

Weight shift again: I can't seem to clear that hurdle and arrive entirely at the hands—because, of course, the two are so intricately connected. Perhaps, when working off a tee in the cage, one doesn't notice how hip-flipping and rocking back pulls the bottom hand laterally and makes the top hand dip; but in a game, where uncooperative pitchers tend not to tee up their offerings and things get very rushed, the hitter's intended vectors of force can be separated from the executed stroke by dozens of degrees. It's a natural reaction to fall back when a pitch gets on you too fast. It speeds the bat up. Unfortunately, it doesn't help to direct the barrel to its objective. The Williams engine proves to be high-maintenance because the least little stress throws its wheels and sprockets out of kilter. It needs time to keep in check its various latent contradictions. Hips are driving parallel to the ground and away from the plate. The bottom hand follows them. The top hand tries to drive down into the pitch and straight toward it: a meeting most likely to produce good contact *before* the uppercut if the pitch is low and almost past the hitter. (Then we might see the towering home runs so familiar to us today: Mickey hit those as well as the topspun bullets.) A heck of a lot of pieces are trying to move in their own distinct direction.

A decisive throw of the front hip, I might add, also commits the hitter in a fashion that allows for little correction in the case of mistiming. At the previous chapter's end, I proposed that Collins, Wagner, *et al.* were really good at getting a piece of the ball even when they were fooled. A swing that is essentially anchored over the rear foot, in contrast, will not have much mobility should the hitter have to reach a bit farther than he anticipated.

I have now spent most of a chapter explaining what the bottom hand did *not* do in the linear "hammer" swing of Cobb and Speaker. What options are left for it?

Chapter Ten

Spread Hands: How to Drive a Whirlybird's Blade

"Power" is not just hitting home runs. With a hands-apart grip, I once hit a pitch by Chief Warhop [sic] of the New York Highlanders that ripped the glove off Harry Wolter in deep right field and broke his finger. I used to love to choke up and smash them at Hal Chase at first base for New York—the kind that carom off the knees of an infielder and leave him limping for days. You can make a ball ring like a bell off the right-field fence with a choked grip, and never doubt it. Again—timing.   Ty Cobb[1]

The [bottle] bat is almost like a paddle with the weight on the hitting end. I don't swing it very much but punch with it, and I can place hits pretty accurately. The handle of this bat is wound with tape. Ordinarily I choke up on the bat, but some times I will slide one hand down to the end of the handle and swing more like a slugger.   Heinie Groh[2]

    We have established that the top hand was the driving force in the compactly hammering, relatively linear DBE swing, but we haven't yet clearly assigned a dynamic role to the bottom hand. It certainly had one: it wasn't just steering the bat like a couple of fingertips rotating a state-of-the-art sportscar's wheel. We spoke of pulling downward at the end of the previous chapter. That's a start. A further clue (and a vital one, in my opinion) lay in Ty Cobb's signature spread of the hands. Photographs abound which show a good three inches of wood between Cobb's top and bottom paws. Indeed, I think he must have showboated his grip for the camera: it appears as commonly with his face as a stare into the clouds after a finished stroke does with the Babe's. I confess that the hand-spread fascinated me from a very early age, probably because I saw baseball cards as a boy that featured Leon Wagner employing the same grip. In those days, kids on the playground and coaches alike would mock anyone who spread his hands. The usual taunt was that it was a "girl's grip." Well, one of the "girls" who used it piled up over 4,000 hits, and another would have finished his career with over 400 home runs if he hadn't tired of being traded and gone into acting.

    There's scarcely any notable hand-spreading in the game today because there cannot be, thanks to the bat's physical specs. A stick of 32 or 33 inches doesn't allow much latitude for the upper hand to "cheat" a little closer to the barrel. It also offers no substantial advantages to the move. Metal bats, especially—but the wooden models engineered to approximate them as narrowly as possible, too—are designed to be whipped through the zone as both hands crowd the knob. With their short length, they need to utilize every stingily created inch of projection to cover the plate; and with most of their weight concentrated in the barrel, they really don't give a feeling of significantly greater control if one hand crawls farther up the pipe-thin handle. Even if any hitter today knew the true benefits offered by hand-spreading a century ago, therefore, he would be unable to access them now, thanks to Space Age technology (unless he could dig up an old-school bat somewhere). Progress claims another victim!

In times gone by, hand-spreading was in fact anything but rare. I cannot account for why it is attributed to Cobb by his many biographers (not including the meticulous Charles Leerhsen: see below) as a unique innovation, unless because so many commentators of Cobb's own day also made this attribution; and for that, I can account even less. Cobb himself would observe to the curious that Honus Wagner would sometimes spread his hands.[3] (Who knows if he ever saw the Wagner named Leon? Since he died in 1961 and Leon was an unknown before the Angels' birth in expansion, it's unlikely.) Was this modest reference to a single contemporary Cobb's way of accepting credit, otherwise, for the stratagem? In the two volumes of *Deadball Stars* produced for SABR, Max Carey is very clearly displaying the spread-handed grip to the All-American Girls Professional Baseball League; Dode Paskert models it on a club with an enormously thick handle; and Elmer Flick features the comparatively restrained spreading of a more explosive hitter.[4] Speaking of explosions… photos of Eighties and Nineties powerhouses like King Kelly, Harry Stovey, and Sam Thompson plainly show the spread, as well as others of singles-punching contemporaries like William "Sliding Billy" Hamilton.[5]

Now, Cobb would not necessarily have been aware of this extensive provenance. A boy from a semi-rural Georgia Southern Baptist household would but rarely have encountered a baseball card secreted in the wrapper of some Yankee distributor's tobacco product. Though many professional practices would likely have percolated through to the hinterland's most remote playing fields, the boys on those fields would seldom have been able to point to a celebrity in Philadelphia or Boston who championed their favorite style. Yet the relative silence both of Cobb and of the Fourth Estate about hand-spreading as of, say, 1910 is a conundrum. One of the photos of Tris Speaker reproduced for this book shows his hands very visibly spread.

Let the preceding remarks, at any rate, suffice to prove that whatever hand-spreading achieved was being or had been achieved by many distinguished players by 1920. I suspect it will shock most readers if I here propose that bat control was not the greatest of these achievements. Ty Cobb, among others, would disagree with me. The hidden advantage I have discovered, however, is one of those "lying in plain sight" solutions to a great mystery—the hardest kind to spot, you might say. In Edgar Allen Poe's "Purloined Letter," the thief of a top-secret document mingles it with the daily mail in a tray at his front door. Would Poe's brilliant detective, Monsieur Dupin, have been able to figure out that hand-spreading can actually enhance bat speed? He probably would have beaten *me* to that conclusion, anyway. I needed years and years to crack the case: a shameful number of years, considering how transparent is the effect.

Back to Cobb. In his vexingly short book, *My Life in Baseball*, the Georgia Peach asks that we imagine ourselves holding a ten-foot pole and being charged with touching its end to a point on an adjacent wall. He observes triumphantly that we would, of course, spread our hands so as to gain better control of the wobbly stick.[6] Being no stranger to analogies myself, I will append another. Imagine that you had to swing said ten-foot pole as quickly as possible (after exiting your house, of course). Picture it as bamboo or something else light and fairly rigid, such that the wobble isn't much of a factor. Would you not spread your hands to do this, too? Why? Is it only because your top hand would move closer to the center of gravity if you slid it upward, thus enhancing control? I think not. I think the major advantage would lie in your bottom hand's being able to drive in a direction more or less counter to the top hand's. With one hand pulling backward at the stick's base as the other hand pushes forward, the increase in acceleration would be dramatic, especially if footwork were restricted; and while a batsman's footwork is certainly not restricted by any *a priori* rule or law, he will need to rely upon his hands as much as possible for acceleration if he's facing a very hard thrower. I don't know what factor or exponent should be assigned to this acceleration—but I or you or anyone would be able to feel the difference, because it's not slight. The more the spread between the hands, furthermore, the greater the factor (at least until the bend in the wrists begins to diminish).

Please note, once again, that one can generate this speed merely by deploying the hands: its production is completely independent of all additional bodily motion. In other words, the maneuver would be ideal for a hitting approach with very little lower-body movement. Heinie Groh was a "punch" hitter of this sort: he describes himself as such in the second citation above. His freakish "bottle bat" (last used by Nellie Fox, as far as I know) was actually thickest just above the top hand's hold, where it flared out dramatically so that the pesky batsman of this variety could fist the ball past infielders. Yet when Heinie occasionally made a bid for a little power, notice the manner of his adjustment: he moved his bottom hand down toward the knob—not both hands, just one. *He spread his grip.*

I'm certainly not suggesting that Cobb, Speaker, and their cohorts likewise made scant use of their lower body. More modest "place hitters" (see Chapter Nineteen) of their day like Groh, however, did little kicking and stepping; and the superstars themselves, as well, probably reduced their striding when down in the count or in critical situations. In this "work together by moving against one another" action, the hands would be empowered to impart to the bat a stunning degree of acceleration within a very narrow window of space and time.

Think of it in the following way (analogy alert): if the bamboo pole that Ty Cobb gave us were shortened to a more manageable four or five feet, and if you were trying to loft the thing into the air with the spin of a helicopter's blade, how would you go about it? Obviously, by pushing with the top hand and pulling with the bottom hand. With a little practice, you could achieve a very impressive "whirlybird effect" even if you were sitting on a stool. The hitting artists who used this technique to greatest advantage must have devoted more than a few thousand reps to getting it down pat.

The proof that the lower hand might be used thus powerfully even among

Golden Age home-run kings is as nearby as my childhood hero Leon Wagner, who clubbed 173 homers from 1961 through 1966 while keeping his average around .275. I have a hunch that Daddy Wags may have been a bit near-sighted. Players of that era who were marked with the stigma of being "butcher outfielders" may often have needed corrective lenses—but their myopia, apparently, would either pass undiagnosed or else be ignored by them out of false pride (or fear of release). Tommy Davis was tagged with the "butcher fielder" label early on, and he eventually donned glasses. Paul Waner, from an era when no star would be caught dead in spectacles, became the subject of several urban legends about his foggy eyesight (some of which had him simply suffering from hangover or a pre-game draught of the time's favorite Performance-Diminishing Drug).[6] How, I ask, could a guy too clumsy to catch a fly ball hit 37 home runs one year (Wagner), amass over 3,000 hits (Waner), or for two straight seasons lead a league in hitting that contained Aaron, Mays, and Robinson (Davis)? I don't know what Tommy's secret was; he eventually wore glasses at the plate, and maybe it started in 1962. But the other two most definitely spread their hands. Quickness and power when you can scarcely even pick up the rotation on the ball... that would be pretty incredible, if it were true. It would mean that hand-spreading could be the most significant secret weapon to have lapsed from the arsenal of the contemporary hitter.

Seasoned ballplayers will be turning their hawk-eyes away from these pages along about now, for all of them know—or think they know—that no mortal human being can possibly achieve success at the plate without good eyesight. But my digression on Great Myopics of the Game is neither entirely facetious nor all that much of a digression. For some reason, a lot of star batsmen struggled with severe sinus problems in the Twenties and Thirties that affected their eyesight and shortened their careers.[7] George Sisler lost a full season to the malady and never recovered his peak form;[8] Jimmie Foxx had some of his teeth extracted because of it and also never fully hit his stride again.[9] Chick Hafey very reluctantly acceded to his doctor's advice and wore spectacles in 1931—resulting in his winning a batting crown; but his sinus-related vision problems persisted and curtailed his career, too.[10] The air of major northeastern cities was laden with some pretty unwholesome stuff during these decades. (Several dozen people in Stan Musial's factory-filled hometown of Donora, Pennsylvania, died one week when a high-pressure system trapped the valley's exhalations.) The science of ophthalmology was virtually in its caveman phase, many a hitter's vision was far less than one hundred percent, and yet... and yet, strikeout rates were still a fraction of what they are today. Sisler actually had a couple of fine seasons even after his eye troubles began.

The only way a hitter could possibly continue to succeed in such circumstances would be to use his hands extremely well: only the hands could make last-second adjustments and generate split-second power to bail out a fellow who wasn't picking up the ball's rotation. The method I am describing now would have provided such resources. The bat isn't really committed beyond the "check" point until the bottom hand pulls the knob into the body; and if the bottom hand executes this move with the top hand poised an inch or two above it, the commitment can be both lightning-quick and very potent. A guy with bad eyes who hits .300, in short, must be doing something really effective with his grip.

Yet the hand-spread remains so dubious to us nowadays that Charles Leerhsen reduces Cobb's deployment of it to a feint—a trick, almost a gimmick.

> He held the bat with a split-hands grip—unusual but not unique—that allowed him to make a last-second decision, to choke up and poke the ball over an infielder's head—or slide his top hand down and swing for the fences (which, in the deadball era, were roughly a million miles away).[11]

I immensely admire Mr. Leerhsen for redeeming Cobb's reputation as a human being from the predations of serial liar and unprincipled sensationalist Al Stump. A writer who does such good work can only be a good person. Yet his book is somewhat mysteriously sourced on points like these, and he has not seen fit to reveal to me where he heard or read the explanation above. Perhaps Cobb himself was the source—or perhaps Cobb's account was garbled by the master of melodrama who took his dictation; for in the text ghostwritten by Stump, the aging warrior supposedly describes his famous three-homer outing against the St. Louis Browns thus: "With the choke grip, I merely slid my left hand down the wood as the pitcher delivered and locked it with my right and took a full swing."[12]

This sentence is malodorous from a number of angles. What is the "choke grip"? A grip where you choke up? Are we to assume that it includes spread hands? Did Cobb, then, also employ a grip with no choking up at all? If he slid the top (i.e., left) hand down, then he still wouldn't be on the knob, because the bottom (right) hand would also have been choked up. Did he wait until the delivery was started (as Leerhsen is convinced) in order to hatch a surprise on the pitcher? But this would only have worked once on that fateful afternoon as a surprise, and supposedly he sprang the move three times. Did the pitcher and the other Browns not "get it"? And why does Cobb uncharacteristically not even give the pitcher's name—for in most of his yarns, his little triumphs are intricately indexed to the habits of the particular hurler. Whatever Cobb did to put Ruth in his place on this occasion, it couldn't primarily have involved a neat but of trickery… or if it did, is the supposedly Babe-envious Southerner conceding that Ruth actually has the better trick up his sleeve? Is that the gist of the story—that Ruth suckers pitchers into throwing him gopher balls?

I find Cobb's self-portraits of his batsmanship often misleading or confusing; but the sample above, honestly, looks more like a bid for drama and even caricature, as the ever-imaginative Stump constructs a scene where Cobb the wily snake figures out a way briefly to rival the Olympian Bambino, and then crows about it in his final days like a Scrooge counting up his coins.

And by the way… you may note later that the "fake 'em out" theory of the hand-spread is incontrovertibly contradicted by a photo in this very volume showing Cobb in mid-swing. The bat and hands are blurry (which is why so few such photos were attempted at the time: the hand was quicker than the camera shutter's eye); yet the spread between the hands has plainly been preserved—neither the top nor the bottom appendage has slid to touch the other. Cobb was *not* joining his hands before he swung.[13]

And by the way... after a swing, almost anyone's hands will be joined on a wooden bat and *sans* batting gloves. The follow-through carries the top hand onto the bottom one. A few sluggers with very dominant top hands might have resisted such slippage, since their stroke was an almost ursine one-paw swat. I've seen a photo of the pre-Ruthian dynamo Gavy Cravath demonstrating this possibility... but we're discussing a more resourceful species of hitter. Sorry, Gavy.

A similarly bewildering dismissal of hand-spreading as a potent tactic appears in Jan Finkel's description of how Honus Wagner made use of it (and I very much doubt that Finkel is the source of this misconception any more than Leerhsen is of that regarding Cobb's spread hands):

> ... he gripped his 40-something-oz. bat with huge hands several inches apart, allowing him to slap an outside pitch to right or to slide his hands together and pull an inside pitch down the left-field line.[14]

At least here we find that the spreading was more than what football players call a "juke": it is the agency of a dynamic undertaking. The only problem is that the undertaking makes no sense. Why would anyone spread his hands to take an outside pitch the other way? Those were the precise situations in which Wagner would most likely release the top hand early. On inside pitches, rather, would he most eagerly want to put that hand to work which was closer to the barrel—and probably *not* to pull the pitch down the line if it was a fastball. Thick handles favored other options, and Ty Cobb confides, "Wagner almost never pulled the ball."[15] These ingenious theories have to me the look of guesses originating in sources that have never actually spread their hands on anything wider than a keyboard.

And despite everything I have written about how inhospitable the shorter bat of today is to hand-spreading, the arcane practice didn't suddenly die out: like an old soldier, it faded away. The late Ernie Banks spread his hands slightly on occasion. So did Andre Dawson. Even Ted Williams would adopt the tactic in a pinch, as one good shot of an actual game-time follow-through betrays (not those spiraling, incredibly "hippy" poses that Ted liked to strike for photographers when no pitch was traveling at him). A few contemporary stars do in fact continue to incorporate a very faint hand spread, though quite difficult to discern on television and beneath batting gloves. Andrew McCutchen springs to mind, and his teammate Josh Harrison will sometimes spread the grip with two strikes. I have lately caught Nelson Cruz in the act, as well. Who knows how many big-leaguers today covertly retreat to the strategy at key moments? Of the three just mentioned, by the way, Harrison and Cruz appear to employ longer-than-average sticks.

I might add that a really good spread of the hands on a fairly long bat (i.e., not the kind of grip we find anywhere today) would likely also have assisted the batsman when he was fooled by a ball's break or its slow speed: in other words, when he had to reach for it. As the lumber moved forward, already committed, the top hand could slip down upon the bottom one before tightening and driving into the Mac Point, thus allowing the barrel to shoot a little farther from the body. In cases of badly deceived judgment, such as I myself often suffer through when hitting off live pitching, the sliding top hand may have released the bat fully during a frantic reach; but it may well have imparted enough juice to the awkward stroke to dump a "flare" just over the infielders' outstretched arms—and that last-instant power surge would come easier with the top hand closer to the barrel. I think such a lightning adjustment would surely have happened instinctively, without the necessity of any rehearsal. Yet the canny hitter would probably become aware that it was occurring because of the hand-spread, and would have been happy to have one more little advantage on his side.

But back to the matter of acceleration for one last point... Coach Brockhoff's "flashlight on the pitch" dictum to young hitters raises the following question that I should love to put to him some day. "Why do you think this 'flashlight' business works, Coach Brock? I agree that it's great advice, but *why* is it so? Is it because the bottom hand guides the stroke with greater accuracy by shedding an imaginary beam on the ball—or is it because the move equates with a pull of the knob into that centered line which the top hand intends to power through?" Of course, I would be asking what attorneys call a leading question. I'm fully convinced that the bottom hand (with or without hand-spacing) pulls as the top hand pushes in any great "wrist hitter's" stroke. Not only that: in such hitters, there is almost as frequently a bottom-hand "mini-load" in reverse direction—a backward-pushing coil of the lower wrist that prepares its hand to pull hard through the pitch's path as the top hand enters the Mac Point. This "back-and-forward" flick of the bottom hand would be a further accelerant; for a lot of movements in baseball (and other sports) involve a preparatory movement in reverse direction that strengthens a driving attack. An arm draws back to throw forward. A foot whips back to kick a soccer ball hard and low. The bottom hand flicks the bat's knob away from the ball for a split second, I submit, because it's about to pull that knob very hard into the ball's path: also known as "shining the flashlight".[16]

Now, Coach Brock—and anyone else with half an eye and an ounce of sense—would agree that our tall, backspinning human pop-up machine never gets his flashlight's beam on the ball. With the handle pressed deep into his bottom hand, whose thumb is fully wrapped around its hold, he must yank down from above his rear shoulder as the top hand throws and releases. Since the top hand isn't driving straight through the ball, the bottom hand cannot accelerate its action with a coordinated pull through the ball. As far as mining the potential of a powerful dexterity is concerned, our tall young man trying to become the latest

Ryan Howard might as well be Captain Hook.

Even though they may not know it, therefore, I would argue that some of today's best hitting coaches are essentially preserving a bottom-hand tactic of the great DBE hitters in resisting the "big throwdown" of the tall, lanky fellows. The "flashlight" image seems merely to dramatize an instant in the critical "snap of the wrists" that accelerates the barrel's linear descent. Now, if today's hitting guru could just introduce his disciples to longer bats and a hand-spread...

Ty Cobb, set-up position with spread hands

Classic Ty Cobb: feet close together, probably touching by the time his knees bend (in preparation for a long, lunging attack into the pitch); arms held out from torso (where the extended bat will roll down and somewhat back to conserve balance once the leg is lifted); hands spread wide (so that the bottom one may accelerate the barrel by drawing back and in just as the top one drives down and through); and top wrist curled (the better to throw an impactful punch into the pitch). The thronged bleachers show that this at-bat is "for keeps." Photo courtesy of the National Baseball Hall of Fame Library in Cooperstown, New York.

Author, set-up typical of 19th-century promo shots

Though my 35" bat (now impossible to find in any chain store's rack) is closer to Ty Cobb's than Sam Thompson's in its "modest" length, my style is otherwise an attempt to copy the set-up position in which late nineteenth-century strikers liked to be photographed for baseball cards and other promotional material. I would have choked up much more if I'd had a few more inches to work with. The bottom hand is poised to "lever" the knob out from the body in preparation for drawing it sharply back in as the top hand drives through the ball. That top hand should remain almost stationary during the load phase. The wrists are loose and curled so as to cradle the bat in the fingers, and thumbs and forefingers are also not gripping tightly at all.

Chapter Eleven

A Shot in the Dark: How Lower-Body Movement May Have Assisted the Downward Stroke (Part One)

Shoeless Joe Jackson, along with Rogers Hornsby the greatest of the right-handed hitters, stood with his feet close together. Joe usually marked a line three inches from home plate and then drew a line at right angles to it. He stayed back of the right-angle line, behind the plate. As the ball approached, he took a slow, even stride, starting his swing in unison with the stride. None of that wide-spread, dug-in stuff for Jackson.   Ty Cobb[1]

[Wee Willie] Keeler could bunt any time he chose. If the third baseman came in for a tap, he invariably pushed the ball past the fielder. If he stayed back, he bunted. Also, he had a trick of hitting a high hopper to the infielder. The ball would bounce so high that he was across the bag before he could be stopped.   Honus Wagner[2]

     As the subjunctive mood of this chapter's title implies, I am entering deeply into the realm of speculation. I'm very certain about this much: DBE batsmen did not employ a single lower-body strategy in firing their crisp linear blow into the pitch. I speculated earlier that hitters like Keeler and Maranville who loved to choke up outrageously would have been dealing sharp smacks to the ball mostly out in front of the plate. They would have met even the low-outside pitch as it was just reaching the dish, surely; for they stood far forward in the box as well as toeing its inside chalk line. At most, they might have administered a "controlled throw" of the bat as an away pitch passed, allowing the sizable length of handle up which they had climbed to slide between their fingers.

    Anything of this nature would have made their stride little more than a bending of the knees, as if to bunt. Using a similar approach with his bottle-bat, Heinie Groh simply set up in the box fully facing the pitcher.[3] This would somewhat obviate the plate-crowding striker's need to open up (or "clear the hips," as coaches say today) on inside pitches. Whether squared to the field of play from the start or by use of a loose-kneed swivel, these authors of many singles would need do no more below the belt than support a presenting of the hands anywhere along a plane more or less parallel to the plate's forward side.[4] They must have been quite proficient at punching hits through holes in the infield. The punches must have been brisk ones, though; for balls struck using an approach such as theirs would need to have a touch of exit velocity, or else infielders would have cheated well in on the grass to cut off their bid for a safety.

    I should imagine that all the batsmen just named were "dusted off" regularly in an age when pitchers insisted on owning the outside corner. Bench-clearing brawls certainly occurred, but not over such "righteous" actions as a hurler's claiming his part of the plate. These pesky strikers, then, would have had to master the art of hitting the deck—and the Rabbit appears to have done so. Keeler was struck by pitches much more often, but probably because that was essential to his game. Groh twice led the league in being hit by pitches, but only with the meager figures of 13 and 11 (further evidence that this generation knew the fine art of dodging bullets). Really and truly, why would you want to drill a guy who choked up almost to the trademark? Why would you want to walk him? Two of these three didn't do much of that, either. (Groh had ten seasons of 50 walks or more, once leading the league.) They reached base by hitting, and they reached base a lot.

Now, I should perhaps have noted earlier that we really can't assume hitters like Keeler and Maranville to have employed a drastic choke all the time (though Sam Crawford's comment about Keeler at Chapter Eight's beginning seems to affirm as much). A few almost comical photos mean very little. I've seen shots of Henry Aaron in the same pose, with hands halfway up the bat—and I don't recall that such was *his* usual grip! If our old-time poster-children for the extreme choke-up didn't always employ said grip in the heat of battle, however, many of their contemporaries must sometimes have resorted to it who were never photographed in so compromising a posture. Let us recognize that even a relative slugger of the day like Honus Wagner occasionally allowed his hands to creep far up the handle, and not to bunt. When players made such a maneuver, they were committing themselves to minimal lower-body activity on that swing.

I think we can also begin this critical stage of the discussion, though, by conjecturing that some of yesteryear's great hitters characteristically had little lower-body movement, regardless of the game situation. It was their habit, their style: they were pretty stationary from the waist down. The strategy is still broadcast occasionally from third-base coaching boxes today: "Lose the stride! Just use your hands!" Such words of wisdom seem especially to fly under the flag of "two-strike hitting"—and in that capacity, I would certainly not deride them. Yet the movement of the feet remains critical (in the sense of decisive) even when eliminated, for its elimination has major consequences just as very active footwork does. Naturally, some things are more critical than others. I stand by my claim that the Mac Point is that vital hotspot of the swing from which all else must radiate.

Let us further recognize, though, that the lower body determines precisely where the Mac Point's dynamic explosion will be aimed. A Keeleresque, bunt-like pivot would allow it to slide virtually anywhere in the strike zone, but would also deprive it of any driving force except from the top hand. I don't think today's coaches are recommending that hitters square as if to bunt by advocating a two-strike "no stride" approach: they're merely simplifying the element of timing (or concentrating it entirely in manual dexterity, to be exact). Yet leaving the hands thus free to react to the pitch—"see the ball, hit the ball"—doesn't mean that even the quickest hands can necessarily put a ball in play from a given location. The lower body holds the answer to such questions. What is a typical hitter of these times, for instance (feet at shoulder-width and toes on a line parallel to plate), to do with a low-inside pitch? Smack it off his forward shin?

For unless he pivots so as to reach that pitch before it crosses the plate, contact may well have some such exquisitely painful result.

Since I'm going to require several chapters, it turns out, to handle issues involving the lower body, perhaps I can best spend the remnant of this one in underscoring the complexity of the puzzle. Keeler and Maranville are "minimalist" cases. Their feet and legs must merely have worked so as to give the hands a straight shot at the ball, more or less as an office-trolley's wheels might spin to let the payload on top—a camera, a projector, a telescope—bear directly on its task. I have reached this conclusion by inference, and the same sort of reasoning has led me to conclude that Cobb and Speaker were doing something much more energetic. All we have for virtually every player of the Deadball Era by way of evidence is photographs: "stills," snapshots, sometimes taken in the heat of battle, sometimes staged for the photographer (and hence prone to the distortions of theatrical posing). The 1909 and 1912 American League home-run leaders—for Cobb and Speaker each led the American League once in that "power" department—have left a photographic record of very active footwork (as well as, in Cobb's case, a precious smattering of video footage). I find the evidence fairly reliable, furthermore, since many of the photos I have seen were clearly taken in the course of either live practice or a game.

In Cobb's case, the feet are extremely close together at one point: almost touching. As the swing proceeds, the front leg lifts relatively straight and stiff… but here's where speculation can take flight (with both legs lifted and wings spread wide) even though one supposes oneself to be studying the physical act recorded on sequential frames. "Movies" of the time (and, as just noted, these were uniquely abundant for Cobb) can be highly deceptive. Their technique is little advanced over that of drawing Mickey Mouse with his hand ever rising for ten times and then flipping the cards to represent "bye-bye." I have viewed what few extent sequences of the Cobb swing I can locate over and over… and still I am bothered by the sense that something has slipped away between the frames. When not artificially slowed down for modern viewers, furthermore, these old newsreels simply speed through the "gaps" and produce the effect of pressing a fast-forward button.

How much emerges with any clarity from such dubious testimony? This much: a) there is no "leg lift" of the modern variety (*á la* Arod—"Get your foot down early!"); b) there is no fluid, sweeping backward dip of the front knee followed by the aggressive hip-roll (*á la* Musial and Williams); but c) there is also no high, knee-locked lift of the front leg that drops it almost in the fashion of a pitcher's stride (*á la* Mel Ott and Vic Daviglio). In fact, what I see resembles B more than C. I had expected to see something more like C than B because, after all, this is the "hammer stroke." It's supposed to be succinct and direct. In Chapter Nine, I attempted to explain in fine detail (and perhaps succeeded in introducing too much detail) why the highly rotational, hip-action Musial/Williams stroke pulls the direct downward chop out of alignment. If this chop was the focal point of what every great DBE sticker wanted to accomplish, how could the greatest of them all (arguably) be selling out the line for the curve to such a degree?

I think something like the following is going on with Cobb. He is attempting to get off his back foot—to shift his weight as decisively forward as possible—by starting with his legs side by side. Were they farther apart at shoulder-width, then retracting the front leg would "cock the hips" (in the Williams phrase), and the stride would function more to open up the front hip than to shift weight fully forward. The result would be more rotational than linear. The foot-to-foot stance, in contrast, allows the batsman to fire off at the pitch like a dart. It impedes the roll of the hips. Cobb assumed this stance with the addition of a bend in the knees—a modest crouch. Knees that are bent tend to straighten out—to move up—if they do anything at all; they are virtually precluded from executing any long fore-and-aft movement. As for holding the hands straight out from the torso, this also seems to me to minimize any swaying, circular motion in the upper body. It keeps the various vectors of force pointing more or less forward. While Cobb's hands did in fact slip down and rearward as he strode (in a bit of a hitch—practically universal at this time), he was allowing the rest of his body to "outrun" them rather than pumping them independently. From some of his comments, one even draws the conclusion that he thought they remained stationary right before his chest until they attacked the pitch: e.g., "You cannot connect with maximum force by hugging the bat—it is exactly the wrong mechanical hold."[5]

I mentioned much earlier an old Stan Musial recording given to me by my father where The Man urges a very modest stride upon young hitters—this from a slugger who measured out most of the batter's box from where he retracted his front foot in a coil. Cobb's "awareness" of his stride's energy is almost as comical; yet at the same time, it contains useful, even fascinating insights:

> As to striding, the fatal error is to over-stride. It causes upper-cutting and fly balls, the upsetting of co-ordination and costs you the freedom to step in or out on the ball. As you stride, the hips and shoulders pivot forward on a level line and the arms come around in synchronization.[6]

I suppose if Ty were comparing himself mentally to teammate Zack Wheat, he might have considered his own forward lunge to be rather chaste… and his diagnosis of how the uppercut may intrude into swings with unhappy consequences perfectly conforms, after all, to our analysis earlier in this book. Though the comments above once again reach us through the unhelpful medium of Al Stump, they have no Ruthian fish to fry and appear to be pretty straightforward. They indicate that Cobb was keenly alert to his method's dependency on a linear stroke for its success, and also that he had calculated why upper and lower body both needed to attack the ball more or less simultaneously if the line was to be preserved. (No emphasis on stretching the rubber band here!) If I might anticipate a key point at this chapter's end, finally, the remark about how uppercutting destroys the freedom to step in or out on the ball unavoidably implies Tyrus's belief in his ability to *step where he sees the ball coming*. More of that later… but notice for now that uppercutting would have no inhibitive affect whatever on stepping in or out *unless the step's direction were being determined as the stride was in motion*. Cobb would reiterate that claim on numerous occasions.

Now, Cobb's "feet together" stance seems unique to us, but it was by no means unfamiliar in turn-of-the-century baseball. Standing straight up at the plate (with or without upper-body crouch—i.e., with feet close together) was almost typical for a time. Ed Konetchy, "The Big Bohemian," was said to assume his position very erectly.[7] Indeed, the classic pose of Eighties and Nineties strikers as they awaited the blaze of the cameraman's flashpan was a disarmingly board-like one, with front foot pointed outward in the pitcher's general direction: not exactly what we call an "athletic position" today. There's a significant difference, however, between standing erect and standing with legs pressed together. From the former, one might simply have lifted hands and front leg in tandem as a "load up," then dropped them—also in tandem, more or less—upon the incoming pitch. Though I have viewed no moving footage of a DBE hitter executing this motion that I can attach to a particular name, solid narrative evidence of it exists (which I shall offer at the present chapter's end); and, besides, I have uncovered no other series of actions that takes us from the "tobacco card" pose to a hammer-stroke—straight into the ball and slightly downward—with a finish close to the body and high over the shoulder.

So was Konetchy another Buck Ewing, or were his legs actually as close together as Cobb's? More to the real point, was the Nineties "lift up, let down" style still in vogue just before Ruth (who, by the way, set up with his shoes almost rubbing one another), or was Cobb's straight lunge from back foot to front becoming the rule of the day? If the latter, then Tyrus could fairly be considered something of a transitional figure between the straight, slightly downward attack and the rotational, barrel-dipping methods that Joe Jackson and Zack Wheat were pioneering. This all leaves Cobb looking like a rather odd bird to me, the least of whose oddities was the celebrated hand-spreading. To launch so far laterally into the pitch and yet to preserve an essentially linear cut isn't easy to do, and wouldn't be easy (I should imagine) to keep in trim.

And could Babe Ruth, yet more shockingly, be less pioneer (as he's so often treated) than throwback? I noted parenthetically above that he assumed his hitting posture with feet side by side. From there, however, his stroke became quite vertical in comparison to Cobb's. His heavy barrel dipped down to balance the weight shift involved in lifting his front leg stiffly (the notorious hitch again): then it lifted as the foot boldly advanced, and both descended with a force that made the Bambino famous. I don't know that most of this picture would have varied significantly from the stroke of Big Dan Brouthers—who, while no harvester of homers in their dozens (nobody else was, either, in those years of the sluggish ball), set impressive distance records with some of his clouts.[8] The sheer ponderousness of Babe's lumber clues us in that he was driving down into the ball rather than rotating toward it; for a heavy bat readily descends into a pitch, but is virtually impossible to sling smartly at it from swiveling hips. Cobb's bat, by the way, was relatively short and light for the times.[9]

Then we have Ruth's well-documented front-foot hitting, which sometimes left the rear foot airborne on contact, and his high finishes, bat snugged up beside or over the front shoulder. If this isn't nineteenth-century power-hitting, then the one clearly distinguishing factor is the grip of the bat down on the knob. For commentators of the time, as we have seen, the grip alone was often cause enough to announce a major news event. One thinks of all the ink spilled by reporters about Henry Aaron's marvelous wrists, as if everything else in the Aaron swing fell out of a cookie-cutter.

In terms of the lunging lateral stride, at least, Ty Cobb is closer to Honus Wagner than he is to Babe Ruth. Honus is the subject of some of the most dramatic and perplexing still shots on record. One represents him as taking a immense, Mays-like stride into the pitch as Hall of Fame catcher Roger Bresnahan almost stands up to receive a high strike typical of the era. Another shot shows the Flying Dutchman completing a swing in a painfully awkward position. His trailing back leg is several inches clear of the ground as the forward leg catches the full weight of his massive, low-bent torso; and the top hand remains on the bat as it carries fully around the front shoulder—but around that shoulder rather than over it in the high finish characteristic of most DBE sluggers. In the excesses of his lateral attack, Wagner could have been the Roberto Clemente or Hunter Pence of his day, less a study in elegant precision than in fall-on-your-face, all-out assault.

We rarely have verbal testimony from the parties involved, to complicate an already complex situation. When we do, it's often on the order of cliché and truism elicited by some publisher who wanted to cash in on a great hitter's celebrity. For example, Jimmie Foxx and Johnny Mize (who, of course, were already decades removed from the Deadball Era) put their names to such pabulum for adoring boys as, "Choose a bat that feels good," and, "Wait for a good pitch." If the Ten Commandments had been so accommodating, none of us would ever have to worry about sinning.

And then, from the other direction, we have on rare occasions some shockingly provocative nuggets from the players themselves. Ty Cobb authored perhaps the most outlandish of these. Some of posterity's baseball minds have concluded that Cobb couldn't have known what he actually did with a bat in describing his swing so implausibly; others, with less charity, charge him with trying to mislead future generations or deliberately claiming the impossible to elevate his heroic status. The assertion that elicited these testy reactions? Cobb's claim that he directed his striding foot to where he saw the pitch coming (see n. 6). Ted Williams would have none of it: yesteryear's hurlers may not have broken the 90 MPH barrier as often as today's; but even at 85 miles per hour, positioning your front foot in reaction to the pitch's cutting inside or tailing outside simply defies belief.[10] The human body is not capable of such rattlesnake-reflexes; and much as certain commentators seem willing to attribute to Cobb several qualities of a rattler, this kind of speed is not on their list.

Personally, I incline to take the Georgia Peach at his word to this extent: I believe that he at least supposed himself to be executing so incredible a feat. After all, Honus Wagner made the same claim—and he added that Fred Clarke had taught him how to do it.[11] We must conclude, even if we remain skeptics about the actual deed, that certain DBE hitters (the best of the lot, in fact) were bringing their hands forward at more or less the same time as they touched their front foot down—for in no other way could they even have acquired the (perhaps mistaken) impression that they were striding in response to the pitch's path. This is vitally important evidence. It rules out the primarily rotational swing, and also any progenitor of the hefty "get that foot down early" leg kick in conjunction with extremely high-and-rear hands. A kick or coil with low hands rising at the same time, in contrast, is a distinct possibility.

And just to finish our sketch of Cobb's stroke... if Ty was following so hard upon his striding foot with his hands that he could believe one to be leading the other directly into the swing, then there's little "stretching of the rubber band" happening in those Mickey Mouse movies. The man wants to get off his back foot quickly and utterly *and* he wants his hands chasing his front foot forward. That must have been what I saw, or what I didn't see that fell between the frames.

Honus Wagner, set-up deep in box

Honus Wagner, one-handed follow-through

Honus Wagner, two-handed follow-through

The Flying Dutchman calls to mind neither an elegant schooner nor a sleek albatross in these photos, but something more on the order of Clever Hans wrestling an ox under either arm. Wagner was a formidable physical specimen, beyond doubt. How much of his dazzling success at the plate was owed to technique rather than to long arms and massive hands of almost superhuman proportions is anybody's guess. The top photograph shows him standing nearly in the far corner of a scuffed-up batter's box (with hands slightly spread, upon careful inspection). Hall of Fame catcher Roger Bresnahan prepares to kneel behind him; and a famous photo (not featured here) of Dutch taking an immensely long stride indeed seems to belong to a later moment of this same at-bat. The middle exhibit reveals an early release of the top hand (and the bottom hand's slipping down to the knob), probably in response to a breaking ball or low-away pitch. Finally, we see Honus (obviously on a different occasion) driving through with a strong top hand and shifted emphatically—almost alarmingly—onto his forward foot, hammering the pitch (perhaps an outside "hanger," perhaps a low-away fastball that he allowed to reach the plate) to the opposite field in the manner for which he was famous. Taking all three pictures together, we can deduce something of the DBE hitter's resources. The objective wasn't to look pretty: it was to get hits, however possible. Photos courtesy of the National Baseball Hall of Fame Library in Cooperstown, New York.

Chapter Twelve

A Second Shot at Footwork: Lower-Body Movement and "Striding to the Pitch" (Part Two)

Ty Cobb and some others used to say the direction of the stride depended on where the pitch was—inside pitch, you'd bail out a little; outside, you'd move in toward the plate. This is wrong because it's impossible. It is only 60.5 feet from pitcher to batter. If the pitcher throws the ball 90 miles per hour, it takes less than 0.40 second for the ball to reach the batter, even without allowing for the four or five feet the pitcher comes down the mound before releasing the ball.   Ted Williams[1]

Tony Gwynn and Larry Walker are two examples of hitters who use the inside-out swing. Successful hitters get the bat head in the plane of the ball early and maintain that plane longer (using good extension), thus increasing their margin for error. If a hitter uppercuts, his bat head is first below the hitting place, on it for a short time, and then above it. If he hits down on the ball too much, he will be above the ball, then on it briefly, and then below it.   Bob Cluck[2]

    Let's summarize the results of the previous few chapters.
    Many successful hitters of the late Nineties probably lifted their hands and forward leg up stiffly and then brought them down again as the ball approached the plate. These movements were orchestrated so as to be very nearly in unison. The hands seldom strayed very far to the rear during the whole process. Their acceleration into the ball was assisted by choking up and/or spreading out on the handle. The downward step was not a hip rotation, primarily, but rather a decisive shifting of the weight onto the front foot. Such a shift would ensure that the hands could make their linear drive into the pitch at a slightly downward angle that offered the best chance of productive backspin.
    How far this style may have carried over into the new century is as yet hard to say. (As we add further pieces to the puzzle, we will be able to speculate more confidently.) Ty Cobb, at any rate, is not a devoted practitioner of the antique style. He still wants to impart a linear cut down into the ball, and he still does this by thrusting virtually one hundred percent of his weight onto the forward foot. His arms are also still rather stiffly projected from the body, implying his intent of having the hands preserve a downward-sloping line of entry. George Sisler (we may add here) also endorsed holding the hands well out from the body.[3] Yet Sisler, Edd Roush, and other high-average batsmen of the time seem to have combined the succinct cut with more lateral movement than one would have observed two decades earlier. Cobb is perhaps the most pivotal figure in this transition, for he added a vigorous, unequivocal forward stride to the mix—quite a long lunge when measured from the foot-to-foot starting point. (Cobb's published censures of over-striding appear to target pulling away from the pitch:

in other words, restraining the weight from a fully forward shift and, thus, introducing more rotation.)[4]

The rotational swing is in some ways much more complicated than any of its precedents. The long strides of Joe Jackson and Zack Wheat suggest that an otherwise Cobb-like lunge into the pitch has here been liberated from any attempt to unify the hands with the lunge; for in these hitters, the hands remained back until the front foot touched down, creating the "stretched rubber band" effect. A bit ironically, though Babe Ruth is credited with ushering in a new era of slugging with a new kind of stroke, he had little more in common with these rotational tactics (his claim of copying Jackson notwithstanding) than a close-footed starting point and a close-handed grip down on the bat's knob. To view the Babe as an exemplar of the Nineties style with peripheral modifications might be more accurate.

One variety of batsman appears to have slipped through the net of the summary above. Even though Honus Wagner has already been mentioned several times, he fits comfortably into none of the brackets just posed. Wagner and Napoleon Lajoie were both front-foot hitters; they both employed an extreme forward weight shift to guide their stick into a linear, downward-sloping attack. Yet they do not seem to have preserved as much control over their stroke, once unleashed, as that most notorious of free-swingers, Babe Ruth. Their long legs also did not stride smoothly into an opening of the hip, as one would have observed in Wheat or Harry Hooper. What exactly was going on with them?

A crucial bit of evidence, I think, is that both usually stood well back from the plate. F.C. Lane writes:

> Honus Wagner had a very awkward position. As Barney Dreyfuss said, "He stands so far back from the plate that it would seem difficult for him to reach the ball going directly over the rubber. But notwithstanding this, he hits balls that are on the outside with apparent ease."[5]

Ty Cobb's description of his beloved rival (legend would have them enemies, but in fact Cobb and Wagner often camped and hunted together in the off-season) concurs and adds some color: "His style looks almost awkward to me as he stands far back from the plate with his feet apart and his elbows flapping from his sides as if he were about to fly."[6]

Lajoie chased after pitches off the plate perhaps even more relentlessly—because he made so much solid contact with them, no doubt.[7] Nap's pose for a photograph reproduced in the 1916 *Sporting News* card set tells the whole story almost as well as a video would have done. His feet are spread as wide as they'll go without the back one's actually leaving the ground, and the front leg has severely closed him up with respect to the incoming pitch—which, in this case, is making an imaginary transit: it's all a pose for the cameraman. What is most obligingly revealed, however, is the mid-swing posture that cameras of the day could not capture clearly in the instant of live execution. Like Hans, the

Frenchman would have been set up very far away from the plate and then have dived into the pitch.

We know that Rogers Hornsby did something very similar. I have seen mobile footage of the Rajah taking a cut (apparently in the 1928 World Series). He was known for hitting the ball to the opposite field (right field, in his case); and the stride from extremely far back in the box—as in far away from the plate—was bound to have contributed to this skill. Lane describes him as a hitter who "stood far back with one foot on the rear line of the box and away from the plate. He stepped forward, however, and toward the plate when he swung to meet the ball."[8] Roberto Clemente (and, to a lesser extent, Pete Rose) would display the same proficiency decades later. Wagner and Lajoie had almost certainly embraced this *modus operandi* at the turn of the century—with far less plate discipline and bat control than Hornsby, to be sure. Outside pitch: release top hand and chase ball the other way. Inside fastball: fist the delivery the other way with the help of the bat's thick handle. Breaking ball or off-speed pitch: one-hand the ball, again, and pull it a long way with the help of the heavy bat's descending barrel, whose momentum will suffice to put a backspin charge into the impact.

Now, honesty compels me to infuse into this discussion Hornsby's firm injunction, "Never hit off the fore foot. Never lift your rear foot off the ground."[9] We know that the previous generation often ignored that advice—and when the outside pitch is chased so aggressively that the rear foot goes airborne, the barrel may indeed lose its straight attack and dip down in too sloppy a curve to stroke a line drive. The advice here is thus not really inconsistent with a hundred-percent weight shift: it only prescribes a *controlled* shift. After all, among the photos and on the dust jacket of the book wherein the Rajah issues this warning is a shot of him finishing a swing lifted erectly over the front leg! As we've seen before, any advice about length of stride, shift of weight, and all the rest must be read in the context of common practice during the time when it was uttered.

Ty Cobb insists that Wagner would wear out opponents by hammering the ball deep to right.[10] One such ambush could account for that famous photo of the awkward finish, torso leaning heavily over bent forward knee. Where Honus (and Lajoie) would have differed from Cobb is in their lunging into the plate from far back in the box and releasing the top hand, more often than not, to let the heavy stick continue powering along a downward slope. The difference, in other words, would not have been in the lunge itself, though many observers would probably have located it there. Wagner and Lajoie had gangly limbs and huge hands; Cobb was tall for his time but regularly proportioned and slight of build. The various adaptations to the energetic forward shift detectible here seem entirely attributable to differences in body type.

For Cobb himself was no stranger to opposite-field hitting; on the contrary, he affirms that he almost always approached an at-bat by trying to hit the ball the other way (to left, in his case).[11] F.C. Lane testifies, however, that the Peach typically chose not to dive toward the plate as Wagner and Lajoie would have done. "Ty Cobb, Eddie Collins, many other great batters, often hit while stepping away from the ball."[12] In the same chapter, Lane informs us that the these two liked to set up very close to the plate, as well. Again, we must be very careful of appearances, which are leading us in opposite directions: Wagner and Lajoie stood far from the plate and strode into it, Cobb and Collins stood close to the plate and strode away from it. If we pay too much attention to directional arrows, we will overlook a deep similarity of method. Consider: all of these superlative "stickers" are taking a forceful lunge from their back foot in a bid to shift weight forward; and they wish to do that, once again, because the bat needs to describe a straight line cutting somewhat downward. The two big boys are content to have the full thrust of that drive pouring into the outside pitch—so torrentially pouring that their top hand often relinquishes the bat and they almost fall headlong (while moving toward first base, happily). The ordinary pitcher probably can't resist trying to sneak one by on that outside corner where they achieve such power, despite advice from veterans. The two slender lads, in contrast, are likely to get worked inside thanks to their crowding the plate. Such pitches are readily dragged for hits, but they can also be fisted the other way for bloop safeties. (In our own era of thin handles, we have forgotten that this is entirely possible.) Striding away from the plate, in fact, brings the meatier part of the handle to bear upon a pitch aimed maliciously at the hands. And for good measure, if a breaking ball or off-speed pitch comes wandering in, striding away from the plate may facilitate its being pulled with power.

What really interests me about this foursome is that two of them explicitly laid claim to adjusting their stride to the incoming pitch. Wagner further extends the claim to Fred Clarke, from whom he learned the technique; and Fred Clarke appears to have been a very similar batsman to Eddie Collins. (The origins of his career in the nineteenth century make his style a little harder to trace—but both were righties who hit left and landed about every fourth safety for extra bases.) Confides the Dutchman to F.C. Lane:

> Fred Clarke, who was one of the wisest baseball players I ever saw and a great hitter, taught me the foot shift as an aid to batting. I have always depended upon the foot shift ever since. I always stand on my right [i.e., rear] foot when I am batting. The weight of my body comes on that foot. But I stand in such a manner that I can shift my left foot around. You can cover a good deal of ground by shifting that foot. You can step away from the plate to hit a ball close up or you can lunge right into the plate to hit a ball that is on the outside.[13]

Now, Wagner is none too clear about just what's involved in this "foot shift." We see a recurrence, however, of those associated with it being practitioners of what I have called a forward lunge—a lateral thrust to shift weight fully forward and allow the barrel's hammer to fall on the ball. If there is any sort of footwork out of which a hitter might be able to make a split-second adjustment as the ball is in flight, this would be it. The lunge might be cut short if the pitch is riding inside, for the foot never leaves the ground in a pronounced lift. The lunge might even be steered outward, if we are to belief Honest Honus, on that inside pitch (a bit of tap-dancing which, I confess, leaves me incredulous). Cobb and Collins, having set up close to the plate, could have slid open a little more on the tight one or have adjusted their stride to run more parallel to the pitch if they saw it riding low and away. (For it seems to me that the hands—they're shadowing the feet all the way, remember—could reach out from the body and check an opening stride far more easily than anything could throw the closing stride of Hans and Nap back open.)

Of course, all of this is speculation; but I would rather conceive of a way in which our remote sources might just be telling us the truth than insist that things could only ever have been done our way and ascribe all oddity to deception, thick-headedness, or window-dressing. Opposite-field hitting actually creates a lot of possible split-second adjustments for the hitter who gets a little fooled (whether or not stride-trimming is one of these). It has always done so. From Orlando Cepeda to Julio Franco to Ichiro, professional batsmen have made a nice living off of letting the ball get deep and, occasionally, reaching out to wallop the one that tricks them into starting their swing early. At the masthead of this chapter, I quoted Bob Cluck on the inside-out stroke of Tony Gwynn and Larry Walker. "Inside-outing" has a lot to do with shifting the weight forward and letting the hands trail behind. That's exactly what has been under discussion here in the context of several great DBE hitters. Coach Cluck opts to celebrate the level plane of the swing... but how does one swing level? The weight shift is a large part of it—but the straight, slightly inclined stroke is, once again, at the heart of the matter; for, paradoxically, "down" is "level" as long as rotation is minimized. Yes, the plane of a falling barrel would intersect the plane of the ball's flight only at one small juncture if we're just doing static demonstrations in geometry class: every hitting guru from Cluck back to Williams has felt the need to repeat this warning to the obtuse.[14] What the great hitter is looking for, though, is *an extended stretch over which barrel will contact ball following a modestly up-to-down vector.* As long as the lower body can bring the weight forward in a lift (recall how Cobb's bent knees straighten in the stride) even as the hands pursue their linear slope, such an extended "happy zone" can be entered.

Personally, I found replication of Cobb's style to leave me feeling quite awkward (just as Tyrus found in Wagner's stroke something reminiscent of an awk trying to fly). Yet it produced results, especially on the high hard ones. Today's player can scarcely imagine what striding away from the plate while trailing a thick handle can yield by way of low lobs to the opposite field. And Cobb would surely have been pitched high and tight very often: pitchers of the day weren't at all shy about "giving a shave" to a batter on top of the plate, particularly when he projected a fearless, arrogant air. Strangely enough, the trajectory of my experimental "Cobb lobs" ended up reminding me of Tony Gwynn's patented "oppo" hits; and Tony Gwynn, short bat and all, bears a certain resemblance to a left-handed Wagner. The closed stance, the one-handed finish that allowed the barrel to continue down through the ball as far as possible... these are significant overlaps in the technique of two hitters occupying far polarities of the century and having very different reputations for selectivity. Cobb's inside-out stroke, then (if you'll forgive me for making a bridge of Tony Gwynn) probably dropped balls into the opposite field on fairly Wagnerian flight patterns, only without the power.

Like Gwynn and Walker, the DBE players mentioned in this chapter were doubles-machines. Cobb ranks behind only Musial, Rose, and Speaker, and Wagner and Lajoie remain in the top ten. Doubles generally find a gap, and they're usually line drives. Those who stroke them tend to hit to all fields—which means that they first must master the off-field. So the elite fraternity that we're characterizing, which runs at least from Larry Lajoie to Larry Walker, can hit hard, low shots from line to line. Joe Jackson actually doesn't break the top forty.[15] Hornsby does. Zack Wheat... no.

Speaker, the chieftain of this clan, came within eight doubles of 800—far and away the highest tally ever. But where, by the way, is Tris Speaker in our discussion of the lower body? I don't think we have yet captured his style with the necessary accuracy. Another chapter must be devoted to that.

Author, alternative sequences of DBE swing

    A   B   C   D

    E   F   G

The Nineties Swing: based on the fragmentary evidence available mostly from baseball cards of the 1880's and 1890's. Though Shot A might almost be mistaken for part of a follow-through in both of these sequences, it instead represents a position which many of yesteryear's batsmen struck shortly after stepping into the box, as the pitcher received the signs. The weight veers forward in order to shift back in the second frame (B)—and the rear foot can also anchor itself somewhere in the box not anticipated by pitcher and catcher as they exchange signals. Obviously I have chosen to draw closed and move back from the plate as the pitcher begins to come set.

    In C, the pitcher has begun his wind-up, and my forward foot is slightly raised, with knee virtually locked. I'm faintly bent over the plate, though still erect. With the low bat as a balance, I can wait out a confusing series of gyrations—tapping the front toes, if need be. Then, in Shot D, as the pitcher starts his move home, the front leg stiffens—still without much lift as the top hand pushes outward and holds the handle in place during the first instants of the forward shift; hence the hands appear to float to the rear. I'm now poised to drive down into the pitch instantaneously, perhaps even adjusting my foot placement to the ball's perceived flight (as incredible as that sounds).

    These movements flow into E, where I have made the decision to swing. Whatever "stretched rubber band effect" occurs is now maximal. Next the front foot is down (F); and hands have almost simultaneously accompanied the descent, working in parallel-reverse fashion (the bottom hand pulling the handle into the torso as the notably higher top hand drives the barrel out and down). Ideally, contact would occur here, at the Mac Point. Notice how close to the linear, with my weight having shifted fully forward, the angle of contact has become. The high follow-through (G) lifts my rear foot entirely off the ground.

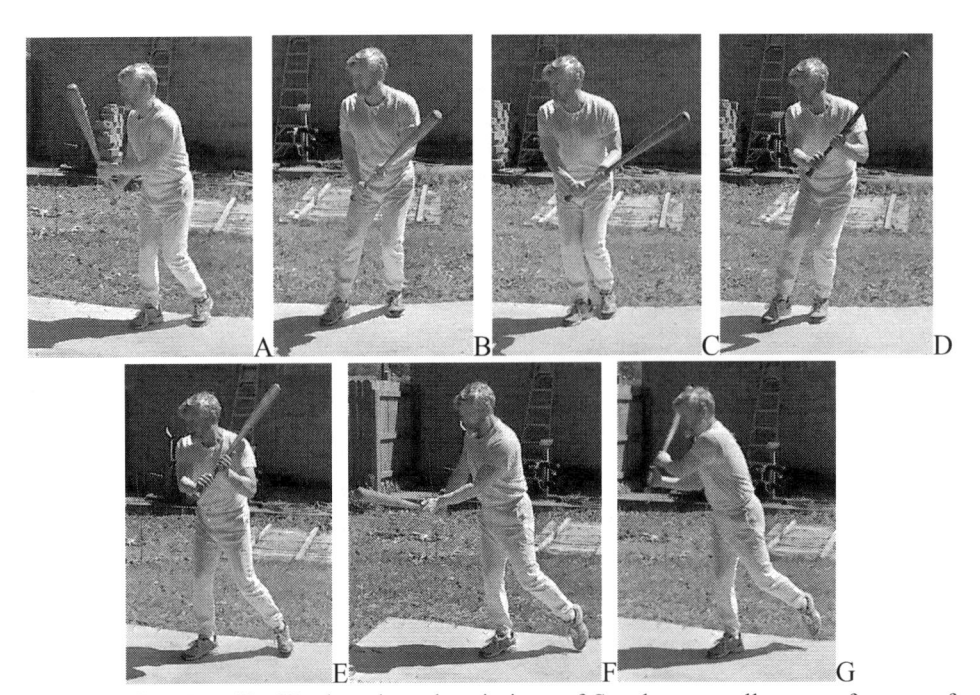

The Tris Speaker Shuffle: based on descriptions of Speaker as well as rare footage of Edd Roush and accounts of other batsmen of the early Twentieth Century. Position A is a little more dynamic and less upright than in the Nineties Swing, because the hitter will literally be running into the pitch. When I recoil into B, I can again anchor the rear foot wherever I want in the space behind me—but much more motion is to follow. In C, I've lifted the rear foot to take a shuffle-step, which is completed in D; and this step, of course, could be toward or away from the plate as well as modest or lengthy. My hands are riding somewhat higher and farther back than the Nineties striker's as I execute my intricate series of movements: maintaining balance requires such manual adjustment. Because of the forward momentum I have created through the shuffle, furthermore, every stage of my stroke down into the pitch (E, F, and G) appears to be somewhat more forward-angled. This would certainly not have been the result in every actual swing. The running attack might have broken down into a crumpling retreat to the back leg if not timed correctly, or if the pitch came riding in hard on the hands. (Roush's bat, besides, was so heavy that he would not have dared to veer this far forward lest he end up like a spinning top: he was careful to stay well back during the final shift.)

   Clearly, this elegant stroke is a close cousin to the more lateral swipes that we see in baseball's subsequent decades. The shuffle needed to be timed so expertly that less acrobatic hitters would probably select it as one of yesteryear's first practices to be jettisoned, thus leaving them with a lot more hip rotation. In the meantime, the very controlled—and successful—stroke of the Nineties, of which I've personally grown to be very fond, faded unnoticed into the settling dust of the previous century.

Chapter Thirteen

Hopscotch in the Box: Lower-Body Movement and the Mobile Rear Foot (Part Three)

The Sporting News remarked in 1906, "[George] Stone crouched down over the plate, with his bat right against his shoulder, took two steps and soaked the ball for all he was worth.... His explanation of the advantages of the crouch is that it gets the eyes in a better position to follow the ball, as they are almost on a direct line with any delivery that comes over the plate."   from John McMurray's research[1]

It's a pleasure to watch a professional like Bobby Richardson, the former Yankee second baseman, when he's about to move the runner on first base around to third. Bobby hit behind the runner better than anybody else, for my money.... The batter, as the pitch is delivered, shifts his weight slightly and steps back with the rear foot a couple of inches [if he bats right, like Richardson]. Then, swinging a fraction of a second late, he just meets the ball with a short, sharp "punch" and bangs it to the right side of the playing field. Willie Mays[2]

    An ample amount of information about DBE hitters that's not mere hearsay has them dancing and shifting in the box. For instance, a scribe for *The Sporting News* wrote lyrically, "[Tris Speaker's] two short, sneaking steps on the pitch… [were] the finest and prettiest attack the game has known."[3] Then we have the evidence of the two opening quotations above, one describing Deadball Era one-year wonder George Stone, the other (from no less an authority than Willie Mays) transporting us into the mid-twentieth century. Willie's portrait of the nimble Yankee second baseman jibes with a video sequence I recall of Phil Rizzuto—a brief bit of footage that must have been shot shortly after World War II. The black-and-white clip was oddly darkened in the background, as I remember it, but fully centered on its subject, as if doctored for promotional purposes. Rizzuto was running up in the box before taking a swipe at the ball—just a little hop, really, before his stride. I had never seen a player execute precisely those moves, and I certainly never saw any such thing again in my poring over many hours of video, mostly from a later time. I'm told that Rafael Furcal used to try running jabs, once in a blue moon.
    For the most part, the Scooter and Richardson were plainly singing the swan song of a technique that was routine half a century earlier. At that time, great hitters were almost always great bunters (Eddie Collins still holds the all-time record for sacrifices, over a hundred ahead of the runner-up); and from a twitch in the hands and feet that feigned a bunt, many an artful hit was "pushed" past charging infielders. Accounts of such play are voluminous. With the support of so much testimony, both on film and in print, verifying the existence of this busy shuffling about in the batter's box, the practice can hardly have been an urban

legend, or even a rarity. We must believe that it was part of the DBE hitter's game. Ty Cobb does not abstain from endorsing it. On the contrary:

> I took a balanced stance with feet close together—not more than 14 inches—and I constantly shifted my feet to adapt to the man on the mound. I was forever moving forward or backward in the box, in or out, erect or crouching, as the situation required. Seldom did I "dig in" and plant myself irretrievably for the heavyweight swing. My idea was to be highly mobile in the box, able to open or close my stance instantly, or to shift into the bunting position.[4]

All citations drawn from *My Life in Baseball* must be pre-treated with several grains of salt; for Cobb's ghostwriter, the unsavory and mercenary Al Stump, would melodramatize any remark that he thought capable of withstanding the pressure of a twist or a warp. The context of this particular utterance places it in a contradictory light that Stump either a) didn't notice, or b) cultivated so as to enhance the image of Cobb the Crazy Old Man; for only a few paragraphs earlier, Cobb had been lecturing his audience about the impossibility of "place hitting" (a mythical skill to which I devote an entire chapter later on). Why would he be saying now that you can shift your feet in the box to steer a hit down one or the other line if he has just decried—with some vigor—the very notion of steering a hit? Quite possibly, too, Stump wanted to stoke the fires of the apocryphal Cobb-Ruth feud by having his informant sneer at batsmen who "dig in."

As I shall argue once we reach the discussion of "place hitting," there's really nothing inconsistent about increasing your chances of (say) an opposite-field hit by closing up while also insisting that such endeavors sink or swim to the extent that the pitcher serves up a certain pitch. Stump doesn't represent Cobb as clarifying this in the least. Nevertheless, any experienced ballplayer would be well aware of it. Mays knew that Richardson was stepping back and away from the plate (Bobby batted right-handed) to increase his chances of driving the pitch the other way.

As for Rizzuto, he was probably skipping forward in the box because he anticipated a breaking ball that could be "ambushed" before it broke—and he didn't want to make his move until the pitcher had started his delivery. According to F.C. Lane, the most recognizable thumper of all time knew and practiced the ploy: "Occasionally a slugger will run up in the box. Babe Ruth used to do this, even running entirely out of the box in his furious rush to meet the ball."[5] If we discount "furious," Lane's claim can be verified through film evidence. A sequence of the Bambino batting against "Wee Willie" Sherdel of the Cardinals in the 1926 World Series clearly shows a forward shuffle before the stroke—a move almost certainly intended to negate the sidewinding lefty's famous breaking ball. The tactic resulted in Ruth's landing a single.[6] I don't know exactly when hitters stopped doing such things... but they were doing them in 1900, and a few were still doing them in 1960.

Here is where I wish to stress that something quite different seems to be happening with Speaker and Stone. Both are described as executing their shuffle as part of their routine approach to the ball. They might well have taken a shuffle-step back or forward, in or out, depending upon the expected pitch and the particular situation in the game—and, in so doing, they might have intended just to destabilize nervous defenders, or they might really have been bidding to place a shot in a certain slot. But a shuffle-step of some kind, apparently, was always in their load. It *was* their load, I believe: it was how they gathered their weight back for a linear, downward attack upon the ball.

And it works! To my mind (and perhaps owing to my body type), it works better than the "lunge" of the previous chapter in the matter of generating low line drives. To today's ballplayers, it must look as alien, improbable, and even laughable as samurai swordplay would seem to someone who had taken nothing but fencing lessons for years. Most of my experiments have involved pitching machines: a distinct drawback in some ways, since timing the delivery of a pitching machine may enlist skills radically different from following a human hurler's motions (and hence useless in a real ball game). The one possible advantage to a machine, in the context of my research, is that it tends to reduce reaction time. I have always been wary of allowing myself too much time in these test flights to load up in some fanciful pose that will eventually carry my weight forward; for while pitchers didn't smoke it in at 95 a century ago, neither were they playing slow-pitch softball. When you see a tobacco-card photo of Dan Brouthers placidly awaiting the pitch with his hands before his buttons, you're tempted to imagine some deep pump of the bat and high lift of the leg reminiscent of Mel Ott. I fought hard to make such gyrations yield results. If the machine was positioned so as to give me the reaction time of a hitter facing a 90 m.p.h. fastball, I could never make any such leisurely hitch work (or only if I accidentally started my load at just the right time, which wouldn't get a professional ballplayer very far: today they call it "selling out").

That Babe Ruth actually did spend a lot of time over his back leg with the heavy barrel drooping earthward—the very snapshot of a softball-league Mighty Casey—suggests what extraordinary balance he must have possessed, and others who practiced a similar style; for waiting over that back leg is an immense challenge. Especially when one desires to shift heavily forward in an explosive movement, merely "playing flamingo" on one leg doesn't hold out any obvious mechanism for launching a quick attack.

The shuffle, in contrast, does. I obtained the best results by simplifying, and then simplifying some more: hold the bat out from the torso about collar-high and lift the forward leg stiffly and slightly (not high off the ground or dipping backward with a bent knee: best of all, in fact, is to have toes pointing down). Even with such a streamlined load as this, where front foot and hands can "fall" upon the ball in virtual unison, I have never managed to index the fall to any vagaries in the pitch's flight. I've tried; but with a reaction time of under a half-second, I just can't make any convincing adjustment. Perhaps a younger body could have done better... or perhaps that claim of Cobb's and Wagner's only ever worked for the "lunge" (if even then).

Keeping the leg stiff in a slight lift restrains it from coiling and then firing out in a rotational manner; for if only a drop is desired, any hint of rotation may risk eating up more time as well as making the barrel's vector a bit "dippy." Yet the temptation to coil, I should note, is very strong, and within it must surely lie the reason for why those stiff, stately poses of the Nineties devolved into the wound-up-spring tension of later stances. You do feel as though you're tapping into more power if you coil... but the barrel has a greater tendency to dip completely under the pitch or else to shoot out too early and top it if you launch without getting off your back foot. A long bat, heavy but very evenly balanced (and hence rewarding the choked-up, spread-handed grip), would seem to allow a calmer lowering of the boom—a mere flick of the wrists. More becomes less, and less is more. I can see why the Nineties stars look so relaxed, and also how they could unleash fury on fastballs despite their show of *sang-froid*.

You may notice that I dropped a "would seem" into my formula above. Against a really good fastball (and in my trials, I was always pressing my reaction time to the limit, fully aware that an old man playing with an old bat would enjoy little credibility), balance continued to be an issue. One wants to be ready to go just a bit early, because everything will happen like lightning; and then one encounters the problem of getting ready too early, and having to wait... and not being able to wait. The front foot comes down before the pitch is fired, and the attempt at perfect timing is utterly spoiled. There's also the physical fact that a mere drop onto a stiffly raised leg stiffly lowered isn't very catalytic. Even the heaviest of bats can only supply so much punch.

What to do about all this? Maybe it didn't matter in the stately Nineties; but when the century turned over, the game was starting to hit the accelerator (see Chapter Seventeen below). How to find more explosiveness?

I had tried out Speaker's "two short, sneaking steps" before, and I had immediately trashed them. If timing a front leg balance was challenging, timing two forward hops was absurdly impossible. Now, however, I felt as though I needed to revisit the Grey Eagle's tactic. What if the stiff leg lift quickly dropped into another, more dynamic one? What if this second lift even had a bit of coil? Since momentum was already carrying forward, a stride out from the coil had little chance of leaving the weight thrown backward. That had always struck me as the problem with coils in the past: striding out of them was more apt to throw your weight back and out (viz., "pulling off the ball") than forward and down.

My conjectural "Speaker shuffle," however, wasn't an ordinary stride: it was a kind of "scissor clip" with the legs that sent the forward foot right back up again, the knee now slightly coiling in a posture actually captured by one of this book's photos of Tris. A batsman who was quick-pitched while using such a technique could attack the ball at once from the first leg-lift. When the pitcher employed a more routine delivery, our striker could practically dance in place and shuffle his front foot back into poise. Indeed, he could do this a third time if the hurler slipped in a deceptive pirouette or two. (The "hesitation pitch" wasn't illegal until Satchel Paige began to humiliate hitters with it in mid-century, the white Major Leagues apparently having forgotten yet another of yesteryear's tactics that the Negro Leagues had kept alive).

A passage that I shall later quote fully (in Chapter Nineteen) reveals that Edd Roush was at least sometimes a practitioner of this style, by the way. Furthermore, and even better, I have happily blundered upon a short clip of Edd's batting practice before the infamous 1919 World Series (or "World's Series," as it was then called).[7] Sure enough, the dour Hoosier charged the first pitch with a couple of steps, practically running his weighty barrel into the ball. On the second (and final) pitch, he appears to have been caught somewhat off guard. This time, he simply folded up on the back leg as a way of bringing the barrel down. Roush's stroke could never have been a matter of rotating the barrel into the ball rather than just dropping it. Not only did he employ the heaviest stick in the National League: he also insisted on gripping it down at the end, close-handed.[8]

Speaker's double-lift, we're assured, was "prettier," and it appears to have been his typical load. I found it very amenable to shooting out line drives, thanks to the emphasis upon vertical thrust that it gives to the lower body. Backspin was produced very reliably in my reconstructions. It's no shock to me that Tris was known particularly for this kind of contact. Reporter Henry Edwards once warbled, "the beauty of Speaker's hits is that nearly all of them have been convincing smashes to the outfield, infield scratches being very scarce articles with Tris."[9] I visualize this technique as a refinement of what had already been practiced at the end of the previous century. As such, its provenance is much more natural than we might think. It wasn't something that a hitter improvised upon discovering a bunch of ants in his shoe: it was a neat little extension of a preexisting style.

After all, George Stone seems to have been doing the same thing, more or less. In fact, what most interests me about the citation opening this chapter is that the reporter was riveted upon Stone's crouch, not his two steps. It's true that McMurray placed ellipsis points right where the sportswriter's column could have told us more; but the flow of the passage does not support the sense that any such critical detail has been left out. Rather, I think we should see here what is "conspicuous by its absence": a mention of the steps themselves as unusual. We must assume, consequently, that they were *not* unusual to the reporter or his readers in 1906—or at least not as unusual as a crouch. More hitters must have been hopping and skipping in anticipation of the pitch than crouching.

I might further note that a cricket batsman often gives a little forward shuffle before striking at the ball to this very day. It wouldn't have been surprising if ballplayers of the nineteenth century had copied the technique used by their British cousins in playing a similar game, especially while baseball was still very much in its evolutionary stage. This book does not attempt to delve so far back; but we have no reason to suppose that what was common for several decades of play suddenly vanished when the calendar turned over to a new century. We also should bear in mind that commentators of any era will record what strikes them as remarkable, *not* what their grandchildren will later consider more remarkable. Contemporaneous accounts of Kansas cow towns don't talk about how many drovers ride down Main Street wearing sixguns—but they do take note if the marshal posts an order that no sixguns are allowed within the city limits. By the same token, Alexander's source underscores Speaker's footwork because it was especially smooth—not because it simply existed.

And in some more remote corners of the baseball world where cricket remains familiar, the shuffle was still being practiced well into this century; it is perhaps in use right now. Here's a fascinating aside from Charley Lau's book that would have referenced a time in Australia of the Seventies:

> In Adelaide, I watched a particularly well-organized and well-coached Little League team taking batting practice, and I've got to say, I didn't believe what I saw. These were ten-year-old kids, and they were executing what the coach called a "quick step." Before the pitcher threw each batter would take a stride. Then as the pitcher threw, they'd come back and stride again in the normal way.[10]

And Lau goes on to compliment the technique as working very effectively for these boys. What Charley didn't know, obviously, is that he wasn't just eavesdropping upon another culture's way of doing things: he was peering back through time to the turn of the century in his own hemisphere and country!

So far, I have made a case that certain DBE hitters kept their rear foot active in launching an attack on the pitch (as opposed to "digging in") by citing documentary evidence, summarizing my own experiments, and describing a smidgen of video footage (which, alas, I can no longer locate). I have one more string of witnesses to call. They are the photographed images represented on the *Sporting News* 1916 set of baseball cards. Curiously, neither Cobb nor Speaker appears on this honor roll of 200 members: they probably wanted more money than was being offered. (This remark isn't intended to be tacky. When Post Cereals ran sets of 200 cards each for the 1960-1962 seasons, the same photo was recycled for many of the biggest names. Aware of how much their success was being exploited, the Mantles and Marises may very well have held out for something over the fifty bucks that was offered.) Now, all of the images in the 1916 set are full-bodied, but many are shown in a throwing or fielding motion. Just enough portray different instants of the swing, however, that we can reconstruct something like the fluid stroke that would have produced those instants.

To begin at the end (where there's least room for confusion), we see a few players whose stick is finishing high over their front shoulder as they stand fully on the front foot, their back leg entirely off the ground. These players are Franklin "Home Run" Baker, Art Fletcher (whose back shoe must be at least two feet aloft), John Lavan (whose back toes are perhaps just grazing the ground), J. A. Niehoff (rear foot slightly cut off from view), and Frank Schulte (also partially cut off—but enough is visible to show a hundred percent weight shift forward). The swing on display here has little of the rotational; and because the players have chosen the pose just for the camera, they most likely consider it the ideal one to model at the end of a good swing. We can be sure that they didn't always end up in quite the same position after cutting down on a live pitch. Shots of this latter sort sometimes show Baker, for instance, finishing with the bat wrapped in a level position halfway down his forward shoulder. This appears to happen rather often to a hitter who wants to shift emphatically forward but gets jammed by a high hard one, or else is deliberately trying to pull the pitch; and, I would conjecture, it's one of those split-second adaptations that the style of the day lent itself to. There's nothing wrong with being flexible! A heavily rotational slugger, in contrast, cannot slip forward to his forward leg if he sees himself reaching the hitting zone far too early. He can only wave at the ball with a weakly ascending hand.

Next is a threesome whose posture fascinates me most of all. Two are straight up over the forward leg and have bent the rear one at the knee to such an extent that the toes are almost airborne. You might protest that this is what we've just looked at; but the feet are not separated as far as in the above group, the body is not slightly bent as if pushed forward in a vigorous thrust, and—most importantly—the bat is not wrapped around or above the lead shoulder. Roger Peckinpaugh is indeed balancing his stick at his rear shoulder, while Fred Williams is pointing his barrel into the ground just ahead of his feet. It might be argued, I suppose, that the two are awkwardly trying to imitate for the camera that most uncatchable of moments: the swing as it passes full throttle through the zone. Yet the third of this triad, our friend Big Ed Konetchy, is unquestionably in a pre-stroke position, with his hands more or less at his rear armpit *but with his back knee also slightly bent.* Ed, I believe, is closest to the load position; Williams, pointing his bat at the ground, is waiting on the imaginary pitcher to come set; and Peckinpaugh is intermediate, beginning a load that will shift his weight back decisively to the rear leg. I wrote in a chapter describing the action of the hands about how it is natural to begin an energetic movement by methodically moving in the opposite direction, as when one heaves backward to throw a ball forward. I'm convinced that these three stars are in various stages of rocking forward so that they may gather powerfully to the rear once the pitcher starts his wind-up. Rotational hitters don't lean heavily forward before shifting back because they're not going to drive with utter commitment from back to front. Many of them like to keep at least half their weight over the back foot as they complete their stroke. They call the result a balanced swing.

Just two more cards to finish up: Armando Marsans and Bob Veach. These two, I think, have not even shifted forward heavily like the previous group as the imaginary pitcher gets his signs. They've just stepped into the box. While the act of merely standing at ease and waiting for the pitcher to make contact with the rubber may not seem to offer many potential clues about a swing, I was struck by how much the pose of these two resembles that of a Nineties batsman. The 1887 Old Judge cards upon which I have often taken my bearings feature many strikers like Roger Connor, John Ewing (Buck's brother), and Paul Hines in almost precisely the same pose. The shoes are perhaps a foot apart, if even that; the front toes are pointed somewhat outward toward the mound; and the hands are held just above the belt, more or less at mid-chest (where a shirt would button up). Again, this is not the widespread position that a rotational hitter immediately assumes after entering the box and digging out a foothold with his rear cleats. Rather, this is the severely upright posture of a batter who intends to prepare a descending attack upon the ball, flipping the barrel down into it along a straight line. From 1887 to 1916, there seems to have been a continuity of style which I would say the *Sporting News* cards well illustrate

That's roughly thirty years. We certainly don't expect Mike Trout to hit in the fashion of Mike Schmidt… and yet, a few important similarities exist. It would be stunning if the teens of the previous century had completely forgotten the Nineties and Eighties of the century before them, especially since the ball was not yet lively. Major changes would come soon and indeed were already under way; Ty Cobb himself was more anomaly than throwback. In hitters like Tris Speaker, rather, do we find the doctrine of the preceding years carried to its highest degree of finesse and accomplishment. Such, at least, is the conclusion I have reached.

A Postscript: I discovered a personal liking for the "lean far forward, then rock back" load which I would never have anticipated, and which came to me of necessity after I'd strained my knee playing Tris Speaker hopscotch. If the rear foot goes firm only as you rock back in a load, you can wait till the last instant to choose whether you want to steer your stance open or point it closed, to slide it rearward or shift it forward; and if your front leg coils as it lifts with your hands, the rear foot has nevertheless been planted so late in the back-shift that you can come fully erect. (Remember Sadaharu Oh?) Now the front leg, in kicking itself straight again, will have to take everything with it in a forward-and-down follow-through: the erect back leg is in no position to "squish the bug" and retain significant weight. The descent can be so explosive this way, as well, that you may *just possibly* be able to direct its force in response to the ball's perceived path. Just possibly.

How often would one have seen such a load among the stars of Nineties? How much of it might Honus Wagner and Napoleon Lajoie have employed? We'll never know… but now I have new suspicions.

Chapter Fourteen

Samurai Training: How the DBE Hitter Achieved and Retained His Balance

I make a major weight shift when I swing, and it's critical to get a smooth first step toward first. To the players here, apparently it looks like I'm already running before I hit the ball. I try my best to start running after I've completed my swing, but they tell me I'm hitting and running at the same time. It's strange, because I don't think that's what I'm doing at all.   Ichiro Suzuki[1]

    Hitting manuals authored by this and that superstar have for decades advised us about how to hold the bat, where to put our feet, how to stride… but few of them ever consider the most complex skill of their art: timing. Bundled up in this skill inextricably is the matter of balance—for good timing is all about getting and holding balance for just the right number of the metronome's beats ("rhythm," hitters will sometimes call it). To say even so much as that is perhaps to create a false impression, since effective hitting and pitching both depend upon not ever reaching a true balance. As online pitching guru Paul Reddick has counseled for years now, the notorious "balance point" that so many coaches insist their young charges find straight over the rubber is the gateway to wildness and arm problems. Rather, there is a critical second—maybe two, in some full wind-ups—when the backward-thrusting drive of the lifted front leg is redirected 180 degrees toward home plate, like a turning of the tide. The tides do not balance at perfect stasis for a few minutes before they start to run out to sea: their swirl imperceptibly but decisively veers from one direction to the opposing direction. The vectors of motion are never at points of zero width.
    So for hitting. The batter must go backward to go forward, go up to go down. Immobilizing the body completely would require that its hands go "from zero to sixty" in a split second if the hitter chooses to swing. Instead, energy is subtly redirected in the load, like water rushing through pipes that needs to exit the spigot at just the right instant. The various ways of channeling this rush are contingent upon so many factors that writers of manuals can hardly be blamed for skipping the subject.
    Nonetheless, you could just about hit standing in a barrel if your hands had the pitcher timed perfectly. I believe that some of the high-average, no-power DBE batsmen were indeed pretty much all hands. The long stick upon which hands could choke and spread would have made such emphasis much more practical than it would be today, with our short and alarmingly top-heavy clubs. Though we have mentioned the Keeler/Maranville species of hitter, however, we have not been focusing upon him. As I conclude Part Two on the mechanics of the swing, I think it might be profitable to put together all that has been said so

far about hands, feet, and the distinctive bat of the era in an effort to foreground the importance of balance.

Let us review the basic characteristics of the DBE striker as he assumes his position in the box. Just for the sake of reference (since no group of human beings is ever completely homogeneous), I have before me the photos of six Hall of Famers as they appear in *Baseball's Best*, a tome published back in 1974.[2] (One of the reasons I love collections and anthologies from bygone years is that they tend to abound in photographs, which could once be reproduced inexpensively and without today's terror of lawsuits.) I might just as well have re-enlisted one of my reprinted card sets for duty here, but the new pool of candidates will enhance the discussion's credibility.

In alphabetical order, and with page numbers referencing photos in Appel and Goldblatt's volume, I am studying William "Buck" Ewing (145), James Galvin (168), Michael J. "King" Kelly (246), Tommy McCarthy (289), Jim O'Rourke (306), and Sam Thompson (361). Now, historians of the game will instantly notice that everyone on my list reached his heyday before 1900, and that most had indeed concluded their careers well before that momentous year. If this observation should lead to protest, I might easily counter that the ball was just as dead in 1895 as it would be in 1905... but my defense would be a little disingenuous. Here's a better justification of my "study group." We have found the styles of so many more familiar stars—Cobb, Lajoie, Wagner, Wheat—to be statistical outliers that I prefer to build foundational generalities upon earlier players who appear to have embraced fairly accepted methods. You can't really understand the Beatniks of the late Fifties until you understand their uncle, The Man in the Gray Flannel Suit. I think the same must be true of our eccentric superstars.

I offer the following list, then, of what I see shared by all six photos of the strikers named above:

- Their bats appear relatively long and of modest taper, by current standards;
- All choke up at least an inch or two, and Kelly and Thompson also spread their hands;
- The hands in every case are held low (again, by today's standards)—a little above the belt and more less over the mid-chest (shirt button) region;
- Their posture is erect—no one is drawn into a crouch;
- Their feet are close together, as the erect posture would indicate—perhaps ten or twelve inches apart;
- The feet are more or less parallel to the plate, describing neither an open nor a closed stance;
- The back foot is perpendicular to the plate;
- The front foot, in every case, is turned slightly outward toward the pitcher's mound.

By the way, all of these six are hitting right-handed except for the mighty Thompson, yet Sam does not differ from the others in any of the particulars above. (He spreads his hands, to be sure, as does Kelly; interestingly, these are the two biggest sluggers in the lot.) The resonant correspondence of styles here is remarkable. I might add that two Negro Leaguers admitted to the Hall by the book's date of publication, James "Cool Papa" Bell and John Henry Lloyd, are also photographed in almost identical postures (pp. 30 and 414), despite owing their careers exclusively to the twentieth century. How many times have we already observed that the Negro Leagues kept Deadball tactics alive for decades!

I can only repeat several hypotheses that I reached earlier by different avenues as I review these eight shared points. 1) The long bat was something of a tightrope-walker's pole, in that it was held before (as in "out from") the body and little higher than the belt—*not* waved about far to the rear and over the shoulder; 2) the only load which would have utilized this distinctive stick's balancing qualities would have would involved the front leg's lifting rather faintly and stiffly, at most swaying back to the rear leg to dangle momentarily; 3) the parallel balance of barrel and front leg could have been translated quickly into a potent attack only if the weight shift were a virtual "fall" (or near-hundred percent shift) forward onto the pitch; 4) such a fall would enlist the barrel into a comparatively straight and slightly downward slice or "chop" into the ball (as opposed to the more rotational sweep with uppercut finish); 5) a stroke of this sort would give us the high, tight, controlled finish over the front shoulder which we in fact find ubiquitous in old photos (e.g., Cuyler, Goslin, and Hafey on pp. 123, 182, and 194, all of whom began their Big League careers only in the Twenties of the next century); and 6) the choking grip, especially when also spread, would have assisted in accelerating this controlled attack in a slightly downward stroke much more than in an emphatically lateral one.

As I attempted to picture all of these elements together over successive months of research, I kept seeing the image—believe it or not—of a Japanese samurai warrior flashing before my mind's eye. I'm not ready to audition for the lead role in a remake of *Yojimbo*... but I know enough about samurai swordsmanship that I find the resemblance striking. (Pardon the pun.) The DBE hitter held his weapon out from his body and accelerated it more with hands and core muscles than with the lower body, perhaps favoring his chop with a stiff, short leg lift. He also often spread his hands. In these practices, he was closer to a surgical samurai marksman (whose hands were always spread on the hilt, by the way: see photo at this chapter's end) than to a Highland gillie with a massive claymore. A sweeping broadsword blow powered by rotating hips might have the good fortune to run into a fastball if Mickey Mantle or Duke Snider were dealing it; but an agile adversary would have plenty of early warning to evade Mick or the Duke, and the scuffed-up, moisture-laden balls of yesteryear were indeed said to have minds of their own. The samurai was light and mobile on his feet: so were the strikers who, legend claimed, could place the ball where they wanted. Of the samurai's many possible cuts, finally, the favorite few all seem to have been quick, straight, downward chops rather than horizontal slashes. This fits our old-school hitter to a "t."

If something is hurtling laterally toward you and you wish to send it back whence it came, I suppose it's natural to plan a lateral reception from the opposite direction. To channel your force into a single point of impact arranged at a maximally explosive angle, in contrast, would demand much planning, practice, and poise.[3] Most of all, perhaps, it would require balance. Sadaharu Oh, invoked parenthetically in the previous chapter, could perch on one leg like a stork for what seemed to be several seconds. (Actually, like the tide, the force loaded into his dramatic lift never reached stasis.) Those of Oh's countrymen who have entered our Major Leagues—Ichiro, Aoki, and an ever more distinguished supporting cast—have at least that much in common with yesteryear's great batsmen: balance. I'm not sure that they have much more, frankly. Ichiro's remark at the present chapter's opening clearly describes more of a fall than a pivot; but neither he nor Oh nor any Japanese hitter that I have seen declines to use the rotational strategy of crowding hands down on the knob of a light bat and then loading them high.

In fact, I have often been left stammering when, after encapsulating what I've learned about DBE hitting, I'm asked by ballplayers if Japanese and Korean batters or certain female stars in college softball are using analogous techniques. I think the source of confusion is precisely that extreme forward weight shift, with its virtual fall upon the ball. The lunge of a Cobb or Collins may indeed have produced some off-field hits very similar to Ichiro's in trajectory, and the two were also like our day's beloved one-name superstar in legging out many an infield roller. Yet I can't see any of my six Hall of Famers from the Nineties executing such a stroke with their stances and their grips. In some ways, theirs was the very opposite of the "slap and run" style. And just because samurai warriors were Japanese doesn't mean that every Japanese is a samurai warrior!

It comes down to this. I don't imagine Ichiro minds topspinning the ball one bit if he can roll it into vacated grass. I do not believe that Ewing or Thompson would have shared that indifference: I picture them as being less than satisfied with anything but a line drive. Again, it's a matter of timing. When Ichiro times something just right, he's out of the box and running almost simultaneously with contact, whether he gives a Gwynn-like flip to an outside pitch that backspins it over the shortstop's glove or a topspin rake to a breaking ball that he beats out to first before the second baseman can make the pick. When Thompson's timing was right, he was a samurai. He hammered the pitch, and it carried low and far. (He was the National League's all-time home run king until Rogers Hornsby passed him, three decades down the road.)

And timing comes down to balance. Ichiro becomes once more an exemplar of the DBE hitter rather than the contemporary version if we only consider his need of shifting forward one hundred percent. For him and for our six hallowed strikers, there's a lot to do before the ball is met. For sluggers like Adrian Beltré or Eric Hosmer who merely pivot on the back foot, the shift seems greatly reduced, and hence simplified. Beltré will famously drop to his back knee occasionally if the ball is bearing down upon him faster than anticipated. (Reggie Jackson was known to do this, too.) I'm sure that yesteryear's heavily forward weight-shifters, when they were "eaten up" by a fastball on the hands, must also have fallen back to fight it off, perhaps without even shifting fifty percent of their load. The resulting swing would look like a prototypical uppercut. It's not what they wanted to do—but it would be what they *had* to do in that instance. Sam Crawford, whom Cobb described as resembling Napoleon Lajoie in his commitment to the same kind of stroke in every situation,[4] appears trapped in one such "emergency hack" as the cameraman snaps this volume's only photo of him (see end of chapter).

I'm trying to build a case for the following claim: the forward-shifting DBE hitter would have found timing a greater challenge, on the whole, than our hitters today who simply raise and lower the front foot in the same spot or spin around on their back foot (a somewhat more Fifties approach). Hence they would have been easier to lure into imbalance... if they didn't develop some strategy for recovering from "too-earliness"—the slippage, that is, of over-eager anticipation. We've acknowledged that just lowering the barrel on the pitch would seem to be the ultimate "minimalist" tactic: move only hands, not feet. As players, Miller Huggins and John McGraw probably poked about for safeties in this manner... and they ended up entering the Hall of Fame for their managerial prowess rather than their batsmanship. A successful sticker would usually have to pack enough pop to keep infielders at a respectful distance; and for such a batsman to punch the ball with any force at all, he would at least need to lift his front leg a little bit.

Might he, perhaps, have tapped that foot's toes lightly up and down to keep from falling forward too soon? Much of my personal experimentation ended up introducing me to subtle tricks like this. The positioning of the hands can also be critical. Ty Cobb recommends the "hands out" posture to slumping batters.[5] The benefits of this "hack" are a bit murky: I observed earlier that I suspected the objective to be a restraint of rotational tendencies, for hands not loaded to the rear are easier to send forward and down into the pitch.[6] It's also true, though, that a bat held directly in front of the torso can help a lifted forward leg find balance for several seconds, if desired. Cobb certainly didn't dangle his leg about in such a fashion... but Babe Ruth did. The barrel of the Bambino's bulky club dipped as his lead foot rose, reaching its lowest point just as that foot had exited its rearmost. Again, this kind of load can be greatly decelerated and orbit a steady balance for seconds at a time—the problem being that shifting immediately from neutral to top gear turns out not to be very immediate. Ruth, by the way, didn't come to a genuine halt any more than Sadaharu Oh, and it's bound to have been for this very reason.

We've seen that Cobb also advocated a bent-kneed stance. I suggested before that this would allow him to lift into the pitch even as his stroke modestly declined into it, creating a generous stretch of the swing when barrel might productively have cut into ball. Yet it has occurred to me that a bent knee can also allow the hitter to "spend time" over the back leg without going static and torpid. In my scenario, admittedly, the hitter would have lifted the forward leg and would be "bouncing" (ever so slightly) over the rear one as he waits; so we're no longer considering an option of which Cobb made any use, as far as I know. But it might just work as a "hair trigger," especially for top-hand dominant batsmen like Wagner who liked to hurl themselves headlong into the pitch.

A more finely tuned version of the foregoing would perhaps be rising up on the ball of the rear foot. If an initial knee bend during the "load" phase had already forced the back heel to lift a little, then the lift could work ever so slightly higher as our striker waited for just the right instant to shift forward. Such a push out of the starting block would powerfully jumpstart the glide and plant of the forward side. It would give a fortified entry into the Mac Point.

I have found, in addition, that the one-legged position with hands held outward can be preserved for dozens of seconds, potentially, if you swing the lifted leg gently back and forth like a pendulum. Something of a gyroscopic effect is achieved. I don't know if any legendary batsman ever did such a thing—and I can only reiterate that he wouldn't want to do it for several seconds if it tended to balance him into a kind of torpor. He would have to be able to get the forward gyre of the pendulum going precisely when he needed it.

All of the past few paragraphs have been highly speculative. To move from personal experimentation to the more objective ground of a newsreel simply proves impossible, over and over again, in the few specific cases where such moving images exist—and not only for the reasons already stated. To those might be added the really annoying habit of yesteryear's editing rooms to clip away everything before the actual crack of the bat (sometimes supplied by a couple of sticks smacked before the audio recorder). Yet there is indeed a source of more objective evidence which, in discussions like this one, is universally either overlooked or misinterpreted: the bat itself. What has the bat to do with balance? Simply everything! I might have added to my eight observations about the half-dozen photographed Nineties strikers that their barrels are all being allowed to dip slightly toward the plate. I withheld that observation until now, when its significance will become clear. A long stick whose higher end is permitted to dip can poise a lifted forward leg, yes (as we glimpsed just above in Ruth's stroke)—but it's also perfectly positioned to cut right down into the pitch, without any further back-loading. Today we cannot imagine that holding so heavy a bat in so awkward a position could bring any advantage to the hitter. In fact, it brings two.

One is that the barrel's sheer weight assists it in accelerating into the ball. Granted, a lighter stick can be accelerated even more—but only in a longer, more lateral swing. Imagine that your hands were thrust through two holes in a piece of upright plywood, and on the other side of the plywood was a sheet of rather tough plastic that you were tasked with shattering. You are given the choice of two tools: a thick-headed hammer or a length of broomstick. Which do you think would more likely do the job? Over a short span with your arm action largely neutralized, the hammer would of course be the better option.

This was the reasoning of players like Edd Roush, who had chronic quarrels with manager John McGraw about ditching his 48-ounce hunk of lumber during his brief stint with the Giants.[7] Edd could be as thick-headed as any hammer; but in these instances, he apparently understood his stroke quite well. His habit of almost literally running the barrel into the ball resulted in two batting titles. The other league's most famous tree-swinger, Babe Ruth, was also plainly falling on his front foot and letting the barrel tumble, at least in his youth. Peter Morris advises us that an aging Ruth, "after using a massive fifty-four-ounce club early in his career... had dropped down to a thirty-six-ouncer by his final season."[8] I have never seen any clips or photos indicating that the ancient Babe had switched to a more rotational swing in his twilight days... so would it be outrageously heretical to speculate that a tiring body might have had less to do with Ruth's power drought than a bat inappropriate to his stroke?

Now, Joe Jackson's "Blonde Betsy" (according to Wikipedia) was a full yard long and weighed in at 48 ounces. That indeed seems a staggeringly awkward object to have swung from behind the rear shoulder, as a more or less modern hitter would do. Perhaps because Jackson began with his feet touching, his long stride was able to carry the barrel down into the pitch almost like Roush's short run. Nevertheless, using a similar lunge, Ty Cobb found 34 ounces quite sufficient—and Cobb was both choking up and spreading his hands. Eddie Collins's bat, which probably came in at about 35 inches and 38 ounces, must have produced almost identical chops and slashes from Cobb-like lateral rushes at the ball; for Tyrus was a great admirer of Eddie's style.[9]

I concluded in the previous chapter that Tris Speaker's attack, in contrast, was likely a little more old-fashioned in being farther from the rotational (with his back foot on the move at every swing). Sure enough, Speaker employed a yard-long stick of about 42 ounces.[10]

The heavier barrels sitting on longer handles could be thrown down with less arm motion than a light model and to greater effect. My experiments have proved this to me repeatedly, despite my resisting the conclusion for some while as illogical. From the posture of the Six Strikers, that is (Ewing, Thompson, *et al.*), you actually generate fewer line drives with a lighter bat. I don't really know why this would be, unless the heavier specimen really is accelerating more with a very curtailed, wrists-and-hands kind of stroke. It may also be true that the lighter barrel holds its line less well, whereas the heavier one puts reliable backspin on the ball by staying on target. Bobby Richardson, at the urging of Bill Dickey, shifted to a heavier bat and transformed himself from a good-field-no-hit utility player to the only Yankee to reach .300 in 1959.[11] Though his biography offers little analysis, I remember Bobby's big bat, choked up and falling straight off his rear shoulder. In that case, surely, the weighted barrel held a straighter line.

Particularly with spread hands working as I have described, a long bat (and the weight of these old sticks mostly comes from their greater length) can accelerate quite dramatically over a short distance. Whenever analysts pejoratively index bat weight to bat speed, they never consider that the hand-spreading technique doesn't work on a shorter bat, and doesn't work as well on a long one swung in Williams style. To make the same observation from another direction, the ideal stroke of a DBE batsman wasn't to get his arms fully extended, as one hears color commentators warble about contemporary sluggers after they put one over the fence; it was to draw a looming bat head in a beeline down onto the ball as wrists moved in unison with weight shift.

That visualization of the ideal draws us right into the second and final point to be made about swings and weight of bat. Heavy bats are hard to hold up, so today's hitters (with their penchant for cocking their rear elbow high over the shoulder) naturally find them cumbersome. My Six Strikers, and those of the Old Guard who would have employed their methods, were holding the heavy barrel close to the upright in letting it dip toward the plate. Their hands sat nearer to their belt buckles than to the top of the strike zone—but they didn't need to lift them, because *the bat's head had the zone's upper reaches covered* (and remember that strikes were called much higher in those days). Their natural stroke was thus "inside the ball," as we would say now. Their clever hands worked the barrel down into the pitch. Though most of them probably lifted the hands at least somewhat in loading, their bat head would either stay or rise (in the case of a hitch in the load) well above those hands, then fall straight in a hammer's blow.

Getting the degree of balance and timing necessary to land this blow just right would have been challenging, since the well-executed stroke (in my opinion) partook of the samurai sword's surgical precision; but the challenge would have been reduced rather than increased by the bat's dimensions. This is what I wish those who scoff at the antique hitting tool would understand.

Samurai swordsman, spread-handed load

The crewmen of a U.S. aircraft carrier little suspect that in watching this samurai display his mastery, they are also taking in the essentials of Deadball Era hitting. The spread hands and the aligned knuckles (with very loose thumbs and forefingers) may easily be noticed; but remark, as well, that the "bat" is held straight before the torso and dipped somewhat downward, so as to apply a lightning-quick stroke with minimal gyration from the rest of the body. This is fully old-school, nineteenth-century batsmanship. If the samurai were to face around toward the camera, he would indeed have no need of shifting his feet to resemble a figure like Dan Brouthers or James Galvin other than pointing his front foot toward the cameraman. Photo courtesy of the online journal *Stripes*, published by the U.S. Department of Defense.

Sam Crawford, bail-out follow-through

Wahoo Sam Crawford on the warpath against an inside fastball. At least one other photograph shows him executing the same very awkward maneuver. One must suppose that Sam was already bailing out in anticipation of a high hard one before actually identifying it; otherwise, he could never have managed to turn his back, almost, to the plate in such a violent act of flying open. Photo courtesy of the National Baseball Hall of Fame Library in Cooperstown, New York.

Part Three

Between the Lines

Informed conjecture about how the Deadball batsman would have handled specific pitches and game situations; applying the swing as constructed in Part Two to such circumstances and observing how it would produce results that correspond to the historical record.

Chapter Fifteen

The Golden Age: Memories of a Perfection That Never Existed

Most hitters who do have slight upswings also have a tendency to uppercut at times. There is a difference between an upswing and an uppercut. The slight-upswing hitter stays in the hitting zone longer than the uppercut hitter. If the hitter can perfect that slight upswing and stay smooth and rhythmic at the same time, then he probably has the optimal power swing. Ted Williams was truly masterful in his use of a slight upswing. Dusty Baker[1]

Now it's the first game of the Memorial Day double-header. The fifth inning. A 2-2 count and I hit the best ball I ever hit left-handed. It was a high drive that came eighteen inches away from going out of the Stadium. Nobody ever hit a fair ball out of Yankee Stadium and the reporters made a big deal of the shot I hit off [Pedro] Ramos. Some years later, I would hit one off Bill Fischer of Kansas City that came within inches of going out of the Stadium, but this one off Ramos was the closest up to that time. The roof was 117 feet high before it was reconstructed and the ball was hit above the 370-foot sign. They estimated that it would have traveled somewhere between 550 and 600 feet if it hadn't hit the roof.   Mickey Mantle[2]

    The top hand cannot drive through the ball in a straight line if the bottom hand is pulling the bat forward in pursuit of a rotating hip. The stroke must describe a smooth, gentle dip rather than a line, even where it is most level—as opposed to the linear chop, punch, or "hammer" blow, which can go straight through the ball before the wrists of fully extended arms roll it into an upward curve. If the rotational hitter catches the ball particularly late in its passage across the plate, this dip is magnified, since the barrel has not yet entered the "gentle dip" phase but is still steeply descending from the rear shoulder (a very steep descent, if the bat is held *over* the shoulder). Outside pitches absolutely must be struck early in the cut, furthermore (i.e., late in the ball's transit), if they are to be reached while the swing still has power and before the wrists roll over; for the roll-over begins immediately after the arms achieve maximum extension, and they extend sooner when reaching either down or away. Pulling the hands into the body, while it results in delaying the roll-over and moving the Mac Point forward, obviously pulls those hands off the plate's outside corner.

    (N.B.: I won't waste more than a parenthetic whisper repeating why extended arms do *not* directly produce long drives. The extension happens *after* the Mac Point—and since it happens very early on the outside pitch, those pitches are really susceptible to being driven only when delivered high. The next time you hear the TV "color" commentator chirp, "Boy, did he get his arms extended on that one!" look at the slow-mo replay and notice when contact actually occurs. The bottom elbow will not be locked if the contact is strong.)

Most rotational hitters, to be sure, adopt the very opposite strategy of the Gwynn/Boggs "hit it late and come down steep" approach. They crowd the plate so that they can be early or "up front" on the outside half (also known as "rolling over")… and then they pull everything on the inner half foul, or perhaps fist the high hard one. I've seen them by the wagonload at tournaments for years, fearlessly armed with metal bats. We're not really concerned with them: we're talking about good hitters in the wooden-bat game.

Dusty Baker deserves a round of applause for his attempt above to distinguish between the "upswing" and the "uppercut"; his struggle to recommend—however vaguely—contact in the swing-hyperbola's ascending curve is common in coaching circles even today, as we have noticed. Yet Dusty, Charley Lau, Ted Williams, and others may only be remarking the limited, if spectacular, success of mid-century sluggers at connecting just after the swing's dip bottoms out. These sluggers had "class," to be sure. Many of us grew up with their photos plastered all over our bedrooms. Their rear elbow was down as they assumed their stance, the bat was hugged into their armpit, their hands were crowding the knob, and they waited in a crouch to launch forward and open. Contact as the barrel descended could be very fruitful for them, but it wasn't understood as such since videos were not yet being picked apart in slow motion. Yes, the barrel's descent was too steep to do more than pop up the high-inside pitch; if they "sold out" and were early on this pitch, they might catch it in the barrel's ascending curve and topspin a double down the line. A low-inside, "off the shoe tops" connection, however, could well finish in the upper deck—*if* they opened up soon enough and contact came just before the dip reached bottom. A misplaced change-up or lazy breaking ball would perfectly fill the bill. Carrying through, the barrel would describe a truly regal uppercut… and the myth of the powerful uppercut swing would draw new life.

The seeds of the legend were deeply sewn in the middle of the last century. Let me attempt to paint the technical picture this way (and I apologize for all the airy references to dips, curves, and hyperbolas: Perry Husband's book [ch. 6, n. 2] has a wealth of charts bearing upon these issues). Williams, Mize, Mantle, and some of the relatively level-swinging rotational hitters of mid-century baseball could keep the Mac Point virtually "frozen" in the inner part of the zone throughout most of the swing-hyperbola, both downward and upward curves. By that I mean that their top wrist was taut and throwing its punch almost from the instant it left the armpit. If they struck the ball's center—on a belt-high or higher pitch—just as the lowered barrel's ascent began, that barrel's direction could still be angled slightly downward with respect to the pitch's. The two opposing forces wouldn't match up evenly like a couple of trains about to collide on the same track. Instead, this slightly skewed intersection would produce mild backspin, despite the barrel's steady rising; and for that reason, the resulting drive would actually carry farther than if you drew up contact to resemble the two unhappy locomotives.

Now, if our golden boys nailed the ball's center on a shoe-top pitch just as the barrel's descending curve ended, then the smitten orb would rise higher than ever as it sailed away (like Mickey's homer off Ramos); for it would have even more backspin, and the stroke would also have fully enlisted gravity to work with muscle as the barrel was flung downward. The naked eye, however, would see the same uppercutting stroke's blur and conclude that the bat had lifted the ball in a mighty, ascending swoosh. At least, that's what the cameras of the Fifties transmitted to an adoring public.

Killebrew, Mathews, McCovey, Mize, Snyder... quite a roster! The constant objective of these human artillery pieces was to get out in front of something on the inner half. Hitting analysts seemed to believe then—and some seem to believe even now—that they were striking the low-inside pitch as well as the high-inside one just as the barrel started to ascend; or that they were doing so, anyway, every time they belted a rocket that made the pull-side outfielder look up and gape. Hence the moniker "uppercut swinger" acquired a kind of epic resonance that made the listener tremble and tingle with religious awe.

The backward tilt in this classic Fifties slugger's torso as he followed through, resisting a rise straight up on the forward leg, was what allowed him to lock his top hand into its stiff-wristed punch so early and freeze it for so long in the swing. Once again, the Mac Point is the key to the whole thing, and here we find it preserving its vigor over a stunning distance. The trouble is that it's also occupying an inflexible track, like one of our ill-fated freight trains: it cannot now be delivered to virtually any part of the zone. In fact, many coaches may not have appreciated that the "lean back and hack" approach's greatest asset was also its greatest liability. They would praise young hitters for "staying back" when the ball took off like a missile and then nag them for "pulling off the pitch" if the delivery came in low-and-away—to be completely missed, of course, or badly topspun. Same swing: different outcome. You lived by the sword and you died by it, with this stroke. To reiterate: though you can restrain your wrists from rolling over while you're leaning back and keeping your hands in, you have to hope that the ball has a ticket on the inside express in making such a commitment. If you take your hands farther out, then your elbows quickly straighten, your wrists start to roll, and your top hand loses its vital punch.

The low-outside location, where hands must reach farthest, is the greatest trouble-maker for almost any swing today, and it was certainly so in the Fifties. Then as now, the rotational swing's only chance for explosive collision at that spot is in the hyperbola's steeply descending curve—and the descent must be very steep, indeed, with the hands reaching so far away. Simply in trying to foul off such a pitch, the rotational batter might transfer practically none of his weight forward—might, indeed, end up falling backward. A ball struck so late at such an angle is very hard to keep fair. It tends to get flicked into the crowd, if touched at all. Among our mid-century super-sluggers, I recall seeing only Mickey Mantle drive the outside pitch beyond an opposite-field wall in fair territory; and I would willingly wager that on all such occasions, the pitch was high. Nonetheless, I believe that Mantle's reflexes, which gave him a phenomenal degree of split-second adaptiveness, have always been underestimated thanks to the concurrent presence of Ted Williams, the era's acknowledged King of the Quick Reflex. If Williams were truly Mick's superior in this department, however, why did he never hit much of anything the opposite way? (His left-hitting teammate Pete Runnels managed to exploit the Green Monster for a couple a batting titles.) Ted's attitude: just let the pitcher have the low-away corner—and good luck to the fellow if he was hoping to toss the beanbag through that tiny spot three times!

Perhaps nothing makes individuality stand out like attempts at generality. Here I sit, trying to represent the dominant slugging doctrine of the period often called baseball's Golden Age. Since it overlapped some of my childhood, I can hardly find the energy to argue with that nostalgic designation. Yet the game at that time was really no more endowed with some hidden formula for success than it has ever been. If Mantle was more than just the hard-swinging, lovable rube that he himself collaborated to create in stereotype, Williams was also more (or less—or other) than the scientifically engineered hitting machine that he gave himself out to be. What hitter besides Ted could have surpassed .300 over and over while pulling everything into a shift? The answer is not to be found in *The Science of Hitting*! Larry Doby, Hank Thompson, and (later) Willie McCovey appeared to model that sweeping uppercut so breathtaking to watch; yet other players who arrived through the Negro Leagues—Aaron, Banks, Mays, Robinson—were making contact after virtually abandoning their back foot, like so many of the DBE batsmen we have studied.

George Altman, a young black player who topped 20 homers and the .300 mark in each of his first two full Big League seasons, was essentially ruined by the "stay back and hack" approach—on Branch Rickey's suggestion, as Altman once explained to me in a personal, handwritten letter:

> Your pressure theory concerning power was partly right in my St. Louis experience. I was batting over .350 three weeks into the 1963 season. Busch Stadium in St. Louis had a short porch [in right field]. Someone from the front office came to me saying Mr. Rickey, the GM or VP, wanted me (a straight-away hitter) to pull the ball to take advantage of the short porch. I mistakenly tried to heed this advice and started "stepping in the bucket" and pulling off the ball. I was pulling the ball a lot but wasn't getting the loft needed to clear the high stands in right. I started to drop my hands and upper-cut. I also was fouling a lot of balls off my right foot. This caused me to have to wear a shin guard.[3]

Happily, George Altman was the kind of man who could make lemonade from lemons. He ended up having a very successful, if slightly curtailed, career in Japan, which I gather was also a personally rewarding time in his life. The passage above, however (and I did not include the full chain-reaction of negative consequences), is a brilliant illustration of how the lateral, hip-throwing stroke—call it uppercutting or upswinging, as you please—spoiled the prospects of many a young Major Leaguer of these times. Black players, especially, were expected to justify occupying a roster spot that might have gone to a white kid by hitting "bombs" at an extraordinary rate. They only dared practice something like front-foot hitting if its results were so miraculous that the coaches simply kept their distance.

Another youngster named Manny Jimenez was tearing up the American League before Charlie Finley ordered him to adopt the same style. One source summed up his career in the following short and not-so-sweet manner:

> Finley's first of many feuds with players and managers commenced at the 1962 All-Star break when he ordered Manny Jimenez, who was leading the AL with a .350 average, to start hitting home runs. Manager Hank Bauer took Jimenez's side and was fired after the season. Jimenez slumped and was sent down in 1963.[4]

How do you "order" someone to start hitting home runs? You mess with his swing: you tell him to use that "uppercut home run swing" that everyone over the past decade had associated with big boppers. Like so many Latin players, Manny turned out to have a leg kick that shifted his weight heavily to the rear so that it would subsequently shift heavily to the front. In other words, he had a significant commonality with our DBE samples. The "wisdom" of the mid-century made short work of his baseball talents and potential.

There are substantial reasons, then, why I have reluctantly concluded that the years which yielded up my first baseball cards do not actually conceal some triumphant mastery of the game's required skills. The gaping low-away hole in the hitter's defenses is but the most obvious of these. Still lacking body armor and even helmets (for the most part), like their DBE predecessors, these hitters could move up on the plate only at grave risk, as Bob Gibson once taught Duke Snider (by way of a broken elbow).[5] I also must wonder, under the circumstances described, how so many of these sluggers could post such flashy batting averages to go with their power numbers. Richie Ashburn was the only player to win the National League batting title (twice) during the Fifties who didn't club over 20 home runs at the same time. Consider the times and the circumstances: many of the old ball-doctoring tricks increasingly hard to practice undetected, some of the mound's greatest masters dulled by years of military service, and the fine art of employing relief specialists as yet largely undiscovered. Is it not probable that pitching shortly after World War II offered a feast of sub-par hurlers to the era's dead-pull hitters? Players were being steadily siphoned off, as well, by the draft as the Korean War heated up; and pitchers, in particular, would have struggled to recover their rhythm after a two years' absence. Ted Williams would once jest in an interview that the slider had forced his retirement; but, all joking aside, his generation of pre-slider sluggers must not have had much to worry about, must they?

As we begin Part Three, I thought it necessary to restore the book's second part to a broader context. Inasmuch as I eventually wish to suggest (in Part Four) that some of yesteryear's techniques might be profitably revived, I emphasize here that they were not nudged out during the twentieth century's middle years—the years of my childhood—by something clearly superior. On the contrary: I now consider the hitting catechism of my youth, such as it was, to have been miserably oversimplified and presumptuous. And how could it have been otherwise? Neither we youngsters nor anyone around us was concluding on the basis of any rational analysis that hitting 40 homers was more desirable than batting .400: it was just plain fact that home runs were beautiful. The guys with the absurdly high averages—Cobb, Speaker, Collins, and whatever their other names were—belonged to the days of running boards and bowler hats. We didn't know them, and we weren't curious.

I saw a snatch of a baseball movie once that purported to represent some the years vaguely but gildedly etched in my memory. A few boys somehow recovered a baseball with Babe Ruth's autograph on it, and all were agog at having an artifact touched by "the greatest ballplayer ever." That's about when I changed the channel. What a fraud! Every kid in my youth would have answered unhesitatingly—and perhaps wrongly, but this was how we thought—that Mickey Mantle was the greatest ever, or maybe Willie Mays. I'm not sure that all of us had even heard of Babe Ruth. He was a fat guy who made a candy bar... right?

The kids today are the same way, of course. George Brett might as well have played ball during the Civil War. Even Albert Pujols is a hobbling old-timer who occasionally gets into one. How soon they forget!

Insofar as is possible, I want to put my reconstruction of the DBE hitter into "between the lines," game situations and speculate about how he would have handled them. We're often told that we can't really compare a Ruth and a Pujols or Cobb and Pete Rose (or Rickey Henderson)... but I wish to attempt doing so on the basis of technique and a little physics. If the old ways died out, *why* did they die out? Did they deserve to, due to their inefficacy... or did we just misplace them? Could a fellow in a sweater and knickers with his hands spread on a yard-long pole held at his belt really do anything with a 90 m.p.h. fastball?

Mickey Mantle, hands loaded tight into body; Roger Maris, hands more high and rear

Childhood heroes of mine—and of millions of kids in my generation. Even in black and white, you can tell that Mickey's photo is more yellowed from years of exposure on my bulletin board… but I idolized Roger, too. Mick's back-loaded hands are hugged into the armpit, from which position the top one will be able to enter the Mac Point's punch immediately. Roger's are loaded more like a contemporary slugger's, high and back— yet notice that his top wrist remains curled in, the better to punch a straight line at the ball. Mantle will have to throw his forward side wide open to preserve the punch's force over a long stretch; and even then, only middle-in pitches will pass into the lethal zone. Maris's more downward-looping stroke was also a pull-hitter's, but his top hand would always release upon contact and incur less jeopardy of drawing the front side open. Many shots of Mick's follow-through, in contrast, show how far his head typically rolled from the plate as he finished.

Chapter Sixteen

Fashionably Late: How the DBE Hitter Would Handle the Fastball

The greatest natural hitter I ever saw was Rogers Hornsby. Hornsby has the best stance at the plate of any of them. His position is as near perfect as any I have ever seen. I would call it bombproof. He stands well back from the plate and steps into the ball. You can't fool him on a thing.   Ty Cobb[1]

  Whenever the chattering class, either in print or on the air, decides to resuscitate for a few minutes the insoluble debate over "the greatest second baseman ever," Joe Morgan's name immediately surfaces, followed soon (nowadays) by Robinson Canó's. Roberto Alomar might put in an appearance. Eventually, someone trawling through the past century's statistics will volunteer Rogers Hornsby—but more as a candidate for runner-up or honorable mention. Eddie Collins will likely be ignored. It isn't that the last two have been airbrushed from the record books... but everyone knows that "that was then and this is now." Today you could find guys playing in a public park on any Saturday afternoon who would have shined on the Boston Braves or the St. Louis Browns.
  So goes the reasoning. Naturally, few of us would dispute that contemporary players are bigger, faster, better fed, and better conditioned. That they have better equipment might be contested in the matter of fielding second base, where a slightly oversized gardening glove could actually be more suited to the task than one of our sleek models with the generous pocket; but fielding stats are rare and unreliable, so the ultimate arbitration in these ranking exercises weighs offense very heavily... and the old-timers just didn't have the pop of today's player.
  In Hornsby's case, of course, that can be called into question, for the Rajah was racking up 20+ home-run seasons at the same time that he kept landing at or near the .400 mark by October. I should like to look at the matter from another angle, however—still offensive, but not strictly statistical. View the challenge from between the lines. You step into the box. Whether Christy Mathewson or Don Drysdale or Roger Clemens is your opponent, a ball is still spherical, must cross the plate within certain parameters to be called a strike, and travels typically between 82 and 94 miles per hour.
  One more thing: perhaps three quarters of the time, the pitch you see will be a fastball. You can bank on it. The fastball is the easiest pitch to throw for a strike. If the pitcher has mastered the art of location, the fastball can function as two or three varieties of pitch. An established fastball threat also leaves the hitter unprepared even for a mediocre change-of-pace or breaking ball. Any hitter,

then, who has ever aspired to success in any era has always needed to demonstrate a competence at handling fastballs.

In a comparative review of ballplayers over the past century and a half, we might ask questions like the following. How would most of today's hitters fare most of the time in a "game situation" where an at-bat's outcome means a win or a loss? How would yesteryear's stars have done? What would distinguish them, and which strategy holds out the higher probability of success, all factors such as foot speed and eye health and diet having been discounted? To a great extent, all of these questions reduce to a single poser: how was the fastball handled in 1915, and did our hitters usually handle it in 2015?

Dusty Baker's manual repeats what is almost a baseball cliché in observing, "Most higher average hitters tend to be opposite-field hitters." The discussion continues a few sentences later: "If a hitter is able to hit to the opposite field, there are other skills in effect. He has more bat control, and he is able to wait longer. He is not as apt to be fooled."[2] The ability to wait longer, if I may venture a well-intended translation, slows down the fastball: you don't have to hit it as early. The ability to resist being deceived is also indexed to the fastball; for the longer you can wait, the better chance you have of detecting an off-speed delivery or a sudden late movement. In a nutshell, we might say that good opposite-field hitters see slower fastballs and have more time to identify non-fastballs.

Dusty proceeds to explain the best methods for driving the ball the other way. Most of these are not of specific interest here, or not nearly so much as which hitter among our chronological prototypes would generally be best suited to execute such maneuvers. Which era is most likely to produce (or to have produced) good opposite-field hitters?

Well, I'm afraid that the era in which I sit writing must be denied the honor. Radical shifts have caused starters' batting averages to plunge far below levels once considered unacceptable for Big Leaguers… yet the hitters affected cannot devise a way to dribble a grounder to the unoccupied side of the infield. This is invariably their "oppo" side. With a bat raised well above the rear shoulder and a style that requires waiting for the ball to pass over the plate, these sluggers are "all in for backspin" on every swing—not the modest backspin of the low liner, but the severe sort that results from driving the bottom hand sharply down with the top hand. This action, in and of itself, largely undermines any possibility of oppo-hitting. For the barrel must trail well behind the knob if the pitch is to be angled away from the stride's direction; that can't happen if knob and barrel are both in steep descent. Or it *may* happen, let us amend, if the pitch comes in so low-and-away that the barrel is indeed distinctly rearward upon contact. Ryan Howard (who has been our stylistic whipping boy once or twice in this book) was really very good at lobbing high drives over the opposite-field wall in such a fashion. Sluggers like Ryan, however, never created line drives from this technique, and also never used it as a reliable means of punishing the shift. They could not recur to it consistently: it depended on the fastball's boring through a certain rather narrow window in the zone.

The group of younger hitters mentioned earlier who drive their raised elbow quickly, violently down in beginning their forward attack—high-average sluggers like Joey Votto and Daniel Murphy—have somewhat solved the opposite-field challenge. Even their shots to left, however (for everyone I can think of who does this well bats left, for some reason), are not exactly "frozen ropes." The curvature of the barrel's descent as it approaches contact remains quite noticeable; hence backspin tends to be a little excessive, and the off-field fly-hawk has a reasonable chance of running the ball down on its humpback trajectory.

The emphatically lateral/rotational hitters of the Golden Age studied in the previous chapter could actually be quite effective oppo-hitters... but few of them worked at it. A benefit of their backward-leaning, "squish the bug" uppercutting in this regard was that the bat's head instantly trailed its handle, and held that position a long way through the pitch's plane of flight.[3] There's no reason why such a stroke couldn't have contacted the outside pitch and sent it the other way *if* the hitter's weight had been allowed to shift forward a little more; but because most of these sluggers wanted to pull everything, they tended to draw the barrel quickly out of its trailing angle and get it even with the handle in an effort to rake that outside offering in their stride's direction. Usually this resulted, alas, in topspinning the ball weakly—what's called "rolling over on it" today.

Interestingly, the one species of opposite-field hitting that pull-happy Ted Williams recommends in his manual seems uniquely suited for the high-inside pitch. Ted counsels "taking my stance a little farther from the plate... [and] striding slightly more into the pitch."[4] Closing the stride helps to keep the angle of contact at the minimal 90 degrees to the ball's vector (measured from behind the bat) approved by Williams. The trouble comes (as Ted himself implies) when the hitter must reach too far for the ball: then that contact angle narrows—or, as I would prefer to say, the bat rises from its descent and topspins the ball to the pull side. The maneuver is tricky, and the Splendid Splinter frankly doesn't appear to have practiced what he preaches here, or even to be preaching it sincerely. He seems rather to be pointing out that the technique is available for those who wish to use it.

Stan Musial was not so persnickety. The Man (as they dubbed him at Ebbets Field) racked up the third-highest total of doubles in the game's history by using the Williams method (before Ted ever wrote it down) as well as by staying on outside pitches. Yet the simple fact is that most Fifties sluggers were going for the downs. In words commonly attributed to Ralph Kiner, and definitely rooted in mid-century baseball, "Home-run hitters drive Cadillacs, and singles hitters drive Fords."[5]

I've observed that a not insignificant subset of the gilded generation who did *not* drive Cadillacs had worked out a thorough plan for hitting fastballs both inside and outside, and were indeed strong to the opposite field. At least two Brooklyn Dodgers, Pee Wee Reese and Billy Cox, would routinely stride open and all but dare their mound opponent to aim at the far corner. The opening up, of course, allowed them to pull inside pitches with authority; but it also, very ingeniously, allowed them to reach the outside pitch quite late, as their barrel was still in its early descent, and thereby to backspin the ball the other way instead of top it into the dirt. I haven't examined his game... but perhaps the notorious Al "Bucketfoot" Simmons had pioneered this technique as he was flying open for Connie Mack's Athletics.

Then there were hitters from just a bit earlier, during and after World War II, who stood the Williams method on its ear. They set up on top of the plate and strode open, confident that they would be pitched tight and, with the help of the open stride, actually getting the fat of the barrel to a pitch aimed at their hands. I was alerted to this technique serendipitously when watching footage of the 1948 World Series. I saw the late Tommy Holmes connecting solidly several times, and always with the same strategy: allowing the ball to get deep and then going the other way with it (left field once again, in Holmes's case). The pitches reproduced in the newsreel footage all appeared to reach the plate high. While it was not really possible to say how far in or out they were, Tommy's routine swing was obviously to stride open and swat the high pitch very late. In 4,992 career at-bats, Holmes struck out an incredibly paltry 122 times, and his lifetime average managed to top .300; so one must conclude, on this evidence, that "bailing out" isn't necessarily a one-way ticket to the baseball bone-pile.[6]

Now, I would incline to say that Holmes's pronounced lateral stride emphasized the hip rotation that became the brand insignia of the Forties and Fifties. It's well worth noting, though, that "bailing" or "pulling off" or "stepping in the bucket" is not necessarily as ruinous a move as all of us alive today were taught. A lot of righty sluggers on that other Boston team—Joe Cronin and Bobby Doerr leap to mind—would set up on top of the plate about the time Tommy's Braves had their last hurrah, and then they would step open to pull for the Green Monster (which only became green in 1947); but if the pitch were too far outside to rake the other way, they would let it get deep and go "oppo." This is pointing us back to Brooklyn and Pee Wee Reese, however. I want to follow the fork in the road signaled by Holmes and pursue it back to the Deadball Era; for that, indeed, is where it leads.

The sequence of striding open from on top of the plate matches up well with one or two rare Ty Cobb swings preserved on newsreels. The link is so surprising and fascinating to me that I will devote all of the following chapter to examining it. Yet we run the risk of digression if we enter that rabbit hole just now, so let us reorient ourselves. We are comparing the overall effectiveness of the hitting styles of different eras in critical situations; and that has led us to consider how those styles handled the fastball, in particular—which in turn has led us to consider how adept each style was at opposite-field hitting. How would a typical batsman of the last century's first years have handled the pitcher's favorite offering, Number One? We know by now that hitting style was no more monolithic in 1900 than in 1950 or 2000; in fact, I'm beginning to believe that it was quite a bit less so. Certainly Cobb was not hitting like Jackson, and neither of them was a mirror-image of Speaker or Wagner. But if I may grossly generalize in the manner of Chapter Fourteen (which peered back into the

1890's)...

The DBE batsman, let us stipulate, took his top hand through the ball in a straight line: virtually no dip to compromise the point of impact until after contact (when the "recovery curve" was not very acute at all until both arms were fully extended, since rising up on the front foot allowed the driving stroke to continue far forward). His bottom hand was not pulling the handle along a vector traced by the opening front hip, but drawing it in a parallel-reverse motion to the top hand's direct line, thus accelerating the bat head. The bottom or lead hand was freed to do this because the front hip wasn't opening much at all: its primary task was to hurtle down toward the ground. (Hence the rise on the front foot.) So the front leg's stepping motion, too, was quite linear.

Now, if the good hitter "stays inside the ball," leading with the knob and following with the barrel, then he should have little trouble hitting to the opposite field. That, in turn, will keep defenses from bunching up on him and create more room for his hits to drop; and it will also allow him to arrive later on a really good fastball without necessarily being beaten by it. To reiterate, that's why I have framed this discussion of hitting the fastball in terms of hitting the other way: i.e., because the best way not to be overpowered by a fastball is to give yourself more time to hit it (also known as "going the other way"). I will not allege that any DBE pitcher could have thrown as hard as Aroldis Chapman or that any DBE striker could have achieved as much bat speed as Giancarlo Stanton. What I would allege, rather, is that anyone employing the technique described in the previous paragraph would stand a better chance against a Chapman heater than most hitters do today, with their light but top-heavy sticks held high over the rear shoulder.

Consider: the hands of our old-school batsman are already positioned almost as if preparing to offer a bunt. Their fingers hold the wood loosely before the torso and rather low. The barrel will strike with very little rear movement in its load, for the weight shift consists mostly of a vertical drop or "fall" onto the front foot. To be sure, the hands are held "out from" the body in the fashion often recommended by Cobb[7]... yet such descriptions may create a misconception that we must now correct. Even Cobb did not straighten and lock his elbows in his "ready" posture: he was nowhere close to that. Besides forcing a bend into the wrists, as was suggested much earlier, this advice seems to me intended to convey that the hands should not drift back beyond the rear shoulder (a "pernicious" load that was already becoming popular well before Ruth).

The hands-over-buttons posture—"out from" the body but not approaching an elbow-lock—means that the arms never really get fully extended as they go at the ball: they do not reach such a point until well into the follow-through, if then. This means, further, that the hands are well inside the ball during their attack and not coming around it rotationally; and finally, *this* means that the ball may readily be struck the other way, or at least up the middle, rather routinely. The barrel is always trailing the handle during the concise linear cut because the bottom hand is leading the bat straight onto the ball, not following the hips in a flip out toward the foul line.

The preeminent exemplar of this opposite-field artistry (at least among the DBE strikers that I have been able to review) may really have been Fred Clarke, whom Christy Mathewson ranked as among the toughest hitters he ever faced:

> Fred Clarke, of Pittsburgh, has always been a hard man for me to fool on account of his batting form. A hitter of his type cannot be deceived by a change of pace, because he stands up close to the plate, chokes his bat short, and swings left-handed. When a pitcher cannot deceive a man with a change of pace, he has to depend on curves. Let me digress briefly to explain why a change of pace will not make a ball miss Clarke's bat. He is naturally a left-field hitter, and likes the ball on the outside corner of the plate. That means he swings at the ball late and makes most of his drives to left field.[8]

The only part of this image that doesn't fit our stereotypical portrait is the crowding of the plate, which one would think might invite inside fastballs upon Fred's knuckles rather than low-away offerings to the plate's preferred outer half. Yet if Clarke were choked up, as Christy describes him and as photos confirm, then he would need to stand somewhat close to the black, even if his stride closed him further, just to reach the far corner; and a thick-handled bat would also assist him in redirecting a fisted fastball over the shortstop's head. Otherwise, we see very clearly here the strategy of going the opposite way by default and then raking the change to the pull side when it surprises you. Mathewson doesn't represent this last contingency in plain English, but he doesn't need to: everyone would know what happens when the pitcher serves up an off-speed delivery to an oppo-field fastball hitter.

Cobb's off-field mechanics were more an anticipation of Tommy Holmes's, I think. Ted Williams refers to Cobb as a "push hitter" in his manual—a term no longer in use (probably because there are no more such hitters).[9] One could certainly describe the DBE batsman's top hand as pushing the ball, in that it is punching straight out at the ball from the body rather than circling around it. Fred Clarke would have been "pushing" when pitched inside and tight. Ironically, Cobb executed this maneuver with a lot more lower-body activity than what I have just portrayed as the norm. In fact, one of my major shocks in gathering material for the present book has been to discover the vigorous "lunge" (as I have called it) that he, Collins, and others apparently took. Lajoie and Wagner were "lungers," too, though *into* the plate rather than away from it. If you distill some of the wildness from their attack and stir in Cobb's batting eye and manual dexterity, you have something like Rogers Hornsby, whom Cobb represents (at this chapter's opening) as the ultimate hitting machine.

And might the Rajah have been just that? Give Morgan, Canó, Alomar, Sandberg, and even Cobb's protégé Charlie Gehringer all the credit that they so richly deserve… but, in the tightest of pinches, wouldn't you still prefer to have the guy at the plate who will go the other way with the best fastball, take a slightly inferior version or a hard slider up the middle, and rip a change-up or a hanging curve into his pull-field? This may have been precisely how Gehringer hit; I've done little digging in his case, mainstream biographies on Hall of Famers are maddeningly lean on information about actual hitting technique, and Charlie's era still remained just beyond the dawn of abundant film footage. So let me cast the question in somewhat more contemporary terms. Would you rather send up George Foster or Pete Rose if the entire season rode on one at-bat? For Pete Rose, by the way, was another stellar example of the "set up back in the box and stride in" hitter who excelled at oppo-hitting. Baker's manual even offers us a photo featuring one of Pete's strokes where (unremarked by Dusty) the hands are spread on the bat![10]

Now, there's more than one way to skin a cat (as some famous feline-furrier once said); and in dropping the remark just above about setting up deep and striding in to go "oppo," I fear I may have complicated the Williams paradigm for fighting off the inside pitch to the other field. Remember: Lajoie, Wagner, and Hornsby were all trying to shoot the outside pitch the other way, whereas Ted and Ty Cobb himself (as well as Eddie Collins) were somewhat-to-very close to the plate and hence more likely to take inside pitches to their off-field. For players who didn't anchor their back foot before the pitcher's wind-up began, however, darting back in the box and then striding in would likely be the preferred way of serving one the opposite way. (For all we know, Fred Clarke may have shuffled back before taking a stride into the plate.) Even Williams admits the possibility of a suddenly adjusted stance when he recounts how he consciously crossed up Williams Shift (maybe once or twice a year)—and don't forget Willie Mays's description of the Bobby Richardson hit-and-run technique. Most of yesteryear's professional hitters have recognized the wisdom of the approach summed up by Kiki Cuyler: "I stand back in the box, far from the plate and step into the ball."[11]

Indeed, let's reconsider Cobb for a moment. Just because he could bloop an inside pitch the other way by stepping away from it doesn't mean that he, too, would not have shot one to left by stepping toward the plate. How could this be? It sounds contradictory. The answer resides in the kind of mobile footwork just described. Ty shares with us that he found it "easy to close my stance by dropping my rear foot back a couple of inches, choke on the bat a bit and punch rather than pull the ball into left field...."[12] Rogers Hornsby confirms that Cobb "was liable to hit from 3 or 4 different places in the box, all during one turn at bat."[13] We can imagine how hard it would have been for defenders to anticipate the batted ball's flight with such a fidgety dynamo at the plate!

This could carry us into a discussion of "place hitting," a topic which I've reserved for another chapter. Here I will only drop the hint that, in addition to positioning his hands so as to hit to all fields, the DBE striker would sometimes even adjust his feet so as to enhance the chances of landing a hit where it was needed. When did you ever see Canó do that?

Adaptability: the greatest of the DBE batsmen had it, and I would argue that it trumps even the most impressive power over the long haul. (And don't discount "doubles power": Pete Rose, that extraordinary throwback hitter, is sandwiched between Musial and Cobb on the all-time doubles chart, where they all chase Tris Speaker. A double will usually clear the bases.) Adaptive hitting begins in the ability to hit the other way, especially as a defense against fastballs. In the Chapter Eighteen, I will try to build a case for how this proficiency against fastballs spread a benign influence over the handling of other pitches.

First, however, I think a seventh-inning stretch may be in order. As a kind of postscript to this chapter, therefore, I wish to devote the next one to the pursuit of the "lunge"—and related matters—a little farther. I'm piling up as many "coming up next" promises as a talk show host teasing his sensationalist scoops, I fear, and I'm keenly aware of the need not to leave too much hanging in the balance at once. Yet the DBE hitter's lower-body motion in an actual game situation has developed in me an almost obsessive curiosity, since it is both the least documented part of his stroke and also—apparently—the most subject to individual variation. I should like to draw a few distinctions more clearly, if I possibly can.

Chapter Seventeen

Hanging Back to Stay On Time: Handling the Fastball (Part Two)

My other mentor was Wilbur "Bullet Joe" Rogan.... Wilbur taught me a lot about hitting. I had problems handling pitches on the inside part of the plate, and it didn't take pitchers long to figure this out, so I was seeing a lot of balls thrown at my hands. Wilbur and I would go out to the ballpark early, and he would throw batting practice to me before anybody else got there. He taught me to stand back in the batter's box and away from the plate. "The pitchers are going to see you away from the plate," he'd say, "and they're going to throw the ball outside, so you can just step into the ball, which is the way you hit best. When the pitchers come back inside, just speed up that bat, swing a little harder."   Buck O'Neil[1]

When hitting to right field, a left hand batter takes a half swing and calls into play all the strength of his shoulders and his arms. When he hits to left field, he pushes the bat more. To gain success as a batter, however, a man must be able to hit to both fields.   Babe Ruth[2]

In Part Two, I attempted to assemble a profile of the successful DBE batsman by employing old photos, newspaper accounts, player interviews, logical analysis of forces and impacts, and experimentation every time a theory was modified. (There were many of these times!) Moving sequences such as newsreels were of surprisingly little use to me even when they were available, which was seldom. I eventually grew quite satisfied with a certain paradigm. It involved a long, heavy bat in a stroke that paralleled—at all verifiable stages—the movements observable in still photographs; and, most importantly, it produced low line drives up the middle in abundance. I had used the tools of the old strikers, I had mimicked their motions, and I had achieved the results attributed to them. I was very pleased with myself.

Yet as I reduced my reaction time to pitches in an effort to thrust myself closer to something like the Big League environment, I encountered more frustration. It wasn't just that the pitching machine offered too few clues for me to time my load properly; I was having trouble, in the best of moments, shifting my weight fully to the front foot on really fast pitches. Especially if the ball rushed inside on me (and I deliberately used an older machine and ragged balls, by the way, so as to simulate late-breaking pitches thrown at somewhat variable angles), I might end up falling backward even as I tried to shift forward. One of the more reliable approaches I found was what I believe to have been Tris Speaker's: a very quick and late set-up on the rear foot followed by an even quicker reset—a little shuffle-step (or scissor-step, as I like to call it). Nothing else brought me down on the pitch with as much speed and explosiveness... and even then, I occasionally ended up fighting one off in retreat.

Over the months, I have begun integrating that kind of experience with photos that had mystified me for years. Hitters appeared to be sloping backward who should have been drawn straight up on their front leg, and their finishing bat would be wrapped around the lead shoulder rather than draped over it. Either the rotational Williams stride had found its way into baseball before Ted was born, or... or something was causing the linear "hammer" stroke to degenerate. Either there never were many pushes, or a lot of them looked like pulls.

Both propositions, I now believe, are true, for both practices were meeting up at the same crossroads. Joe Jackson never did use the "samurai approach" to hitting: he was always too rotational to suit my model. Yet neither was he ever Ted Williams. There was a heck of a lot of body weight being shifted forward on his swing. (For that matter, I think this was also true of Ted—compared, say, to Killebrew or McCovey: no bugs were getting "squished" under the Kid's rear foot.) Now, Jackson really had to swing as he did because of his massive bat. It needed his whole tall, rangy body (including hips) to be set in motion; and on certain photos of his follow-though, Betsy appears to be spinning her dance partner rather than the other way around. Edd Roush is of interest here, too—another timber-tosser. Though Edd started low with his club and thrust or ran himself onto the front foot in order to heave it into the pitch, he would also (like Shoeless Joe) finish low, leaning back on his forward leg rather than rising straight up over it.

Entering the intersection from another angle would be Ty Cobb and Eddie Collins. I don't know if the latter set up with his feet virtually touching, like the Georgia Peach (and like Jackson and Ruth); but both seem to have taken a healthy lunge forward rather than simply lifting and dropping the front leg, in High Nineties style, or hopping and skipping into the pitch like Speaker. Yet, by the standard of their time, it wasn't as if they were swinging especially heavy bats. On the contrary, theirs were among the lightest sticks used. So... wherefore the lunge?

Some of my elegantly intended lifts and hops in front of the pitching machine had also morphed into lunges (into forward-shifted but rearward-inclined strides, that is). One very likely explanation of Cobb's long stride from a feet-together position could be that it was his defense against the fastball. Again, this was not a classic Fifties swivel-hipped approach: Ty was not keeping his hands back, but bringing them forward more or less with the stride so that he could plant his foot where he saw the ball coming and lower the barrel on it in one motion. (At least, he was so convinced of his doing this that the hands must have chased the front foot pretty closely.) I think he had worked out a way to fall back and fight off a pitch instantly if it chanced to be bearing in on him, yet to continue the stride and carry his hands far forward if he recognized the pitch to be traveling slower or veering away. His primary concern would have been (as it has always been for every hitter) the fastball... and then he adjusted outward, you might say, from the tight defensive strategy that he had developed for the high hard one.

I can see Tommy Holmes's patented inside-out stroke (described in the previous chapter) developing from this kind of strategy. I can even see Frank Robinson's extraordinarily daring style as sharing some Deadball DNA in this regard (see n. 6 for ch. 16). Any hitter's setting up on top of the plate constitutes a dare flung at the pitcher: "You can't beat me on the outside corner. It's mine. Go ahead and try to chase me off the plate, if you think you can." Naturally, the next pitch will likely accept the dare… and if the hitter's default stride is away from the plate (as with Holmes and Robinson), or if he can channel his lunge to fall wide open (the feat of incredible adaptability to which Cobb laid claim), the high hard one might actually end up catching a lot of a trailing barrel and taking off to the opposite field. It wouldn't damage the batsman's cause, either, if his stick's handle were unusually thick. Elmer Flick fashioned his own bats so as to meet just such specifications. Perhaps the technique of smacking fastballs over the infield that struck scarcely above his hands motivated the boast, "I loved to hit against Cy Young and Walter Johnson, because they were fastball pitchers and they couldn't fool me with that inside stuff that everyone today pops up in the air, or breaks his bat."[3]

I can't prove it definitively, but I would wager that pitching was making substantial gains in velocity by the turn of the century. Plain facts (such as the decline in pitching both games of a double-header or in making fifty starts a season) would indicate that mound-craft was being refined beyond a mere lobbing in of strikes. Indeed, deliveries were made exclusively underhanded until 1884; and although, "during the next couple of years, pitchers began to throw overhand with running starts,"[4] the mid-Eighties spate of altered rules obviously rushed along a few that were soon discarded. A period of stabilization consumed further seasons. Only by about 1900 were pitcher's mounds a standard feature of the professional game.[5]

As much as anything, a rise in average fastball speed would have explained why batsmen were being inhibited from passing comfortably onto their front leg and cutting down on the pitch from that royal perch. The game had accelerated. Though imparting a mild backspin to the ball remained (and must always remain) the best way to make it sail far and fast on a line, the hitter's lower body had to become more creative as a delivery system for the hammer-blow. In doing so, those nether limbs veered toward what would inevitably become a more rotational direction, whose influence would spread to the hands and transform the samurai's lethal chop into an aggressive but vaguely aimed saber sweep. Such, at any rate, is my current theory. The amazing thing to me is that so many hitters were able to balance along the transition's halfway point for so long.

Babe Ruth, for instance, had a balancing act at least as dazzling as Cobb's. No lunger he, but a batsman of the old school who still finished his stroke straight up over his front leg and dangling his back toes a foot or two off the ground. The quotation below this chapter's title carries an invaluable clue: the words "half swing." This is Nineties talk—1890's! Like Jackson, Ruth pressed both feet together in loading and put the forward one into motion by dipping deeply—almost to the dirt—a huge barrel as a counterpoise; but unlike Joe, the

Babe shot the bat's head straight up, whence it could fall down heavily on the ball without his having to "muscle up" on it excessively much (though he seems to have liked attributing his success to brute sinew, in this remark and others[6]). For all his *avoirdupois* and his grip on the end of the bat, the big fellow was still coming at the ball with a very linear, controlled cut. That he could speak approvingly of "push" hitting shows that he was also familiar with staying inside the ball.

Cobb's teammate Sam Crawford was no doubt more like Jackson than was the Bambino in this regard: that is, he appears to have used a more lateral rush into the pitch. Still eager to get his weight forward, Wahoo Sam had nevertheless leveled off his stroke, apparently, to the point that he pulled rather than pushed. Or perhaps, as Cobb implies, he himself and Sam had very similar strides, but Crawford simply didn't like to alter his step's direction:

> I tried swinging at a ball in the Crawford style and discovered I could hit it all right, but it occurred to me that if Crawford would change the position of his feet at the bat he could hit the ball in another direction with the same swing.
> Crawford never shifted, however. Like Lajoie he had acquired a definite stance at the bat, and it is likely that if he changed he would have lost the rhythm of his swing.[7]

It's fascinating how similar Cobb's reflections are to Bullet Joe Rogan's advice at this chapter's opening. Negro League stars were thinking along the same lines as the wiliest Deadball stars were about half a century earlier... but Crawford, unlike Buck O'Neil, would have nothing to do with retreating in the box, letting the fastball get deep, and taking it the other way. Only the final bit of Rogan's counsel would have appealed to him: beating the inside pitch to the draw. Whether or not the heaters were getting hotter, sluggers obviously existed by the turn of the century who loved to pull and lived to pull. I refer the reader again to the one photo of Sam in this volume. It represents almost an impossible follow-through—something I can only imagine a hitter corkscrewing himself into if a high, tight fastball has chased him off his stride yet not dissuaded him from taking a shot at it. That's Wahoo Sam for you.

Lou Gehrig sits well beyond the purview of this book. The ball wasn't dead when he strode to the plate in the mid-Twenties... and if it was, he tended to resurrect it. I wouldn't have said that Gehrig's stroke was beholden to the previous decades for much of anything before I began to ponder the lunge to the front foot studied in this chapter. Frankly, I had long wondered just what was going on with Lou. His bat was clearly a heavy, long model in all the accessible photographs; so that much, if nothing else, he had inherited from the days of Joe Jackson and Edd Roush. Yet his body appeared shifted back decisively over a steeply bent rear knee as he made contact and carried through... and yet, that rear leg also appeared to be airborne at the instant of contact in certain photos. From one angle, he would appear to have been an extreme "bug-squisher"—but how do you damage the insect population when your foot isn't even on the ground?

I believe now that many of the factors just considered account for the unique Gehrig swing. Like Roush and Jackson, Lou hurled such a ponderous piece of lumber that it bent his back side low in the load (Roush) and had to launch off a lowered shoulder as he began his attack (Jackson). Both his muscular thighs— and Lou possessed as much lower-body strength as anyone ever to wear cleats— and the barrel's great mass carried forward a virtually complete weight shift: hence the rear foot might leave the ground during the climax of the swing. Because the body had fallen so low to the rear, however, in the act of launching the bat, it was unable to rise with the barrel's transit forward; and also, I suppose, weight probably needed to be held back to preserve some semblance of balance, or else the follow-through would have sent the hitter whirling like a top toward first base.

One must wonder how such swings (and I'm now classing Jackson's and Ruth's with Lou's, and also Roush's and Crawford's) could ever be held back just a bit to accommodate a change-up. Did these hitters build up so much momentum in their great sticks that merely letting the top hand slip off would still deliver a forceful impact to the ball? Or did they simply look for fastballs every time, getting their tree limb started early and then hoping for the best? Of the four mentioned parenthetically above and Gehrig himself, only Crawford never won a batting title (thanks largely to Cobb—a professional eclipse that may have motivated Sam's willing encouragement of the "Southern Satan" stereotype).[8] The overall strategy, then, must have worked, improbable as that may seem. Heavy bats, faster fastballs, aggressive/defensive lunges... the recipe sounds almost like a formula for rocket fuel. And it cannot be accident, surely, that the photo of an outlandishly contorting Crawford turns out to have a Gehrig version as like to it as an identical twin.[9] Two hitters cannot have gotten themselves into that position unless they were waging the same muscle-racking war against the high hard one.

Also not accidental: Bryce Harper is the only hitter after Gehrig that I have ever seen to follow through while leaning far back and yet having his rear foot off the ground. Harper, it seems, has a Gehrig-sized bat that he wields during batting practice.[10]

Wistfully, I wonder if another of my childhood favorites, a fellow named Johnny Callison who was no bigger than I would grow to be, might also be a grandson of this group. From a relaxed, straight-standing pose, Johnny would launch himself into a furious lunge that, for three years or so in the mid-Sixties, produced more total bases than Aaron or Mays or Mantle could tally. I don't think he hit those low liners all over the field by squishing bugs: I suspect his weight shifted forward almost completely and that his stroke was quite linear for the day.

Yet Johnny didn't achieve longevity. It might have been an injury of the sort that ballplayers play through and reporters don't write about... or it might have been the slider. Having geared up their game so well for ambushing fastballs, just how do good hitters stay off the throttle when something else flutters at them? How did the DBE batsmen do it?

Chapter Eighteen

Adaptability in a Pinch: How the DBE Hitter Handled Pitches Other Than Fastballs

Remember that the pitcher depends upon the breaking of his curve ball and the jump of his fast one to fool you. By stepping toward him you can rob him of this advantage. In other words, the trick of batting is to play the ball instead of letting it play you. Be on the offensive. Never allow yourself to be on the defensive at the bat, in the field, on the bases or in any walk of life.   Ty Cobb[1]

Stan Musial and Ted Williams—and I subscribe to their greatness—insist that what I call a dinky curve, the slider, is the big thing that has cut down on batting averages. But can you compare the addition of the slider to what they have taken away from the pitches? I mean the pitches we used to have to face. There was the emery ball, the shine ball, the spitball, and the duster, which everybody feared. Infielders would load the seams with dirt, or scuff the ball or stain it with tobacco juice. Catchers were known to have sharp grummets on their gloves to make it easier to scuff a ball.   Frankie Frisch[2]

    The first quotation above requires a bit of excavation. For instance, by "stepping toward him," Cobb does not mean that the batter should move up in the box aggressively on every hurler and in all counts and situations. Indeed, Ty describes a few pages earlier in the same source how he would set up farther back to confuse Carl Mays, whose low, sharp breaking balls would now come in below the knees and not be called for strikes.[3] It is also basic physics and common sense that a sticker should not edge closer toward a hard thrower (or in a fastball count) if he wishes to pull the ball; yet he might, as detailed in Chapter Sixteen, stay forward a bit if he wishes to shoot for the opposite field, which will require his contact to be a little late.
    In contemporary parlance, then, Cobb probably would have written, "Be preemptive," instead of, "Be on the offensive." He is counseling forethought, not aggression without regard to circumstance. The chapter following this one will underscore how much emphasis he and most of his peers placed upon shifting one's set-up from one plate appearance to the next, and even from one pitch to the next—and I may anticipate that chapter now by stressing that artful DBE hitters conceived of no single spot as the correct place to stand. Here Cobb's objective is to portray a state of mind, not a particular position in the batter's box.
    At most, there may be the following modicum of positioning advice in the quoted remark. If the batsman can handle a fastball from a forward location in the box, then the task of hitting off-speed and breaking deliveries will become that much easier. And Cobb himself may have embraced such a strategy. He doesn't appear to have numbered among the extremely mobile strikers like Roush and Speaker who would routinely shuffle their feet as the pitcher was

winding up. If he was daring his mound-adversary to throw hard inside by standing on top of the plate, then moving farther up in the box would have "doubled down" on the dare; and if he had a bail-out, opposite-field exit strategy (described in the previous chapter) ready for execution in case a high-and-tight one really did come at him, then he would also be well positioned in case the offering were a "drop ball," instead—for the ball would drop less to a hitter stationed farther forward. Remember, too, that the Georgia Peach insisted on his ability to control his rather lunging attack from the foot-to-foot set-up so that it could go toward the pitch or away from the plate right along with his bat.

Except for this final element (which remains a little hard to accept as fact for many of us), the approach just described was in use as recently as the late Forties and early Fifties, at least among a few elite hitters. Hall of Famer George Kell (who once beat Ted Williams out of a batting title by thousandths of a percentage point) describes his practice of it thus: "I stood very close to the plate and up front so I would be alert for the fastball or be able to hit the curve before it broke too much."[4] I don't know when I last saw a Major Leaguer settle into the forward part of the box rather than dig in over the rear chalk line—unless, perhaps, against a knuckle-baller; but when hitters were somewhat more creative, such "fast on fastball, get to curve early" thinking showed transparent logic. Kell's old-school habits, by the way, didn't stop there.[5]

Whether or not Tyrus Raymond Cobb could actually deliver his stride to the point where he saw the flying ball headed, it's safe to say generally that the best DBE hitters devised an approach to changes and breaking balls off of their approach to the fastball. Well, all good hitters do that, of course—even several who, alas, will never hear the name of George Kell. The strikers in our study, however, had many an exotic species of non-fastball swirling around in 1912 that today's hitters needn't worry about. Spitballs, scuff balls, dirt balls, emery balls, shine balls, grease balls... practically nothing was outlawed, and even an undoctored ball was usually as pock-marked as a battlefield and as furry as a kitten by the late innings. Frankie Frisch reviews the infamous inventory in our second introductory quotation; and Frisch began his Major League career over a decade after Cobb, just a year before Ray Chapman's fatal beaning by none other than Carl Mays. Immediately thereafter, the tide of ball-abuse began to be stemmed by new rules. Today, every soap-smelling baseball exits the game as soon as it's fouled into the dirt. A split-finger pitch or a sharp slider is the worst deception that our hitters have to fear. With two strikes, sluggers wave at and miss a slider that never had the corner, even before it broke, their 32-inch bats coming up about a foot short. How would these young men have fared in the days of Burleigh Grimes and Three-Finger Brown?

Not well, by my estimate. The problem has little to do with how long the bat stays in the plane of the ball's flight during the standard, well-rehearsed stroke. We've already considered this formula, popularized by the Lau/Hriniak school of hitting philosophy and still widely repeated in professional circles. Even if today's prototypical hitter could be said to keep his barrel in the collision-rich zone for most of its severe sweep downward from over the back shoulder, the pitch's plane turns out to be no very fruitful plain in safeties. Contact at spots removed even a bit from the Mac Point—whether before or after it—is often counter-productive. A less-than-fully accelerated stick tends to generate weak pop-ups and weak ground balls. Unless they have two strikes, hitters may well be better off executing a clean swing-and-miss than putting a "bleeder" into play.

I mustn't draw the contrast between then and now so starkly as to distort it into a falsehood. The happy accident known as the "swinging bunt" was probably at least as prevalent in 1915 as in 2015—indeed, probably much more prevalent, considering what a stigma was formerly attached to striking out. Weak contact can indeed be as good as a perfect bunt. Like bunting, it may even represent a lost art—an ingenious but forgotten response to a challenging set of circumstances. And bunting itself, to be sure, is a Deadball skill. Omar Vizquel is the highest-ranked player in sacrifice bunts who is not of DBE vintage, coming in at Number 35 (along with Johnny Evers and Edd Roush).[6] Today's sabermetricians, while paying close attention to walks and on-base percentage, seem surprisingly indifferent to the basic facts of situational hitting, preferring to refine new methods to measure the exit velocity of ball off bat. Yet if "a walk's as good as a hit," as the baseball cliché maintains, then why is a Texas Leaguer not as good as a line drive in a critical spot? Weak versus solid contact is not the issue: the issue is whether the hitter can make a kind of contact at a given moment that the pitcher doesn't want him to make and angle the ball in a certain direction where the pitcher doesn't want it to stray.

Or so goes that side of the argument, which is not without merit. Yet I would now return to the "exit velocity" side of the issue, as well, for I think the greatest of the DBE hitters win the battle on both fronts. That is, they had mastered the art of shooting low liners off the barrel with their "samurai stroke"; but also, and precisely because of the forward- and downward-shifted nature of this stroke, they had a better chance of turning swing-and-miss pitches into swinging bunts, twelve-hoppers, and dying quails. Most weak contact today that stays in fair territory happens on the steep ascending curve of the swing's hyperbola as the pitcher frustrates the slugger's relentless bid to go deep. Contact of this sort imparts to the ball a brush of unenergetic topspin. Yesteryear's batsman could certainly be lured out of his timing, as well; yet because he was shifting heavily forward, in any case, and because his barrel was being sent in a linear path toward the ball, he might still reach out one-handed and stroke a change-up rather sharply. Such was his confidence in being able to get a piece of the ball that he and his buddy at first base would frequently exchange nods and put on a hit-and-run play (for batter and base runner made those arrangements at the time).

Naturally, our antique striker would also want to land solid hits, some of which could roll a very long way in the day's huge ballparks. (Most homers were of the inside-the-park variety; and big, lumbering Owen Wilson's single-season record for triples [36] owed a heavy debt to Forbes Field.) The DBE hitter could go after evasive pitches that lured him forward or broke down or away from him with all the aggression recommended by Ty Cobb, and he wouldn't necessarily end up with a "ducksnort"; for the same motion that allowed him to put dribblers in play rather than strike out could also turn a dribbler into a "blue darter." Let us imagine that motion in detail. Our batsman's "stride" displays little real rotation of the hips, favoring a straight-down launch upon a forward leg that had been lifted stiffly in its load. That leg, essentially, becomes the bottom half of a more or less vertical axis. The hitter plants it where he anticipates the pitch being, or where (if you believe Cobb, Wagner, Clarke, *et al*.) he actually sees the pitch coming. Then his torso rolls up erectly on the planted prop and his top hand punches down and through the ball—all in a fluid set of motions that are close to a single motion.

The top hand punches too early if the pitch is misjudged. In that case, it slips off the handle, and the bat continues its downward-angled forward drive. Because the barrel isn't yet coming up in its ascending backswing, little momentum is lost. This means that contact, even if one-handed, can be very solid. Since change-ups and, especially, breaking balls are also dropping as they near the plate, the barrel's continued path downward may just carry it right into the deviously spun orb whose design was to pass untouched with a dip and a duck.

I have executed this kind of swing (i.e., the bad kind—very ill timed) so often in my own modest experiments that I will boldly advance the following claim. I think a great many out-of-the-park home runs were probably struck in exactly this manner, with the barrel arriving "too early" and the full force of its blow just before the ascending finish imparting a formidable amount of backspin to the ball. This "oops" kind of contact can produce a majestically soaring shot that's pulled a great way right down the line. The more usual trajectory, occurring when the barrel is "right on time," would be a low bullet somewhere between the power allies. In other words, with the hammering DBE stroke, the consolation prize for "being fooled" and getting out in front can be very generous.

(By the way, through my own tinkering around, I managed to validate a formula that I have read in several transcribed interviews with Negro Leaguers: aim for the middle, and then if you're early you pull it hard. Never aim to pull. The physics of the line-drive swing so favor of this strategy that I'm shocked to find it almost dissolved into something like a lost oral tradition.)

Now, the rosy scenario just described would most likely happen if the pitch broke into the hitter (as when a lefty throws a curve to a righty) or when the off-speed pitch wanders toward the middle of the plate. Yet even well-executed pitches that stay to the plate's outer half can be "poled" (as reporters of the time used to describe it very aptly) with full, admittedly awkward extension: weight transferred heavily forward, top hand slipping off, and front arm reaching all the way out. I am convinced that at times when the striker was really in "scramble" mode, as well, the bat could suddenly grow several inches in his bottom hand as all that choked-up space came sliding back through the fingers. I cannot overemphasize the value that releasing the top hand for an "emergency hack" and letting the handle slip through up to the knob would have had for a scrappy hitter's adaptability. I see Eddie Collins, for instance, as being very much this type of contact artist; for of the few photographs I've ever found of a swinging Collins all seem to bespeak a "sticker" who would make any adjustment to reach the ball.

Indeed, I think the awkward-looking swings of several hitters that have been captured forever (somewhat unfairly) in black-and-white are best explained by the final contingency above. That is, they show a batsman collapsing on his front leg in an effort to rush the top hand up over a deceptively slow pitch. George Sisler appears to be grimacing painfully in one such photo, his forward knee deeply bent yet his top hand having successfully clung to the bat in a strong follow-through. (George's grimaces can be misleading, I might add; after sinusitis affected his sight, he would regularly squint at the plate.) The pitch must have broken inside and low; on an outside pitch, the Sizzler's top hand would likely have released the handle. Sisler, Collins, and many of the other more photographed exemplars in our study would clearly follow through both two-handed and one-handed, depending on the adjustments demanded by the pitch. As long as the two-hand finish was the default setting, the top had could easily be allowed to slide off in a pinch.

I am inclined to place Honus Wagner on the same list. Yet hitters who stand well off the plate, stride into it, and look to drive an outside pitch the other way are almost always one-handed finishers. (We have already mentioned Lajoie and Roberto Clemente in this context.) Furthermore, when the top hand is the stronger hand (as was also suggested earlier), it might routinely leave the handle early, even on inside pitches: e.g., Willie Mays. This obviously isn't the same thing as losing your grip on the handle because you're fooled. The hand comes off in these "strong top hand" cases only after the Mac Point has been reached, and does so because its strong burst is throwing the stick through the zone, so to speak. (Charley Lau must have had something of the sort in mind when he recommended an early release: that is to say, I think he associated the quick release with a strong follow-through.) The final photo of Wagner in this volume, while certainly capturing him in an awkward pose, shows the top hand staying firmly on the bat—yet the photo just above it highlights the one-handed finish. Maybe Dutch's right released its grip in the characteristic Wagnerian fashion on an outside change-up or a dipping curve—and maybe it retained its grip in the other photo to power through an outside fastball that took Hans somewhat by surprise. I would acknowledge, in other words, that *keeping both hands on the bat could constitute a split-second adjustment* for some hitters.

In light of how much verbiage has been expended for how many decades disparaging down front-foot hitting, it's pretty amazing that so many batting champs have displayed a greater-than-usual forward weight shift, especially before metal bats introduced a taste for short wooden facsimiles in recent generations. Harvey Kuenn hit off his forward foot (as Coot Veal testified to us a while back); Aaron and Clemente showed pronounced forward weight shifts. Even Miguel Cabrera will as often as not have completely retracted his rear foot from its dug-in position when he makes contact. The potential in this kind of mobility to accommodate all kinds of sudden, erratic behavior in the target was a large part of the secret behind the DBE batsman's success. Why the secret remains so well concealed is itself something of a mystery to me.

While we began this chapter by analyzing how Ty Cobb might have positioned himself in the box, we have ended up devoting most of it to abstracted elements like weight shift and the "chop" stroke without paying any further attention to where the batsman might set up in a specific situation. Let us make one more stop in Section Three, therefore, to study how altered positioning in the batter's box could collaborate with a linear cut and a fall or lunge forward to create opportunities for the hitter. The claim was often made that a brilliant few, upon executing each intricate move in a certain magical style of choreography, could serve up the ball wherever they wanted it to go. The magic was called place hitting. Were the claims made of it fact, or legend?

Tris Speaker, high follow-through

Tris Speaker golfing a low pitch—probably a breaking ball or change-up, to judge from the catcher's attempted scoop and the contact made evidently well in front of the plate. Like Ruth and other legendary hitters of the time, Speaker never finished a swing with fingers and thumbs locked around the handle. Here his digits have the complex arrangement of a flutist's, suggesting an intricate and expert application of manual force at the point of contact. That "Spoke's" hands have not finished in a "spread" position does not necessarily indicate that they did not begin so. Hands rarely remain spread on a wooden handle after you put a brisk swing (especially a downward one) on the ball. Photo courtesy of the National Baseball Hall of Fame Library in Cooperstown, New York.

Tris Speaker, load with spread hands

Speaker might have been about to take his distinctive forward hop into the pitch—or might already have done so, and now is poised to swing. Of course, here we see an excellent example of a DBE hitter who spreads his hands when actually hitting, even though photos of Speaker at more casual moments often don't reveal the grip. Note, too, the bend in the top hand's wrist which has thrust up palm and thumb. Photo courtesy of the National Baseball Hall of Fame Library in Cooperstown, New York.

Chapter Nineteen

The Phantom Clue: How "Place Hitting" Hides Major Evidence in Plain Sight

Now, another thing—never try to place a hit. In the first place, you can't do it, and it is not a good idea, anyway. Very few batters ever successfully acquired the art. I never try to place hit. I have tried simply to meet the ball solidly and let hits find holes for themselves. They usually will. Most boys have an idea that when the infielders or outfielders spread apart, and leave a wide gap, that they can hit the ball right through the gap. Don't fool yourself that way. By centering your mind on that open spot you ate taking it off he ball.   Ty Cobb[1]

If I went to bat every time it was my turn [this afternoon], and put my whole attention into meeting the ball, and hit it hard, I might very well make a couple of healthy hits. But I shan't ever try to do that. Instead, I shall try to place my hits, and because I am none too sure of myself [in spring training], I shall be lucky to make even one hit. So far as today's game is concerned, I would be better off if I didn't bother with place hitting at all. But today's game is not the big thing to consider. If a player can really place his hits, he has a long advantage over the men who cannot. He can cross up the opposing pitcher and outfielders almost at will. It's difficult, if not impossible, to work any combinations against him.   Ty Cobb[2]

Before I try to follow Ty Cobb's laconic prose into yet another labyrinth, let's understand first exactly what "place hitting" meant in the early twentieth century—which was probably far less plain than what it meant in the late nineteenth century.

The accomplished place hitter is supposed to be able to drop any pitch, delivered at any velocity, into just that part of the field which he has identified as desirable, either because it allows a prior base-runner maximal chances for advance or because the hitter himself anticipates making maximal progress on the bases by serving said pitch into said real estate. (In an ideal world, a competition predicated on an exercise of this sort would replace the annual Home Run Derby.)

One notices a kind of buzz about place hitting in the years leading up to 1900, just as one would hear a buzz at the century's other end about juiced balls before the steroids scandal broke. The place hitter was a genius. His approach to batsmanship was rigorously scientific—and pre-war, electrified-and-automated America had all of our present faith in science with none of our misgivings about it. More skeptical minds, to be sure, wondered if any substance at all had ever existed at the legend's core. Yet their skepticism was restrained and good-humored, for the paying public wanted very much to believe that such a superior being could be flesh and blood. The place-hitting maestro was baseball's answer

135

to the cerebral Monsieur Teste, creation of French pre-war poet Paul Valéry; or, to stay on our side of the pond, he was Nikola Tesla. He was Harry Houdini. He could turn a dewdrop into a flying machine. In an immortal phrase attributed to Wee Willie Keeler, he could "hit 'em where they ain't." A decade or two later, and he would have had his own comic-book series.

Here's what *Spalding's Official Base Ball Guide* had to say on the subject in 1890:

> Under the rule of the swift pitching which has been in vogue for several years past, there was a general idea prevalent among batsmen that it was next to an impossibility to *place* a ball from the bat in the face of the swift pitching batsmen had to encounter; but this rutty idea has been got rid of by headwork batsmen, and last year saw many very successful attempts made to place a ball against the fire of a swift delivery.[3]

The author of these reflections, one Henry Chadwick, had employed the generalities above to preface his celebration of Ross Barnes as a "scientific batsman"[4]… and the legend was off and running into the twentieth century, where every batting champ who hit to all fields was now written of as an alchemist wielding a magic wand.

The present chapter, to be honest, was a late arrival to my plan for the book. My method has been to take what scraps of real evidence I could find and combine them with my own experiments, logical analysis, and observations of contemporary hitters. My original exposure to place hitting did not dispose me to view it any more seriously than I would have the very painful superstition, current in the early twentieth century, that a hitter could recover his batting eye by having teeth pulled. Stirring pixie dust into my efforts at reverse-engineering could only compromise them, as I thought, by making the DBE batsman at once more mystical and—from an analytical perspective—more preposterous.

Yet as I ran across the two-word phrase ever more frequently in my reading, I began to fear that another researcher might question why I had overlooked such "significant" evidence that yesteryear's stick-wizards really had developed a science of hitting. At this nearly terminal point in my presentation, I believe I may be able to demonstrate why the background chatter about place hitting, while somewhat silly on its surface, also offers valuable clues about how yesteryear's striker went about his business. I shall be relying heavily on F.C. Lane for source material, since he devotes an entire chapter ("The Theory of Place Hitting") in his little book to interviewing numerous stand-out hitters on the subject. In the complexity of the testimony, I think, hides a treasure-chest of implied information about the amazing things these hitters were doing in the box.

Yet even before I call such expert witnesses, let me follow my usual method of examining the "place hitting" assertion logically and with common-sense physical observations; then I will go "between the lines" and review what players of the era said about themselves and their peers with regard to this legendary (or imaginary) skill.

An hour's worth of dithering with a tee in your back yard should suffice to convince you that the proposition in its purest terms is indefensible—and here we have even removed the element of motion. When the tee is erected on the low-inside corner, for instance (i.e., right beside your knees), the ball cannot be struck effectively to the opposite field. You can get to it early and pull it (tee out in front), or you can let it reach your hands and pop it straight back, or you can hit it very late (tee behind you) and—with a "bailing" kind of swing—perhaps bloop it down the opposite foul-line; but this last is an extremely unlikely result. More to the point (since those who "believe in" place hitting as if it were an article of religious faith always emphasize the severe rigor of training needed to do it), the technique of being late on an inside fastball, such as I described in Cobb, Tommy Holmes, and others, is not place hitting *per se*: it's a defensive tactic to be used by a hitter who would probably rather have the ball over the plate but finds himself down in the count. Such a batsman would be responding to the pitch and the situation; he wouldn't be announcing to himself (or to the world, in the manner of Ruthian myth), "For my next hit, I shall drive the upcoming pitch deep to the opposite field."

For what if that pitch should happen to be a curve on the outside corner? Plant your tee on that corner, lower it, and slip it ahead of the plate (the latter two in order to simulate break and velocity): then try hitting a strong drive to the opposite field. With good luck or great skill, you might lob the orb over the shortstop position (hitting lefty); more likely you will "roll over" and hit a weak grounder to your strong side. Now, weak grounders can serve a purpose, as we've conceded. I once heard Mike Shannon speak admiringly on a broadcast of how Roger Maris prophesied—correctly—that he would pick up twenty RBI's simply by rolling over on the outside pitch and producing a weak grounder to second. This sort of thing might qualify as place hitting in some minds: that is, an "ineffectively hit" ball can be very effective in a certain situation. Today we see some sluggers beating the radical shift by topping hop-along dribblers to the infield's undefended side.

Such, however, doesn't seem to be the intended meaning of place hitting in its more ancient and exalted form. I'm sure that Maris (who was one of the most underrated ballplayers of all time)[5] would have forgotten all about the dribbler to second if the pitcher had elevated a fastball on the outer half. Making the best of what you're given in a critical situation isn't the same as calling your shot and then dropping the next pitch there as if by divine intervention. The mythical place hitter is supposed to be able to position his stance with a slide-rule, position his hands with a protractor and compass, and then plop the next delivery within five feet of his calculated landing spot. Well… in batting practice, when the pitcher is feeding in mediocre fastballs down the middle, that might just be possible. Not in a game.

Rogers Hornsby saw it my way and, of course, said it much better than I ever could:

> I have heard a great deal about place hitting, the knack by which some players claim that they can dump the ball about where they want it to go. I never took [sic] much stock in such stories myself. In my opinion, batters who make such claims are talking purely for effect. But even if I believed all they say, I wouldn't recommend their system to anyone else. I surely don't follow it myself.
>
> I am a right-handed batter. Suppose the pitcher put one on the outside of the plate. I can drive the ball with great force into right field. I could hardly pull that ball around into left field, if I tried. But suppose I did try and was successful. I surely couldn't get as much force behind my blow. In other words, I could not make the ball travel any where so hard or fast even though I could govern the general direction. And the speed with which the ball travels is, nine times out of ten, more important than its direction.[6]

If, therefore, the place hitter's claim is that he can send any specific pitch during an at-bat to a specific spot, then the Rajah's reply is that 1) no such feat is consistently possible, and 2) if it were, the cost of executing it would be greater than any dividend it would pay. We still haven't unearthed what I consider to be the single most important revelation about DBE hitting that nestles within this debate, but we're drawing closer. Let us try to unravel more of the subject's mystery.

Some commentators of the past would dismiss place hitting as a curious relic of the mid-nineteenth century. Until a couple of decades after the Civil War, pitches were required to be thrown underhanded. Strikers would stand almost facing the pitcher in something very similar to what we would call a bunting posture, though probably less crouched. The bat would be held before their chest, typically with extreme choke. In such circumstances, a well-rehearsed batsman could no doubt reach out and poke at an offering delivered to practically any part of the zone in such a manner as to direct it to right field, center, or left. (By the way, during these years the hitter also got to point out to the pitcher where he wanted the ball served up.)[7] The "flick of the wrists" which our genteel striker would then execute in driving the barrel through the Mac Point, dissected so thoroughly in this book's earlier chapters, would likely suffice to send the ball beyond an infielder's grasp much of the time. Wee Willie himself seems to have represented such a style very creditably into the following century.

There could not have been many like him, however. The accelerated speed of overhand pitching would have spelled doom to minute finessing of this kind. In F.C. Lane's chapter, witnesses such as Honus Wagner will commit themselves no further than to say that Keeler might have pulled off the caper, with an honorable mention to Cobb. Still others define place hitting in that slack sense which would cover Maris's run-producing dribbler to second. Harry Heilmann, for instance, testifies that he never place-hits except on a bunt or hit-and-run, and Tris Speaker reckons that only about ten percent of hitters can resist driving the ball where their natural tendency dictates (these happy few, apparently, qualify as place hitters). Such terms are very generous. The bunter, after all, really isn't swinging the bat at all; and if to place-hit is to let the outside fastball get a little deeper so that you drive it to center rather than pulling it, then the ratio of place hitters among professionals should be closer to nine out of ten, one would hope.

Edd Roush, an avowed place hitter, attempts a helpful elaboration for Lane:

> There are, theoretically, two ways you can place your hits. One is by shifting your feet, the other by timing your swing. The easier of these two methods is by shifting your feet. You can step into a ball when it is on the outside of the plate or you can step away from it [when it comes inside?]. Sometimes infielders will get on to you by the way in which you hold your feet. You can then fool them, if you are artful enough, by changing the timing of your swing. If I stand at the plate, a left-handed batter, and hit late at the ball, it will go to left field. If I hit a little quicker it will go through the pitcher's box or to center field. If I swing still quicker, it will go to the general direction of right field.[8]

If these details are helpful to Lane's endeavor—as he certainly seems to think—they remain little more lucid than Cobb's juxtaposed, all-but-contradictory remarks at this chapter's opening. Most specific are Edd's comments about striding into the away pitch, presumably to strike it to the opposite field; but such a move could also produce Maris's roll-over pull swing—while we've seen, too, that striding away from an outside pitch can produce an oppo-hit. (Remember Pee Wee Reese and Billy Cox?) Whatever Roush intends at this point is supposed to illustrate the efficacy of good footwork: let's leave it at that. Why, however, would infielders have sufficient time to key on such footwork unless the batsman were setting up in a closed or open position rather than stepping as he read the ball's flight? If Roush were doing this latter, by the way, he would be offering yet further testimony that DBE hitters tailored their stride in response to the ball's movements... and I believe that he is indeed making such a claim, for his statement literally describes how the stride's direction follows the pitch's vector. So, again, I must pose the simple question: how could fielders be taking advantage of any clue in footwork that occurs a few milliseconds before contact?

The only answer that makes sense to me is that *Roush is switching around his back foot's position to assist in the forward foot's anticipated stride.* He is shuffling—not setting up open or closed, but actually executing some version of Speaker's "pretty" dance as he loads up. We had already deduced that Edd was apt to make such moves, even if he didn't shuffle-step all the time. Infielders could get enough of a tip-off, in these cases, that they could break left or right, in or out, just before contact was made: even that much of a head-start might give a distinct advantage. One would think that if back-foot movement were a significant part of place hitting, it would have drawn far more comment in Lane's lively chapter. But then, as I have had occasion to suggest so often before, you don't remark upon things that an angel or a Ouija board tells you may interest people three generations down the road; you confine your remarks to what interests you and your peers here and now. If shifting the back foot was relatively common in 1910, even among hitters who didn't claim to place their hits, then why underscore it?[9]

To me, this rare glimpse of the mobile back foot is easily the most important find in the whole place-hitting discussion. Because "digging in" has become an unquestioned ritual in our style of batting, we cannot imagine its not having been so at any stage of the game's history. Yet for strikers of the Deadball Era, shifting the back foot in various directions (and Roush, notice, speaks of "shifting the feet" instead of "striding") as the pitcher enters his wind-up must have been so unexceptional that it failed to merit a descriptive sentence or two.

Edd's final remark about speeding up the hands to override the message in the feet teaches how to fool the infield rather than how to place the ball expertly, it seems to me. Does he truly mean to imply that speeding up or slowing down the bat is a sufficient strategy in and of itself to determine pinpoint placement? George Sisler appears to be of that dubious opinion… though one must wonder. He originally explains to Lane that "the first essential of place hitting is a proper position at bat. Have your feet right and your arms will take care of themselves." Yet Sis, too, implicitly contradicts himself by elaborating, "you must stand in such a way that you can hit either to right or left field with equal ease. The secret of good strategy is to keep your intentions to yourself." In other words, the stance assumed in the box must be squared up and totally non-committal. Then the hands deliver the real magic, because "the timing of your swing" determines if the ball goes to right, center, or left.[10]

This is frustrating stuff. Sisler's commentary appears tantamount to saying, "The feet are most important because you have to make sure that they don't do much of anything; otherwise, they'll give you away." A thoughtful, college-educated type, George would hardly seem a likely source for so inane an "insight." I'm convinced that something isn't coming through in translation. I have no reason to suppose The Sizzler one of those footloose types who moved all over the box as the pitch was being delivered. He nearly belongs, after all, to the next generation: his career didn't end until 1930 (and was prematurely cut short by health problems, at that). I believe, rather, that he is advocating a medium-deep set-up in the box, a stride toward the plate when bidding for an oppo hit, a straight stride to hit up the middle, and a somewhat opening stride with a quick bat when bidding to pull. But even then….

Even then, we have no indication of what to do when you stride into the plate, looking to go the other way, and the pitch rides in on your hands. Take it, one must suppose. If the pitcher works you inside for the whole at-bat, however, can you be said to be a place hitter because you watch a third strike or draw a walk and then come back next time looking once more for that outer-half pitch? Or if you wish to pull the ball and are fed nothing but low-away pitches all afternoon, are you a place hitter because you never get the bat off your shoulder?

Edd Roush, too, had nothing whatever to say about how to handle a pitch that crosses up your intended direction. Could Roush still go to left (his off-field) with a low-inside pitch—or would he even want to try? He and George Sisler appear to have told us how to hit the ball where it's pitched instead of how to place a hit; and, in some respects, that is essentially the contrary of place hitting. Rather than imposing your will upon the ball, you would be letting the pitcher call your spot and then trying to beat him through solid contact—the Hornsby way.

Now, if you were employing a shuffle-step, you could counter the pitcher's refusal to give you anything outside by shifting away from the plate as he went into his wind-up. Then a pitch on the inside part of the plate would be outside relative to your bat's reaching barrel. You could also set up far away from the plate and then dash forward after the hurler began his motion in order to pull the outside corner. Guess-work would still be involved, obviously—the more so once you acquired a reputation for relocating your back foot; then the pitcher would be fully expecting you to move your knight if he moved his bishop, and the chess match would be on. But one can well imagine how a hitter who pulled such tricks would come to be revered as an artist, a scientist, or a magician. Viewed from this perspective, place hitting begins to make a little sense.

Let us return at last to those two inaugural Cobb quotations that seem, at best, mischievous (or, as some Cobb-haters would insist, malevolent). The Georgia Peach appears flatly to contradict himself: "I never place-hit and wouldn't recommend it, because it can't be done. The only times I do it are when I want to outfox the opposition and take control of the game... which is always." Gee, thanks for the advice.

Now, a little scene-setting here would be beneficial. Cobb's extolling the virtues of place hitting took place as F.C. Lane was observing him at spring training. One might speculate that Ty was playing the age-old game of "pull the reporter's leg"; or, alternatively, that the Cobbian ego had gulped down the offered bait of being the One and Only Last Great Place Hitter; or, as yet another alternative, that Cobb the strategist was feeding the gullible Lane a bunch of tall tales in order to intimidate his adversaries through the newspapers. Yet I think we must acknowledge this much of the occasion as unstaged: Cobb really did proceed to put on an impressive place hitting-demonstration before his one-man scribal audience on that golden spring day. Lane describes how Tyrus landed hit after hit in spots that he had predicted, one at-bat after another. It isn't unusual for a master stick-artist to play a little game-within-the-game during spring training so as to tweak his timing. I have heard Lou Piniella speak of how, when manager of the Mariners, he would grow worried at spring workouts when Ichiro would hit everything to the opposite field, day after day... and then how he came to realize that, slowly but surely, the man who would wrest away George Sisler's record for hits in a single season would start pulling in his own good time, once his complicated stroke had stabilized.

Cobb was at spring training. The games didn't count, and the pitchers were throwing nothing but fastballs (they would likely get into trouble if they tried to throw anything else).[11] Naturally, there would be situations during the regular season when being able to take a certain pitch a certain way could prove extremely advantageous. One would practice that skill in the spring; and a hitter like Cobb, furthermore, would practice it until it was truly ready for deployment. Wagner, Sisler, and several other worthies in Lane's chapter conceded that Cobb had managed to acquire the mysterious knack of placing his hits. None of this amounts, however, to claiming that that Cobb could drop any given pitch into any given spot at any given time. As Ty himself explains to Lane, "Naturally I depend mostly on fast balls. I couldn't be so sure of a curve."[12]

One final point, since I made so much of Edd Roush's foot-shuffling earlier: to whatever extent Ty Cobb may have been a genuine place hitter, he was not so due to any scurrying around in the box just as the pitcher started home. I have discussed what I call his "lunge" elsewhere; in effect, this highly variable step of the forward leg would have taken over the role of "skipping" while also rendering any sort of a hop impossible. For you cannot shuffle your feet lightly if they begin pressed side-by-side together—the front foot must be able to fall down briskly (if only from a slight lift) for the rear foot to catch the shift and lift, in turn, before relocating itself. Yet the whole point of such split-second shuffling is merely to concentrate a forward, downward momentum. Cobb, with his bent knees, had substituted for this movement's falling motion the more horizontal thrust of a sprinter firing out of the blocks. That didn't mean, however, that he couldn't fire out either toward or away from the plate, and either for fifteen inches or a yard. Indeed, even if he were deluded in his belief that he stepped where he saw the ball coming, he would necessarily have had much mobility in that step just to have sold himself on the proposition.

In his role as a place hitter (or would-be or sometime place hitter), he had riveted his attention on what his hands were doing, probably because the highly flexible stride had become second nature and needed no surveillance. Likewise for Sisler: the younger man makes clear in Lane's chapter that he admires Cobb and has tried to copy him, so George must also have been employing the adaptable, emphatic thrust off the back leg (though I have found no evidence that he set up with both feet together). The difference between this style and contemporary hitting is far less noticeable than foot-shuffling, but it remains significant. Today's hitter practices hard to achieve the same stride, over and over and over. The Cobb/Sisler approach, as I read it (and add Eddie Collins, for my money), would have been precisely to avoid locking in the stride without any reference to immediate conditions.

We know, furthermore, that Cobb assumed different static positions in the box all the time. We have seen his recipe for befuddling Carl Mays, and he writes elsewhere of such strategies as moving back to catch lefty curveball specialist Doc White's offering after it broke.[13] Once again, the era was so inured to lower-body mobility of this sort that no one, I must conclude, thought it worth mentioning in the specific context of place hitting. Nevertheless, you wouldn't have stood the ghost of a chance of stroking a ball all over the field on various pitches if you were rigidly wedded to an immutable stride and merely varying the arrival time of your barrel.

Let me attempt to summarize my verdict on *place* hitting. In contemporary parlance, I think, all of this would boil down to the following formula: 1) learn to hit to the opposite field—it can win games at critical junctures; 2) let the ball get deep on those occasions when you want to go the other way; and 3) wait for a pitch on the outer half, or else inside-out the high-and-tight fastball—don't try to execute an inside-out swing on a pitch that won't accommodate it.

To the extent that there's anything more to place hitting than the capsule of imperatives above, it has to be in the shifting of the back foot or in a highly adjustable stride: in lower-body movement. Now *there* is a set of techniques as forgotten as our old friend, the coelacanth! They allow you to turn an inside pitch into an outside one, and vice versa, with the pitcher and his defense having virtually no leisure to make an adjustment. Such skills would be well worth the trouble of dusting off… but that proposition will carry me into the odds and ends of my final section.

Ty Cobb, straight drive into pitch

If you pause to consider that Cobb would set up in the box with his cleats virtually touching, then this stride has to measure about four feet: that's why I have labeled it a lunge. The rear foot is already taking leave of its hold in the ground, and contact has not yet occurred; so a very vigorous, more-or-less complete weight shift is ongoing. Note as well that the spread of Cobb's hands is preserved as his top one carries the bat head down into the ball (though this particular pitch appears to be coming in high, probably out of the strike zone: maybe an inside fastball, with Ty striding a bit away from the plate to draw the barrel into play). Some commentators have mistakenly alleged that the hand-spreading evaporated as soon as the Peach started to swing, or even before. It may often vanish during the swing, especially on a low off-speed pitch… but to place the vanishing point before then amounts to declaring the spread a flashy gimmick. That's just plain wrong! Photo courtesy of the National Baseball Hall of Fame Library in Cooperstown, New York.

Part Four

Turn It Over to the Bull Pen

Evaluating the consequences and ramifications of this study: what aspects of the Deadball Era stroke might productively be revived in contemporary hitting, and how recent or current players hearken back to certain elements of the Old School; individual profiles of legendary DBE hitters; a defense of experimentation and inference from the perspective of historians and the historical record.

Chapter Twenty

The Usable Past: Elements of the Deadball Style That Deserve Revival

How you approach tasks, challenges and risks, successes and failures… will affect, therefore, the way a hitter approaches the ball. Clear vision or clouded vision? Relaxed or tense? Does the hitter hold himself responsible or does he hold himself "at fault"? Or does he make excuses?... The starting point for a healthy perspective is clear and simple. Think instead of feel. Be rational, rather than emotional. Step back (out of the frame) and use your brain. Emotions such as frustration, anger fear, resentment, and jealousy—to name a few—distort your perceptions.   N.A. Dorfman[1]

In my opinion catchers do not ordinarily hit well because they know too much about pitching. They've exhausted their ingenuity in trying to circumvent opposing batters. When they become batters themselves, they picture the opposing catcher as having worked all the regulation tricks and invented a few new ones. Their minds are not free and centered on the task in hand. They are thinking about curves, batter's weaknesses and a lot of things. Hence they magnify the difficulties which confront them and usually they don't shine at the bat.   George Sisler[2]

    Personally, I find the past always worth knowing in its own right. Like a strange plant in the rainforest, it may harbor vital secrets or encode miraculous remedies in its DNA that we cannot now appreciate. Burned bridges have a way of proving necessary about the time that the last charred beam falls into the abyss.

    The past also keeps us humble, both by reminding us that we are not giants but merely sit upon giant shoulders (to paraphrase Bernard of Clairvaux) and by warning us that many a vain fool has fallen to his death while reaching for the stars. History is morally improving and morally sobering.

    In the specific context of hitting in the game of baseball—a.k.a. "batsmanship"—however, I fear that our immediate opportunities of applying the wisdom of the past are severely limited, thanks to equipment changes. And when I say "equipment," I mean "bat." As long as the contemporary bat dominates the mass market (and its metallic version will most certainly continue to do so for the foreseeable future), practicing the striker's art as Cobb or Speaker did will remain as quixotic as trying to learn the samurai's craft with a steak knife. That is, some modest degree of carry-over may be discovered, but the exercise for the most part is bound to create many puzzled impressions.

    Virtually all of the suggestions below, therefore, will require imagination and ingenuity of anyone wishing to act upon them. There's no point to testing out a technique on an instrument not made for that technique. Students of hitting who are willing to experiment may very well have to customize a bat somehow or other if they truly wish to sample the Old School.

And then, having run an experiment, they must be very honest with themselves about the results. Both of the opening citations above alert us that we can think ourselves into a state of unthinking; or, to be a little more accurate, Professor Dorfman would have us purge our calculations of those traitorous thoughts known as emotions, while George Sisler urges us to consider what's in plain sight rather than fantasizing about an alternate reality. What attracts me to the statements is their fairness—their scientific integrity, I might almost say. There's no place in an objective evaluation for "soft spots": a young hitter can't ignore persistent failure just to continue imitating his favorite player's leg lift. Likewise, I don't think a fair-minded analyst can keep trying to crowd extrinsic considerations into a simple undertaking. An example of this (analogous to Sisler's over-reflective catcher) might be the boy who protests when asked to try hand-spreading, "But nobody does that now! Show me one successful hitter who does that today!" If it works, do it. The objective is to get good results. Getting those results while also copying the style of a current All Star is not a sensible representation of the task at hand.

Yet I must repeat—with all due respect to The Sizzler—that imagination is required when testing out the techniques of yesteryear: something resembling an old-school bat must be found. A metal model of this sort would be rarer than a Moon rock; but a younger boy or girl, at least, can try out a bat that everyone insists is "too big." A fungo bat is also an option, though what it bestows in length and balance it takes away in feather-lightness. I have not yet learned how to make my own bats effectively, but those with the necessary skills may pursue that option. Maybe the key to reviving old-school hitting is a revival of carpentry!

At any rate, here are my "take-aways" from having studied master batsmen of a century ago. If I ever have the chance to coach another boy or girl, these would be some of the arrows in my quiver.

1) Reach the point of maximal acceleration with the barrel driving in a linear, slightly downward motion.

If a young ballplayer could just accept in principle the notion that giving a straight, slight slope to the stroke is the best way to drive a pitch, then he or she would already be well beyond my starting point, almost twenty years ago, as a concerned father. I explained earlier my struggle to find a way through the miasma of "uppercutting" versus "swinging in the ball's plane of flight" versus—most repellent of all, originally—"backspinning" the pitch. As it turned out, the single option of these three that I resisted long and fiercely (mostly due to the kind of emotion that Dorfman warns us about) was the correct one. If the novice, then, could embark upon a study of hitting with the clear understanding that correctly executed backspin produces line-drives rather than pop-ups, then subsequent lessons will rise upon a foundation of granite, not of sand.

The irony is that the stance and stroke emphasized today as the surefire way to impart backspin are a very poor means to that end. Lifting the bat over your rear shoulder, cocking your rear elbow high, pumping your forward knee, then hurtling down on the plate (in hopes that you may find the ball there) by yanking knob with bottom hand and driving down bottom hand with top one, then "squishing the bug" and letting the handle fly out of your upper paw... all of this may produce a few homers for a tall body-type playing in a small park, but it conceals several vulnerabilities, even then. The barrel's angle of descent is too steep. There's a brief instant where the swing levels off before charging up an equally steep ascent (led now by the bottom hand alone). At that moment, the hitter might achieve something like the proper angle of entry to drive the ball. Earlier, and he pops it up; later, and he weakly topspins it.

Now, youngsters with exceptional height can get so much acceleration into the stroke with this "hurl down" method that initial feedback may be very positive for them. Let's admit the truth: to young players and their coaches alike, one homer per every three or four games counts as positive feedback, even if each dinger is nestled in an assortment of unproductive at-bats. The "ceiling" looks high for these budding sluggers. Just imagine how many home runs they'll hit with a bit more growth and drilling! As for other kids, swinging the short, top-heavy bat in such a manner makes them clearly inferior at what has become a tall guy's game. Hence my excessively emotional response to the notion of backspin: I viewed it almost as a conspiracy for keeping shorter children off the team.

I have a suspicion that if young hitters would just get the image fixed in their heads of slicing the ball in two while the barrel is still headed mildly downward, they would find their own way of performing close to potential. Boys of my day were told to lift the ball with their uppercut swing. They understood intuitively that this would require a jet-propelled start at the pitch, since the front hip needed to open—according to the Mantle/Williams paradigm—before the hands went forward. Hence they shot out of the blocks with their after-burners flaming. They often reached the pitch too early and topspun it, especially if it came in below the belt. The "highly trained professional" (or his weekend-warrior clone) observing from the third-base coach's box would diagnose a "pulling off" resulting from excessive ferocity in the attack—probably over-striding. The boy would be told this, take a more restrained stride resulting in a more tentative swing, arrive late and pop up or strike out, and at last conclude that he had no talent for the game.[3]

Now, if the young hitter gets it in his head that he doesn't have to lift the ball before it crosses the front of the plate, then he can relax a bit. He can let the pitch come to him. He can attack it before rather than after his stroke emerges from its dip (though this would favor riding up on his front foot, a tendency which many coaches would be sure to red-flag for him). He can be patient, in other words. And if the ball is consistently contacted as the bat remains in the hyperbola's downward curve, then the length of the stride doesn't matter, and the finishing position of the head doesn't matter, and the front foot's stepping away from the plate at a sharp angle doesn't matter. Swings are for hitting baseballs: the ball isn't thrown to provide a pretext for showing off an elegant pirouette.

To hit well, you need to create an effective metaphor of how hitting works. *You hit with your mind before you hit with your hands.* You visualize. An improper visualization will lead to perception misaligned with bodily movements. "See ball, hit ball," is admittedly about the most productive thought you can have running through your head as you await the pitch in a game situation (as Dorfman concurs in his fine book's first chapter)... yet it would also be naïve to think that any human hitter could ever reduce his craft to so robotic a command. The combined motions required are too numerous and intricate. Practice is needed; and to practice, you must have a paradigm—a picture running over and over in the back of your mind. Practice without a good plan is worse than no practice at all, for then you commit flawed motion to muscle-memory.

The DBE hitter's explosive chop into the pitch is the best video, the best paradigm, that a young hitter could possibly keep reviewing in his imagination: that's my considered opinion. George Sisler warns that the hitter's mind can be too broadly focused, guessing feverishly at the coming pitch's variety, location, likelihood of nicking the strike zone... all the things that a good catcher would assess as he scans the current situation before flashing his signals. This is too much for the hitter. See ball, hit ball—but hit ball hard. Smack it through its heart. Make the barrel explode through the orb's spinning equator.

2) Grip the handle in the fingers—do not lock the thumbs around it—and keep the wrists bent.

It's presumptuous, in a way, to volunteer this advice as an insight provided by studying DBE batsmen; for the same advice has appeared in every hitting manual published since that gilded era (some of which I've cited in this book) until, say, about twenty years ago. On the other hand, it's sad to reflect that such a venerable continuum of advice now leads to a dead end. The handles of today's bats are so thin that they snuggle deep into the palm no matter how hard you try to keep them out. A Big Leaguer could naturally order his bats made to whatever specs he preferred; but even this star was once a Little Leaguer... and where would he have learned to hit with a thicker-handled bat in the late twentieth century? Perhaps in Venezuela, with the cast-off shaft of his *tio*'s shovel....

If you can't get the handle to nestle securely in your middle knuckles, then you can't bend your wrists dynamically; and without the bend in the wrists, you can't lead the barrel through a linear attack upon the pitch. Handles locked up in fists describe a distinctly rotational stroke. There's no other option: it's anatomical destiny.

I have mentioned in passing before now Albert Pujols's preparatory technique of thrusting the bat outward to work the handle into the fingers. (Come to think of it, this is not unlike Ty Cobb's sacrosanct ritual of thrusting the bat out from his body, though his hands were much lower.) I also occasionally observe a contemporary hitter pressing his back elbow in to force some bend into his top wrist. As for a grip where both wrists are lithely bent... *that* I have not seen for perhaps two decades. Those of us who have been around a while can ramble off the names of a few hitters that were always associated with great wrists: Williams, Aaron, Banks... and Billy Williams, too, by the way... Clemente, Cepeda, Carew.... Boys of my generation loved to imitate Rocky Colavito's dramatic pointing of his barrel right at the pitcher just before both of them drew up into readiness. This, too, was a way of settling the handle into the fingers.

Where are those hitters now? Name one hitter who is known in the twenty-first century as a great wrist-hitter. Our fractious adolescent might nag, "See? You can't! That must mean that it's not such a good idea, since nobody does it." Not necessarily, O Inheritor of the Omniscience Gene: it may mean that your generation no longer has bats that allow for maximally effective wrist action. The great wrists are still there, but they lack tools that allow them to work effectively.

And "nobody," by the way, is probably a bit strong. Martin Prado deserves an honorable mention, and several of the young Latin players are promising. Boys, in other words, who are not raised in our system using our sophisticated hardware appear to have a much better chance of learning to operate their hands dynamically.

I will have much more to say in the next chapter about characteristics of DBE hitting that linger in our own time. Perhaps there I can convince certain young people who find today's players clearly the best and brightest that no great mountain has ever been climbed without ropes.

3) Consider choking up and/or spreading the hands.
Oddly enough, choking up has not yet passed entirely out of vogue. Barry Bonds may even have brought it somewhat back into style. A major resurgence in popularity is a little hard to imagine, however, when many Major Leaguers are using 32-inch—or even 31-inch—bats. What remains to choke up on?

Mother Nature seems to persuade some kids that it's a good idea, even with their "brick on a string" metal-alloy models. I once observed, from the outside looking in, the ultimate know-it-all coach ordering a boy who had come to him as an exceptional hitter to stop choking up and get down on the knob. The boy's hitting efficacy started declining immediately. To my certain knowledge, this man was responsible for turning at least a few youngsters away from baseball permanently. In his "manly" mind, choking up was an indicator of weakness, and probably "girlishness." I'd like to have seen him express that sentiment to Bonds, Joey Votto, or Hunter Pence!

Nevertheless, even with Mother Nature whispering words of encouragement and a great many color commentators extolling the virtues of choking up on broadcasts, I don't think the real advantage of the maneuver is generally appreciated; and, again, the shift to short sticks isn't going to shed any light on the question. With the grip raised, the bottom hand actually has something substantial beneath it to leverage. Old-time hitters (and by that I mean hitters as recently as twenty years ago) routinely used to leave the thumb and forefinger of their bottom hand very loose on the bat, applying most of the pressure with their pinky and ring finger. On a short bat, the pinky may be engaging nothing but thin air while the ring finger curls over the knob. Not much "lever" action can possibly occur. The choke-up provides a solution, even though it superficially appears unnecessary on a light bat and also decreases the already much-curtailed reach of the barrel. I suspect that boys (and men) who opt for choking up must surely have "clever" hands, and that they understand as if by instinct the benefit they're getting by letting the bottom hand work the handle like a hammer.

Now, as for hand-spreading... if certain cerebrally challenged coaches find something feminine in the choke-up, I suppose they would consider a hand-spread tantamount to playing with Barbie dolls. I confided early on in this book that disparaging remarks were made about a boy's masculinity when I was growing up if he dared spread his hands. The good news is that there's absolutely no room for spreading on the contemporary bat, where choking up with closed hands can just barely be accommodated on some of the longer models.

The bad news is that the defunct hand-spread would have enhanced all the advantages of choking. The quick, strong swat that becomes possible when the bottom hand pulls in as the top hand punches down is magnified in proportion to the distance between the hands (up to two or three inches, anyway). Now, to be sure, in a swing where the overriding rule is "stay back," such a linear stroke works against the rotation in the lower body and must inevitably degenerate into something more compatible with a circle; but for hitters who have a pronounced forward weight shift, the use of a longer bat conducive to choking up and to spreading the hands would release stunning reserves of power, I am convinced.

At the very, very least, hitters fond of practicing the so-called slap-bunt, where the show of bunting is a feint and the hands are drawn back together for a chop at the pitch, should remember the truths above about hand-spreading. A chop with spread hands working properly together would be both more accurate in its aim and more potent in its impact. Why not pick up a dollar that just happens to be lying on the sidewalk? If you ever use the chop-swing, why not reinforce it? You don't even have to bend over: the pay-off is literally sitting in your hands.

4) Consider keeping the back foot somewhat mobile rather than digging in inflexibly.

Here, at last, is a strategy that doesn't depend almost completely on the use of a longer bat. And yet, employing a shorter bat on a swing that shifts weight emphatically to the front foot might prove a little awkward. This is because of balance. Let me try to explain.

The main reason you might wish to keep your back foot somewhat unmoored when you set up, with your weight leaned heavily to your front side, would be to transfer all of your weight to the rear when you load. As we have often noted, to begin a strong movement in one direction, you gather your energy in the reverse direction. Now, once you had positioned that rear leg where you wanted it and had backloaded your weight upon it, your front leg would need to lift and also veer backward. Following the principle that you make a strong move toward Z by preceding it with a move toward A, the raised forward leg is destined to come down and catch virtually all of the weight that was gathered to the rear. With so much weight-shifting occurring on feet so close together and a frame so erect, the bat would play an essential role in preserving balance throughout. The front leg might even remain airborne for a second or more, so… the longer the stick, the greater its balancing effect.

You could say that there's a rocking motion—a pendulum effect—brought into being whenever one of the two props upon which the human body stands is lifted up. The sluggers of the Golden Age, with their breathtakingly fierce strides, would go forward so hard precisely so that they could plant the front foot firmly and throw their weight back to the rear. (For the Williams release of the hips is throwing weight backward as well as channeling energy outward: uppercut hitters actually desire this about-face of energy. Only a very few sluggers consistently executed the Gehrig style of drive that would achieve contact while force was still traveling somewhat forward and not yet cycling decisively rearward. Williams himself may have been one of these, as well as Mickey Mantle.) The more contemporary method of using a high leg kick, as opposed to yesteryear's lock-kneed or modestly coiling lift, does a better job of keeping weight forward than a Fifties coil-and-lunge; but the forward vector tends to point steeply into the ground before home plate, and the desired *slightly* downward cut of the swing becomes excessive.

We're going over old turf now. What I would highlight is this: a loose rear foot that suddenly digs in for the load would be ideal for legs that stay pretty close together and erect—which in turn would be ideal for a controlled fall into the pitch, with very thorough forward weight transfer. Both the Fifties coil (if I may call it so, for convenience) and the Arod leg kick (more shorthand), however, require that the feet be somewhat-to-very widespread, because both are throwing weight partially backward-and-down and not exclusively forward-and-down. (In other words, both "stretch the rubber band" between front foot and trailing hands.) This means that the front foot has to get so far out ahead of the body that the forward shift remains modest… and (need I repeat) it also means that such swings are going to be proportionally more rotational and less linear.

With his erect, relatively close-together feet and his controlled forward fall, in contrast, the old-school batsman with the mobile rear foot really needs a longer bat, especially to stay balanced just before the fall. The only alternative would be to carry the light bat far to the rear, emulating the style of a Japanese hitter like Ichiro; and the problem with that adjustment (from a Deadball point of view) is that, yet again, it produces a very rotational kind of stroke that I have called sabering. Our DBE striker, remember, played it pretty close to the vest as far as how upward and rearward he held his hands. He needed them at the ready for a concise, slightly downward blow that stayed linear.

So, even here, I suppose that the longer bat is almost a "must" for those who would borrow something extremely productive from yesteryear. Too bad… because the ability to plant the back foot quite late would allow the hitter to achieve something in the vicinity of place hitting, magnifying the likelihood of pulling the pitch or stroking it the opposite way—or of catching the slider before it broke. In an era when shifts are shaving fifty points off of batting averages, it seems to me that the game could well use an adjustment of that order.

Where, then, are the manufacturers and marketers who will bring us a "new old bat"… and where is the outcry from players for their services? He who hath ears, let him hear.

Chapter Twenty-One

"He Could Have Played With Us": How the Old School Has Lingered in Certain Recent Swings

If you're balanced and you're back, you should be able to take batting practice on one leg. And some players have even approached doing that in regular games. If you've ever seen pictures of Japan's leading hitter, Sadaharu Oh, you know that he lifts his front knee and brings his thigh up when he strides. Vic Davalillo used to do something similar, and Mel Ott used to kick his leg out a little. Unusual as they are, I think these moves are all mechanically sound. They all have the effect of getting the weight back on top of that rear leg before starting it forward.   Charley Lau[1]

I say that Ty Cobb was the only white ballplayer that we observed who played somewhat like we played on the American Giants. None of the teams in the major leagues in those years—and up to now—really concentrated their attack against the opposition. The batters come up and they swing away and okay, it's a double play or a triple play—or a home run. But they so often fail....   Dave Malarcher[2]

    Ty Cobb was a tormented soul, it seems. On the eve of his first big break in baseball, he received the news that his mother had shot and killed his father; and as he was beginning his first full season in the Major Leagues, the Widow Cobb was standing trial for manslaughter. She was acquitted, arguing that she had mistaken her husband for a burglar in the dark... but that didn't give her eldest child back the one figure whose approval he claimed ever to have valued, and who had been very skeptical of his son's dallying in baseball. It was at just this time in his life that young Tyrus was treated to steady doses of what might variously be called teasing, hazing, harassing, or bullying. By all accounts, he didn't respond well.

    A certain contempt for people who drawl lingers north of the Mason-Dixon Line to this day. I can only imagine what slurs and obstacles must actually have come Cobb's way as the Civil War smoldered in the memory of many a player's father or grandfather. Lives and limbs were lost on both sides. A boy from the Deep South, stigmatized by an accent (the word "athlete" came out "a-tha-lete" in Cobb's radio interviews), would certainly have faced challenges in a progressive northern city. In fact, no small degree of the illiterate Joe Jackson's complicity in the "Black Sox" scandal may well have been motivated by a desire to appear clever, for once, in the eyes of his northern teammates.

    The baseball "historians" that I hear cited so often on television, especially, have made Ty Cobb (with lots of rhetoric and straw) into the evil Other that they love to slay.[3] Many continue to take Al Stump's discredited book (published over thirty years after Cobb's death, when even those who had known him personally were gone) as their gospel on the subject.[4] Until recently, the MLB

Channel contributed to the greater good by re-running incessantly the Tommy Lee Jones movie based on Stump's sensationalist fantasy. *Field of Dreams* also receives lots of playing time, naturally. The film's single reference to Cobb has an absurdly Yankee-accented Joe Jackson explaining that the all-time hits leader hasn't been invited to the games because "none of us could stand the bastard when he was alive"—a particularly ungrounded sneer to place in the mouth of someone assisted by Cobb in his later life's reduced circumstances. It's simply inconceivable that the real Shoeless Joe would ever have said anything of the kind. Well, what can you expect from a movie whose "research" failed to turn up that Jackson threw right-handed?

To some commentators nourished in these elite circles, any praise of Cobb at all—even as a hitter, a technician with a bat—will appear a moral outrage, as if one were to compliment Adolf Hitler's landscape paintings. I should like to make it clear that I do not consider myself a judge of the man as a human being. The people who might most justifiably have refused ever to utter Cobb's name often mentioned him with admiration, like Dave Malarcher above. The basis of this admiration was professional, to be sure. Yet Malarcher must also have realized a) that Cobb's social prejudices were a product of his upbringing, and b) that the North was a long way from being free of those same prejudices. Read Leon Wagner's boyhood recollections of the Detroit Riots in Jackie Robinson's *Baseball Has Done It*.[5]

And as for those prejudices, I would refer anyone interested in the subject to Charles Leerhsen's stunning review of the evidence.[6] I read Leerhsen's insightful book a year after writing the words above in a preliminary draft; I had already been convinced by the tenor of Cobb's own writing and by deep contradictions in the testimony against him that a gross injustice had been done. Mr. Leerhsen only confirmed several distinct impressions.

One of these was that the man who had said admiringly of a young Willie Mays, "He could have played with us"—a man who very seldom made such remarks even of white ballplayers in the Fifties—could not have been a rabid bigot.[7] Indeed, having been born and raised in the South, Cobb would have known much better than any Caucasian from the North just what someone like Willie must have endured in the Sally League. This is precisely what Leon Wagner said of his white teammate and friend, Bill Moran (another Georgian), in Jackie Robinson's book.[8]

I have begun the present chapter by clearing the deck of "politically correct" encumbrances because, first, I want all those who have such reservations to know that we are not now, and have not been in the preceding pages, concerned with nominating anyone for sainthood; and, second, because it's an inescapable fact, once you look into the matter, that among recent hitters, minorities are far more likely to preserve certain DBE techniques than WASP types. Call it an irony, if you will: it is that, no doubt. (Tris Speaker, who came into this world a few miles down the road from my own birthplace, was rumored—on scant evidence—to have been a Klansman.)[9] Personally, I don't find the explanation of this oddity to be dark or bitter or conspiratorial in any way. It runs as follows:

kids from "fringe" environments, in Middle American terms—fatherless kids from the Projects who learn baseball in some park riddled with dope-peddlers, kids whose dads labor in a Third World mine or factory all day and half the night, kids in more well-to-do but culturally eccentric settings whose buddies prefer basketball or soccer—are not processed through the same channels as the typical high-school player. As youngsters, they don't have metal-alloy bats, organized little leagues, batting cages, or Buck Stormgard's Miracle Swingmatic Hit-a-Flick (batteries not included). They just play. They swing what they have by way of a bat and throw what they have by way of a ball. They teach themselves. And while what they learn this way isn't foolproof, it is at least *them*. It comes natural. They have a chance to build upon the instinctive rather than to be drilled in some paradigm until it becomes their second nature, rendering them incapable of ever finding their way back to their original inclination. They have a hammer that they can swing like a hammer: nobody is forcing them to pretend that it's a wagon wheel or a set of bolas.

Certain characters in baseball's ongoing epic have had a way of wielding a bat that I shall never forget, even though I only saw it on a grainy black-and-white television screen one time as a kid. **Leon Wagner** and **Wes Covington** fall into that category. I have already mentioned Leon's Cobb-like spread of the hands; and Covington, whose coil resembled Stan Musial's with a little extra bend everywhere, suggested the DBE tactic of keeping the bat low and away from the body. I was privileged to have slightly more and better views of **Vic Davalillo** at a slightly older age, so I can recall what Charley Lau is talking about above (though, having seen many a clip of Mel Ott, I can't imagine what Charley's basis of comparison is in writing that Ott would "kick his leg out *a little*"). The stiff forward leg-lift clearly hadn't died out with the running board and the high-top shoe: Tiger second-baseman **Dick McAuliffe** also employed it in the Sixties.

In further proof whereof, I offer the fairly recent hitter who seems from my recollections to embody perhaps the most old-school techniques: **José Cruz, Sr.** Spending most of his career as an Astro, Cruz collected 2,251 hits—and he did it with a panache only partially attributable to the disco-do that flowed from under his batting helmet. His feet were rather close together, as Cobb had recommended; and though he stood relatively erect in the box, I believe his knees were slightly bent. Hands were held out from body and at about the height of the armpits. As the pitcher delivered, José's forward leg would lift high and straight and his lower hand would draw the knob back into full cock. Once the leg descended, the barrel would follow it down almost immediately. I recall Cruz shooting a lot of balls up the middle, and pretty much on a line. In an era that saw few 30-HR sluggers, he was a very successful middle-of-the-order man.

And then there's **Harold Baines**, of whom one could make many of the same remarks. Harold is almost the final hitter highlighted in Lau's *Art of Hitting .300*.[10] One can find a very helpful sequence of photos there that reveals the low and outward-held hands again, a leg kick with notably less height than Cruz's and more of a knee coil, and then—at last—a transfer of weight so emphatic that the back foot leaves the ground. Baines tallied almost 2,900 hits and 500 doubles. He would probably occupy a space in the Hall of Fame if he had not passed much of his career under the "shadow" (as it has proved to be) of designated hitting.

One can observe these tendencies tailing off at different rates and in different directions, of course. The hand-positioning and the all-out forward transfer of weight appear in **Rod Carew**. **Tony Fernandez** was Carew on a slightly less dynamic scale. I'm pretty sure that Rodney spread his hands on occasion, as well; and I remarked earlier that several contemporary players still employ a trace of that strategy, often semi-concealed under their batting gloves. Among slightly less recent players who have distinguished themselves, add **Bill Madlock**'s name to the hand-spread list. Madlock was a batting champ rather than a wall-banger; yet in all of these cases (and recall that they include Banks, Dawson, and probably current star Andrew McCutchen), I'm convinced that the spread permitted the bottom hand to pull in as the top hand drove forward, providing a subtle but significant source of late acceleration. Depending on the hitter's size, strength, lower-body movement, and other factors, the enhanced contact might mean more hang-time and distance or more exit velocity in a low line-drive... but the hitter's "game," whatever its specific parameters, was indeed enhanced.[11]

Is it possible that certain tricks of the trade have embedded themselves covertly in certain organizations? In mentioning Madlock above and then dropping McCutchen's name parenthetically, I recalled having seen the versatile Pirate Josh Harrison spread his hands on one occasion; then I smacked my head and cried, "I've forgotten **Jason Kendall**!" Kendall's hand-spreading was both distinctly noticeable and fairly routine. It must also have been effective, for not many catchers ever surpass 2,000 hits. Is this a tradition taught to Pirates as far back as the Waners, and even Honus Wagner himself and his mentor Fred Clarke? (Kendall doesn't mention the technique in his otherwise intricately revealing book about how he played the game [see ch. 16, n. 2]; perhaps every Pirate is sworn to conceal it on the sword of Captain Blood.)

I haven't the space to catalogue all recent hitters who have come up rather heavily on their front leg during the weight transfer; but this strategy, as well as preserving the stroke's downward angle for a longer stretch, would have allowed them to reach more breaking and off-speed pitches by making their vertical axis more mobile. Such sluggers could "go out and get it," often taking difficult pitches to the opposite field with great power. The names of **Julio Franco** and **Mike Piazza** leap to mind.

Those two, of course, used very long bats by current standards. To class Albert Pujols, Miguel Cabrera, and Mike Trout as adherents to the same style would require a squint of the imagination's eye; yet Paul Reddick, through his online *90 MPH Club*, posted some videos not long ago exposing that all of these superstar hitters actually depart from their back foot on contact when they deliver an effective swing. Reddick even eased his way out on the Limb of Controversy and revealed that Trout doesn't (or, at the time, didn't) practice his stroke under the tutelage of instructors the same way as he executes it in the heat of battle.[12] Paul has featured several videos by hitting guru Mike Ryan, as well, who advocates a powerful stride shifting weight wholly forward instead of the "balanced" fifty-fifty paradigm popular in the Nineties—*our* Nineties—and the early twenty-first century. Other online coaches are picking up the theme.[13]

    I would love to know where **Steve Garvey** came by his extraordinary swing. A figure so muscled-up around the forearms that his nickname was Popeye, Garvey in fact used rather little in the rest of his linebacker's build to drive the ball. A very quiet lift and then drop of the forward leg, with minimal bending of the knee, allowed his hands to descend into the pitch in that linear fashion highlighted throughout this book. Steve is also featured in Charley Lau's classic manual.[14] I'm not entirely sure why I have not volunteered him as the most instructive recent example of the DBE stroke: perhaps because he hit right-handed, or perhaps because his massive frame makes one think in Russian proper nouns like "Kalashnikov" rather than "Baryshnikov." Indeed, Garvey's impressive physique has probably worked against him in Hall of Fame balloting, for the disappointment at his not having hit for more power always surfaces. Yet he topped 200 hits in five seasons, many of those safeties falling in the opposite field. Such accomplishments reflect the DBE artist's skills—skills suddenly devalued, even a century ago, by the Babe's explosion upon the scene.

    If you were to take Garvey's approach and give it some sharp tugs—really sharp—around the edges, you might end up with **Gary Sheffield**. Both of these stand-outs were affected by the Steroids Era in very different—but perhaps equally terminal—ways, as far as concerns HOF voting. Perhaps if the voters understood the degree to which technique contributed to Shef's success, they would reconsider their reluctance. It will sound odd to reverse the Garvey argument now and claim that DBE methods actually created one of the most potent sluggers of the Nineteen-Nineties; yet recall that Babe Ruth, though perceived by Cobb as the antithesis of elegant, artful hitting, embraced vastly more of old Ty's tendencies than he rejected, especially if we cast our eyes forward twenty or thirty years.

    I notice two things, in particular, about Sheffield: the very active and finally straight leg lift and a bottom hand equally active in its load. Spectators who saw far more of Gary in uniform than I ever did will insist that his forward knee bent vigorously—which I do not deny; but these naysayers have failed to notice how the leg stiffened well before landing. The redirection in its vector of force just before touchdown from "out" to "down" allowed for a more linear, downward stroke, with the hitter's shift now being able to ride up emphatically on a stiff front side. (All of the foregoing, by the way, was true in spades of **Ruben Sierra**'s famous leg-kick.) As for that signature—and unforgettably violent—flicking back and forth of the bat in an impatient load, it makes me imagine a bottom hand yelling at itself to go out and away so that it will go down and in during the swing: a "levering" action being prepared by reverse motion.

    If little of the above appears reminiscent of Steve Garvey, perhaps **Darryl Strawberry** would make a more convincing precursor to Sheffield. Straw Man also featured forward leg movement with premature straightening by today's standards; despite the high leg kick, Darryl more or less glided into a plant of the front foot. Although his hands were far less nervous than Gary's, I suspect that the lower one was again entrusted with the mission of working out and back as the top one remained relatively still—a load intended to catalyze that "parallel-reverse" collaboration. **Hanley Ramirez**'s technique has preserved some of the same style. What strikes me as making Sheffield more old-school than either Strawberry or Ramirez (and more like Garvey, ultimately) is the strong top hand that stays on the handle throughout the follow-through. This is important. Just as a knee that coils backward supplies a constant temptation to rotate the front hip unless the rear leg is stiff and straight, so a top hand that routinely surrenders the handle early is probably on the path to less-than-complete transfer of weight forward before contact. The amazing **Miguel Cabrera** usually manages to do both: to release early and to hit from the front foot. For most body types, however, this seems to be an uncomfortable combination that tends to break down.

Picking out specific tendencies in your favorite players' swings is an entertaining parlor game, but it is perhaps more amusing than informative at last. Though I have dedicated this chapter to answering the protests of my here-and-now-fixated adolescent in the previous chapter, I don't know how many of my exemplars can fairly be alleged to have Deadball DNA in them—especially those who arrived on the scene after bats began getting radically shorter and lighter. At some point, drawing such parallels risks becoming as subjective and fanciful as Hamlet's twitting of the obsequious "yes" men, Rosencrantz and Guildenstern, by having them admit to seeing various shapes in the clouds. A cloud, finally, is just a cloud… and Aaron Judge is not Babe Ruth.

A couple of current players, then (current as I write—and long may they continue in uniform!), must suffice to fill out this list. Perhaps no player today keeps the Deadball Era more alive, in spirit as well as style, than **José Altuve**. I notice few players' bats going more linearly into the ball on a slight incline. A leg kick that largely resists hip rotation allows this straight descent of the barrel. The clever hands are also working in parallel-reverse fashion to accelerate the downward drive. A documentary aired by MLB Channel showed the diminutive warrior at home in Venezuela getting in some off-season practice by beating on an old tire with a sledgehammer;[15] so we seem to have come full circle back to the carnival! José's size may actually work in his behalf, in that he sees—and hits—a lot of pitches that would correspond to the upper limit of a DBE batsman's strike zone, though probably not strikes by today's measure. (Yet he is often forced to attack such offerings, I believe, because the umps have grown conditioned to taller players.) The linear punch is ideal for cutting into the heart of a high fastball. Our day's dominant stroke is singularly ill suited for handling high hard ones—but they're right in Altuve's hammering wheelhouse.

Nolan Arenado is also exceptionally adept at driving straight into a high fastball at a slight incline. Though quite tall in comparison to José, of course, Nolan has an old-school trick that I've observed in no other hitter of this generation—and, frankly, cannot recall seeing in any other hitter during my long lifetime: he resets his rear foot. It's a small movement, and probably no one who hasn't been trying to reverse-engineer Tris Speaker's stroke would ever notice it; but just before the swing starts, the back foot picks up and settles in again. No doubt, this is a technique (conscious or otherwise) to load backward strongly so as to prime a strong forward weight shift. As such, it would possess the extreme advantage of reducing the time that a complicated leg kick would consume. Front-back-front: then down come the hands along a straight, mild, extended slope. In preparing the swing, the front foot stays very busy, too, by initiating minute but incremental back-and-forth shifts. Fascinating!

No more examples: just a couple of quick anecdotes. On the afternoon of August 10, 2016, Johnny Cueto was twirling a no-hitter for the Giants against the Chicago Cubs. Yet as the game edged its way through the sixth inning, a couple of Cub runners somehow reached base. Since the score was nail-bitingly close (I believe San Francisco had a one-run lead: I am writing from recollection and a few notes), every pitch was critical. Chris Coghlan was at the plate, with two strikes. Aware of the stakes and probably tensing up, he had called for time out… but had not received it. Who knows if Cueto perceived his confusion and hastened the next delivery, as only Johnny can? Caught completely off guard, Coghlan hadn't time to load up in his usual manner or even set his feet. He quite literally had to hop back into the box, shuffle into the pitch, and protect the zone… which he did well enough to stroke the Cubs' first hit and bring in a crucial run.

I recall rearing back as if a ghost had silently flitted across my TV screen. Had I just witnessed the Speaker Two-Step?

Exactly one month later (maybe the haunting conformed to a regular cycle, as I'm told they do), on September 10, Yankee catcher Gary Sanchez was being intentionally walked when he decided to reach out and stroke a rather-too-careless wide one to deep center field. The fly barely stayed in the park and was easily sufficient to bring home an important run from third. Once again, the hitter had abandoned every element of his well-rehearsed swing and simply executed a shuffle-step and a simple stroke.

Neither of these hitters, nor any of their peers, is likely ever to reenact such a swing for the rest of his professional career… but in both instances, the shuffle appeared to get the job done. So why is it an inviolable law of batsmanship that the back foot must be dug in and kept immobile?

Chapter Twenty-Two

Snapshot Album: Brief Profiles of Deadball Era Swings

Back at the turn of the century, you know, we didn't have the mass communications and mass transportation that exist nowadays. We didn't have as much schooling, either. As a result, people were more unique then, more unusual, more different from each other. Now people are all more or less alike, company men, security-minded, conformity—that sort of stuff. In everything, not just baseball.   Davy Jones[1]

    This chapter could as easily have been an appendix, except that its contents should really be viewed as something more than a postscript or an addendum. In a way, they constitute the nucleus of everything the book has sought to communicate—for here are actual players who embodied some or most of the techniques represented in the previous pages. Indeed, I thought seriously about placing the material far earlier in the book: that, too, could easily have been justified. My method, however, has been to reconstruct a broad paradigm through a kind of reverse engineering, sometimes stumbling and lurching as I go, occasionally having to admit major mistakes made along the way that required doubling back. It was through the paradigm that I was able (with some success, I believe) to understand specific styles of the time. Even when I discovered that a player's style decidedly ruptured the paradigm in some ways and left me a bit shocked (and this was nowhere more true than in the case of Ty Cobb), I found the novel style at issue more comprehensible against the backdrop of certain bedrock assumptions generally applicable to Deadball hitters.

    Now, to have planted descriptions of particular players' practices beneath my bedrock assumptions, as it were, doesn't sound like good architecture. Putting the particular first would have disrupted everything. It would have belied the actual order I followed and also have made the whole presentation harder to understand than it already is. And I hasten to add that I still don't know what's going on in the productive strokes of these immortals beyond certain parameters. In each case, I have tried to assemble a workable whole from an array of stray pieces. I should love to blunder upon new sources of evidence that would give me enough fresh insight to write another edition of this book; but, for now, the descriptions below are my best guesses at how the batsmen named went about the business that made them legends.

    For the most part, I have abstained both from any new footnoting and from recycling notes already used. The objective here is just to leave a final clear, succinct impression of the practices that I dismantled and put under the microscope in the previous chapters.

    To that end, I should begin with the strikers of the late nineteenth century whose suspiciously calm poses confront us most often from the panels of tobacco cards. Without doubt, their posture is somewhat staged; but a major assumption I made here was that it was not entirely so, and could in fact be studied for important clues. Since the method of these batsmen became a large part of the paradigm off of which I worked to reconstruct swings another ten or fifteen years down the road, I should like to have found out much more about it... but there wasn't more to be found, in the form either of recorded accounts or of photographs. I was unable even to resolve a generalized picture into usefully individualized portraits, and so I have merged all of my impressions to make a profile that I call Nineties Style, for the sake of convenience.

Obviously, once we pass the century's milestone, all of the players are alphabetized by last name. No sort of ranking is implied.

"Nineties Style"

Entering the box... Feet squared to the plate and relatively close together (probably within fifteen inches) to create an erect stance, front foot angled slightly outward toward the pitcher; shoulders may be slightly bent in the hint of a crouch, but just as often the shoulders are thrown back and the head very upright; hands choking up on handle and—about half the time—spread noticeably, positioned less than a foot above the belt and at mid-chest ("over the buttons") without more than two or three inches of separation from torso; bat either tilted toward rear shoulder and allowed to rest there or else positioned to "droop" slightly outward and rearward, with barrel veering over plate.

From this set-up, the striker would be positioned to initiate his swing with a modest, stiff leg lift, in coordination with which the bottom hand, especially, would lift in preparation for a downward chop upon the ball. The hands would not stray too far to the rear or climb much higher than the set-up, for their task was simply to bring the barrel down upon the ball in a straight line as the body's weight fell upon the lowered front foot. The crispness of the chop and the weight of the barrel would backspin the ball beyond the infield, ideally, on a low line. The barrel would finish over the front shoulder and close to the body in a controlled, two-handed follow-through.

This profile appears to approximate the technique of Dan Brouthers, Roger Connor, Buck Ewing, King Kelly, Tommy McCarthy, Jim O'Rourke, and Sam Thompson, among many others. Yet all of these seven probably managed to apply the stroke with somewhat more vigor than my representation above. I would love to have more particulars!

Max Carey

Entering the box... Shoulders slightly slumped but body otherwise fairly erect and relaxed; feet close together but probably less so than in Nineties Style, with hands also setting up (and no doubt loading) a little more to the rear; the grip chokes up on both sides of plate, but hands are spread more often from left side than from right (power) side;[2] bat long but not particularly thick for era.

Though not often mentioned in this book, Carey was a Hall of Famer whose switch-hitting style, overall physique, and offensive game have very much in common with the slightly later Frank Frisch. Carey—and Frisch—featured the controlled, two-handed follow-through of Nineties Style and were probably very conscious of reaching base, above all else. A slightly more rearward load and occasionally lower follow-through may indicate that Max's stroke was growing somewhat more rotational than the classic Nineties version. He was a patient hitter for his time, logging many at-bats and also many walks, striking few extra-base hits but able to move up a base via the steal with great regularity. The succinct chop would have been well suited for driving darters through an infield that was probably often drawn in to defend against his considerable bunting skills.

Fred Clarke

Entering the box... Perhaps closest to Nineties Style of anyone on the twentieth-century list—not surprisingly, for his career began in the Nineties; a righty who batted left, choking up and spreading his hands; feet close together in set-up and squared to plate, or perhaps slightly closed toward plate, with the hint of a crouch in knees and shoulders.

Clarke was a manager of and mentor to Honus Wagner, reportedly responsible for teaching him how to step where he saw the ball coming. This would require the front foot and the hands to move virtually in unison, so Fred's grip could not have loaded very far back from the set-up position. His forward leg movement was likely rather stiff and controlled, and he followed through high and two-handed over the planted leg. Yet he seems to have done more than merely slap the ball out of the infield, for his percentage of extra-base hits is about a quarter (compared to Collins's, which is closer to a fifth).

Ty Cobb

Entering the box... Feet set up nearly or fully touching and knees bent in a crouch, hands held directly before torso at about a foot's distance; hands choking up on handle and also spread two or three inches.

From this highly original, distinctly tense, and uniquely awkward-looking position, Cobb would launch forward, apparently (so he claimed) trimming the direction and extent of his stride to the ball's flight path. The role of the hands was key in this attack, and deciphering it from so much movement is amazingly difficult, even with the aid of moving footage (of which two or three good clips exist). Since Cobb's hands must have fallen almost in unison with his front foot (see Fred Clarke above), he could not have allowed them to separate very far to the rear. They certainly did not ride statically forward in the strained set-up position, thrust well out from the torso (unlike anything observable in Nineties Style). What the motion footage allows one to glimpse is a straight drop of the hands—surely a balancing maneuver that allows the striding foot a vital few instants to direct and measure its step. Then the hands seem to come more or less straight up rather than loading farther back as the foot falls; this allows them to complete a somewhat downward stroke over the foot rather than rotating away from the plate as they drive through with an opening hip. They would not, however, have been able to descend upon the ball at the same time as the lead foot touched down; so Ty's claim about striding just where he saw the ball coming must remain very dubious…

Except for one thing: because Cobb seems to have driven fastballs the opposite way and pulled breaking pitches (speaking in generalities, of course), a slight tardiness in the hands would have served his purposes well. F.C. Lane writes the following paradoxical description of Cobb handling a fastball: "Ty Cobb, though he regarded place hitting as the secret of his success, developed a tendency to *pull the ball to left field* [my italics]."[3] My initial reaction was that Lane had simply misspoken—since a left-handed hitter definitively cannot pull a pitch to left field—or that the typesetter had made a gaffe. I'm not so sure now. In fact, I noticed belatedly that Cobb himself "misspeaks" in the same way at one point (see ch. 16, n. 12). It seems to me entirely possible that Cobb, crowding the plate in his crouch and then lunging open, was drawing a lot of high-and-tight pitches in upon himself (the response that plate-crowding is wont to elicit from pitchers) and then firing them off the other way in a stroke that "looked pull." Maybe the opening stride itself sufficed to create that impression; or maybe the fact that the top hand was punching toward right field as the barrel trailed behind it rather than pushing outward in a stroke that scarcely reached the front shoulder was part of the odd impression.

Whatever was happening, Ty Cobb's approach was at least as unique for the time as Babe Ruth's—which, as we shall see momentarily, had more than a little in common with the Cobb method.

Eddie Collins

Entering the box… Very little evidence available; used moderately light bat for his day, but with notably thick handle, held with slight choking up but no observable hand-spreading; poses resembling a set-up position all appear extremely relaxed and lacking in tension.

The man who is ninth in all-time hits garnered has left behind an incredibly meager stock of clues about how he amassed them. Perhaps that spareness is itself a clue. When photographed with a bat, Collins seems either to be casually handling it as an absent-minded professor might finger an umbrella or to be finishing a swing that has brought the stick to an almost haphazard position. There looks to be nothing "signature" about his stances or motions: just a batsman with some lumber who wants to put the ball in play. This Eddie did with remarkable regularity. He was a superior bunter, and the thick handle indeed suggests that he would have been able to produce a good little bounce from any part of his stick that found the pitch. His free and easy poses further hint that his footwork could have been quite mobile in the box—for a hitter who wants to bunt and slap has no need of digging in. The variety of finishes in the photographic record likewise implies that Collins was more invested in getting some part of bat to ball than in dealing a sharp, straight blow through the orb's center. Eddie's stroke was probably not a thing to admire. If he was given to lunging at the ball in Cobb fashion (as I have speculated earlier in the book) rather than dropping down upon it in a neat, lethal attack, then even his lunge was apt to have been more improvisational than finely tuned.

Sam Crawford

Entering the box... Extremely modest choking up without any hand-spreading; feet spread perhaps a little wider than usual for the time; bat probably larger and heavier than average.

Crawford almost appears to have been a more sedated version of Joe Jackson. He was a pull hitter who loved to take full swings with both hands pretty close to the knob (which must account in part for why he is the all-time triples king, with 312). Yet Sam did not employ the foot-to-foot approach that launched into a long stride, adopted by Jackson and Ruth as well as Ty Cobb. Rather, he leaned forward in the box with his barrel almost touching the ground and his rear foot very nearly lifted clear of it, then swung all his weight back on that foot with a vigorous back-and-up sweep of the barrel, and finally launched into the ball. In the photographic record, his strides look neither especially short and controlled nor long and wild, by the day's standard. Indeed, the stride's dimensions (direction as well as location) appear to have varied quite a bit, pointing us toward the conclusion that Crawford was another batsman who allowed his step to respond to movements of the incoming pitch. As the photo reproduced in this book suggests, his strokes could be very reactive, as if he would make up his mind to swing and then be forced to let the ball play him once he found it.

Joe Jackson

Entering the box... feet nearly or fully touching, body bent at waist; hands held together and close to knob (but with slight choke) on a distinctly large bat.

Jackson's swing was universally admired as a thing of natural beauty, though not recommended for imitation with the same unanimity. The heavy bat must have played an important part in the dynamics of his stroke, as it did with Roush's and would with Ruth's. Hefting the massive barrel from his shoetops all the way to the rear of his back shoulder must have allowed Joe to counterpoise a fairly stiff front leg lift (with a little coil) that would leave his forward hip "sitting on the pitch," as it were. By throwing this hip open in a generous stride, Jackson could hurl the barrel down from his shoulder, into the pitch, and through a finish that would wrap it around more often than not over the front shoulder. One can well understand why he was noted for taking the same swing every time, regardless of count or situation: with so much lumber coming off his shoulder and so much rotation (unlike the era's common practice) coming from his front hip, Joe's style would not have allowed for much fine-tuning around the edges.

Wee Willie Keeler

Entering the box... very much Nineties Style, though exaggerating some elements: feet close together in erect posture, front foot pointing slightly outward; stance assumed as far forward in batter's box as rules allow; hands joined and choking up almost half the length of a thick-handled bat, resting calmly over chest.

Inasmuch as his career began with the Giants in1892, Willie's old-school habits are scarcely a throwback. The extreme choke-up on the bat, however, invites caricature, and may blind us to the variety within Keeler's attack. Certainly he often made contact well in front of the plate simply by thrusting the barrel into the ball and then instantly releasing the handle with his top hand... but the photographic record indicates that this was not the extent of Wee Willie's game. The choke-up could just as well be a feint that would draw infielders to the grass. Both hands could suddenly slide down the handle as Keeler's feet beat a mild retreat into the box, allowing him to deal a healthy stride and full cut to the pitch (a style of attack imprecisely but frequently attributed to Cobb); or perhaps some of these photos of a full swing also suggest that he would occasionally allow the bat to run through his fingers down to the knob—in effect throwing the barrel at the ball—on certain pitches.

All in all, Keeler's offensive game must have been the most diverse and ingenious thing going in the new century's first decade. Peers spoke of him as the ultimate place hitter. If Eddie Collins would send his stick through just about any improvised move to put the ball in play, Willie featured the same resourcefulness within a well-rehearsed repertoire of strokes and adjustments.

Napoleon Lajoie

Entering the box... Stance slightly closed and well back from the plate, with feet spread moderately; perhaps not as erect as Nineties Style, with a slight hunching over at the waist anticipating the long stride into the plate; hands usually choking up to some degree—but rarely if ever spread—on a large, thick-handled bat.

The natural grace of Lajoie's stroke drew almost as much admiring comment as Joe Jackson's; and like Jackson, he was a rather indiscriminate hitter, notorious for chasing balls well off the plate—and doing so effectively; for "the Frenchman," a big man for his time with a long reach, clearly loved to be worked away. His default stroke involved striding aggressively into plate after rocking his big barrel up from the ground and gathering his weight back for the plunge. He had developed a one-handed follow-through which was considered highly unusual, if not unique, among his peers. This surely assisted him in getting another inch or two out of the barrel's stretch over the plate. Allowing the choked-up portion of the handle to slide through his fingers might also have extended his reach—although, since "Larry" employed a peculiar bat with a second, higher knob that he briefly sought to market commercially, he must not have considered such slippage part of his regular game.[4]

One wonders why such an approach didn't draw inside fastballs consistently to keep the formidable Frenchman off the outside corner. Perhaps it did. The bat's thick handle would have permitted Lajoie to fight off such offerings if he felt compelled to swing, and even to drive them over the infield. The second knob may have helped him to pull the bat in on an emergency swing.

Edd Roush

Entering the box... Feet somewhat close together but not inordinately, stance probably a bit closed most of the time; knees slightly bent and upper body hunched over more than usual for era; hands together but modestly choking up on an exceptionally heavy, thick-handled bat.

Players who wielded really large bats generally constructed the swing around them; and Edd is not only no exception to this broad truth, but perhaps the preeminent illustration of it. I have described elsewhere how he virtually ran the barrel into the pitch. His feet would necessarily have begun spread to balance his weight but also close enough to execute several rapid, shifting steps. The barrel, loading from a position almost in the dirt (as was very common during this period), was not so much rocked back on a planted rear foot in Joe Jackson fashion as "run to the rear" by shuffling feet. Then it would be practically dumped forward on the ball, creating a forward weight shift as pronounced as any in the game; yet its mass would likely prevent a high finish unless it had descended upon a very low pitch. The body was extraordinarily bent throughout the swing in order to manage its mobile load.

Roush might have devised a more stationary approach with his lower body that could have yielded something like Lou Gehrig's stroke—but he was quite content to engineer less-than-all-out collisions that resulted in two batting crowns.[5]

Babe Ruth

Entering the box... Feet touching, knees unbent and legs erect; bent over at waist, shoulders slightly slumped; hands together at end of bat, which was massively large (though scaled down in later years).

Technically, Babe does not belong to the Deadball Era: it was he, indeed, who rang in the new era. Yet he is too generally credited with having innovated a style the like of which had never been seen under the sun. He himself attributed many of his stroke's characteristics to the influence of Joe Jackson, and this seems highly plausible. The touching feet that broke into a stiff forward leg lift (somewhat stiffer than Jackson's) as the barrel dipped in counterpoise, the closing front hip that the rear-shifted bat allowed to gather for a launch, the all-out transfer of energy to that front side which brought the huge barrel slamming down into the pitch's path… all of these instants were vintage Shoeless Joe. The difference, as far as I can tell, lay mostly in Ruth's rising up entirely on his front foot as he made contact, more often than not, and hence finishing with the bat high over his forward shoulder and close to the body. It does not appear to me, in other words, that his lateral lunge at the ball typically equaled Jackson's in length—or, for that matter, Ty Cobb's (all three of whom set up with their feet touching). Hence it could be said that the Babe, in coming down on the ball slightly more than the other two, was that much less rotational in his swing and that much less adrift from the heritage of the Nineties.

We tend to forget that a) Ruth made enough routine contact to win a batting title in 1924, b) Yankee Stadium was constructed expressly to assist some of his drives in clearing the fence, c) the spitball and certain other trick pitches had lately been outlawed, and d) the livelier ball of the Twenties was a reality independent of one man's great bat. The press played up the Bambino's homering prowess, and he naturally did his best to suit the role; but a Jackson, or even an Ed Delahanty, might have performed very similar feats in similar circumstances.

George Sisler
Entering the box... Moderate distance from plate, feet squared and moderately separated; hands choked up perhaps three inches on an average-sized bat for the time; knees relatively straight but shoulders slightly bent over plate; elbows hanging easily near chest to create a relaxed grip, but bat clearly a little farther back (leaning on rear shoulder) than in most Nineties styles.

Everything about George Sisler (in case the wording above concealed the fact) was moderate. A great admirer of Cobb's who claimed to imitate him in some respects, Gorgeous George nevertheless eschewed such extreme practices as the touching feet and projecting hands of the set-up, the crowding of the plate, and the lunging stride. We have seen how he described to F.C. Lane his preference to be very non-committal in positioning his feet and to let his hands make all adjustments necessary for placing the ball. This claim actually appears to be borne out by the photographic evidence of the Sisler follow-through. After a weight shift which comes mostly forward but does not draw the back foot from the ground (moderation, yet again), the hands may finish high and snug over the shoulder or wrap around the shoulder in very level fashion or part company and leave the bat trailing far out in the bottom hand. I believe these different finishes must obviously have been determined by differing pitches, or maybe by a differing intended destination for each pitch. The Sizzler's were clever hands, in short, that worked their magic upon a very regularly moving lower body. After all, George began his baseball life as a pitcher and actually beat Walter Johnson in his first start: the fellow was talented!

More than any other hitter on this list, George seems to me to provide the link between the Deadball Era and the Thirties. His forward leg lifts rather than coils—but its stiffness is perhaps softening with a view to throwing the lead hip more than his predecessors did; his weight is shifting forward—but not in an emphatic way, and perhaps not one hundred percent; his barrel is cutting a slightly downward path to the ball, more often than not—but the slightest of uppercuts may be working into a little midway dip.

Tris Speaker
Entering the box... Close to a typical Nineties Style set-up, with a little more bend in the upper body and the hands resting perhaps a little more back and up before the torso; usually a mild choke and often a spreading of hands in the grip, bat somewhat larger than the average; position relative to the plate highly variable.

Speaker's approach is my personal favorite, for I have found no other in my experiments that produces low line drives so reliably. It seems as sure as any such claim of this kind can be without photographic proof that "Spoke" shuffled his feet in loading up. Such foot shifts would have given him the option of arranging his angle to the ball so as to maximize the chances of handling a certain pitch in a certain place. Mobile feet also defeat the pitcher's best efforts to disrupt timing (efforts that were quite crafty during the Deadball years), for one small hop can always lead into another if the weight starts to drift forward too soon. It must be added that commentators do not write of Speaker as skipping wildly about, and he declines to designate himself a place hitter in F.C. Lane's discussion; so I must not overstate the case for his lower body's being extremely active. Yet I would reiterate that a subtle shuffle of the feet is well designed to bring the weight down upon the pitch in virtual unison with the hands, and the Grey Eagle's follow-throughs do indeed vindicate the supposition that he had fashioned a "forward and slightly down" linear cut into the pitch. Seldom does one find any photographic evidence of a one-handed finish, a tilt backward onto the rear foot, a bent forward knee, a barrel ending belt-high, or any other hallmark of lunging, slashing, and emergency tactics of the sort.

Honus Wagner

Entering the box... Also a fairly typical Nineties Style position, with feet a little more widespread and hands holding bat a little farther back than the norm; stance assumed very far back from home plate; hands often choking up and/or spread on handle (grip widely variable, dependent on situation); bat about average for the day, perhaps slightly larger.

The Dutchman's unique body time allowed him to adopt a style equally unique—or at least not approximated by anyone other than the powerfully built Napoleon Lajoie. Both men routinely strode into the plate from very far back in the box and drove pitches to the opposite field after getting their long arms fully extended. They also shared a love of free swinging and an unusual (for the time) indifference to striking out. Yet Hans (as F.C. Lane always styles him) appears to have had a Plan B in his hip pocket. With his changeable grip, he could have prepared to whip the choked bat around on an inside pitch and then let it slip through to the knob if he were fooled; his enormous but nimble hands were quite capable of such adaptation. He also appears to have released the top hand early or followed through with it strongly, depending (we must assume) on where he attacked the pitch. Lajoie had no such versatility. Furthermore, Wagner is also among those batsmen who claimed to be able to adjust their stride to the path of the incoming pitch. His famous bowed legs, long and flexible, may have been up to the task of stopping short on their stride toward the plate. The photographic record commemorates some very awkward-looking finishes that suggest Dutch's ability to execute incredible contortions as his barrel descended. Whatever it takes to get a hit (as a much feebler Eddie Collins might have nodded)!

Nevertheless, especially with his hands riding so far up as the barrel was loaded from knee-level and with so long a typical stride following the leg lift, one has extreme difficulty picturing front foot and barrel falling at almost the same instant. Whatever Honus had learned from Fred Clarke about stepping where the ball was pitched was probably trimmed down to fit some kind of outside/opposite field strategy.

Zack Wheat

Entering the box... Feet spread a little wider than the shoulders and squared to the plate, the front foot pointing slightly outward; posture fairly erect, with mild bend into plate at waist; hands raised to the rear armpit (left-handed hitter) and held almost a foot out from body; bat of average length and weight but with unusual amount of flair from handle to barrel.

Wheat is a curiosity, if only becomes he retains so little of the Nineties Style. Though he entered the Big Leagues in 1909, even his set-up in the box appears more like a modern hitter's than like the rituals of our ancient batsmen. With feet spread relatively wide by the day's standard and hands held well aloft, he seems unlikely to have pumped downward with the barrel to balance the front leg in a stiff lift (at least not in the exaggerated manner that we associate with this period). That his stride was of breathtaking length may be more legend than fact; the photos and period baseball cards showing him with the rear knee on the ground and the front knee bent to keep him from falling may put us in mind of a Reggie Jackson or Adrian Beltré swoosh, but these images were probably staged. Nevertheless, there had to be a lot of lateral movement and rotation in "Buck's" swing. It was not a lunge after the Cobb or Jackson (Shoeless Joe) fashion, either; for Cobb was bringing his hands forward rather quickly and at a downward angle, while Joe was also forward-shifting enough to get off his back foot and finish on a fairly straight front leg.

Zack's style sufficed to rack up almost 2,900 hits, but neither he nor Harry Hooper (a more elegant practitioner of the rotational stroke) showed extraordinary power. Their proto-Williams science of hitting obviously left them feeling comfortable, but it did not pay clear dividends in terms of extra bases.

I had considered finishing off this chapter (and hence, very nearly, the whole book) with some tidy little evolutionary sketch of what brought strikers out of the Nineties into the new century and thence into the Thirties... which decade, of course, was the granddaddy of the Golden Age. As we look back over the very brief list above, however, we already see numerous distinct styles displayed. Evolution of some kind is surely taking place—but not everything occupies a step on an inexorably ascending staircase. Sometimes old ways hang around and act stubborn: the Coelacanth Phenomenon! Sometimes several competing ways putter along from one era to the next without a clear victor being declared. Sometimes a completely original way will appear from nowhere and then, just as suddenly, disappear.

The Deadball Era seems to me, if anything, to feature a much wider variety of styles than we find at other points in baseball history. In this chapter's opening citation, Davy Jones (with maybe the faintest hint of a Welsh lilt in his "you know") cannily notes that we have grown more conformity-minded—"in everything, not just baseball"—thanks to the mainstreaming effects of mass technology. Of course, that observation itself, whether made of the Sixties when Ritter's interviews were published or of our own time more than a half-century later, speculatively traces an evolution. If we postmoderns have indeed preserved enough independence during the universal march toward digitalization, however, to protest that we haven't all "evolved" into robots, then we should be capable of recognizing at least as much eccentricity in earlier times, when pockets of population were much more isolated. Strange to say, most of us, especially the educated, appear instead to believe that our ancestors trudged lockstep through their puny lives. Why would any thoughtful person dismiss daily life before 1910 as regimented, when you could still see the Andromeda Galaxy from your farmhouse's porch on a clear evening and when even radio didn't yet exist to blare the day's news?

Nothing can justify the facile summation of all turn-of-the-century culture with the clownishly mechanized crates of the Wright Brothers and other aviation pioneers. That is, not everything done in 1900 was just a comical series of leaps, flaps, and flops that we had to blunder through before we could coast far above the clouds and, today, plan trips to Mars.

But academics, I've often remarked, are prisoners of the evolutionary paradigm. It's as if they (and I might as well be honest and write "we") know no other way to make sense of things. The cosmos cannot simply be a fairly stable system running in accord with certain laws: it has to be *becoming*—to be veering into something else. An old Sanskrit saying runs. "Learned men call the One by many names." I don't think that's intended as a compliment, but rather as a mild rebuke. Is true understanding essentially to see beyond the many and find one… or is it to look at a grand, enduring unity and proceed to dissect it into a thousand volatile pieces?

Whatever the reader may feel about such metaphysical questions, I hope that he or she will at least emerge from this book with the suspicion that old ways are not necessarily, automatically inferior. It's true that we advanced from the kite to the Space Shuttle… but it's also true that most of us can't start a fire or tell north from south. The caveman was pretty clever about a lot of things—and our great-grandparents were a long way from being cavemen.

Chapter Twenty-Three

A Postscript on Validation: One Last Look at Our Proposals From a Historical Perspective

The method of science depends upon our attempts to describe the world with simple theories: theories that are complex may become unstable, even if they happen to be true. Science may be described as the art of systematic over-simplification—the art of discerning what we may with advantage omit.   Karl Popper[1]

    As an author, I made an early decision to introduce this inquiry just as it evolved—in the more or less narrative form of hit-and-miss probes—rather than to organize my findings retrospectively and artificially so that they resembled dominoes falling in a neat logical row, each chapter replete with supporting documentation. Later on, I indeed added as much documentation as I could find or recover; but I also ended up preserving a somewhat subjective entry into the subject, for its initial draw upon me was very emotional. A little-known truth is that even the most rigidly empirical sciences often advance by hunch. Karl Popper (than whom no one better understands scientific method) hints at both the hunch and the *ex post facto* clothing of respectable objectivity in his remark above. The poetic notion that a draining basin of water behaves very like a whirlwind is inspired, and as a metaphorical association it overlooks certain unpoetic, tedious details (such as that water is not air). The theoretician will formally explain later, however, that liquids and gasses act similarly under pressure—and he will indeed lead off with the explanation, as if his theory about weather systems began in a graduate seminar rather than in the bath tub. The punctilious review of previous research, the formation of an hypothesis, the testing and recording, the assessment of data, the revision of the hypothesis… all of that is a tuxedo for what may have been the most accidental of discoveries.

    In the classic baseball movie, *It Happens Every Spring*, a professor of chemistry (played by Ray Milland) chances upon a substance that repels wood while he cleans up after a baseball has come crashing into his laboratory. The residue of several destroyed beakers lies stewing in a basin—and everything that has soaked in the strange liquid runs away from wooden implements on the counter! Of course, upon realizing the magical properties of the mystery brew, the professor resolves to take a sabbatical and revive his dream of pitching in the Big Leagues (with the help of an impregnated sponge that nestles in the palm of his glove).

    Comedy aside, this is how most creative investigators operate, whether they admit it or not, and this is the *modus operandi* I chose to project in my book. I knew that, in doing so, I would be violating the paradigm of historical baseball-writing; but then, historical research is almost impossible to conduct in this area, for reasons I have enumerated more than once. Chronicling the zigzag progress of my reasoning therefore seemed a more honest approach. Though I performed experiments—many, many experiments—the inspiration for these arrived at odd, sometimes inconvenient moments. I had no particularly logical plan of attack. I employed logic, I hope, in connecting the dots, but I had no dot-collection strategy. Evidence was rare and widely scattered.

The obvious liability of so undisciplined a procedure is that one may overlook what little useful research has actually been done. I was so intent on trying to glean scraps from various sources in the distant past that I neglected to lift up my head and look right before me. Several excellent resources have emerged just in the last few years. Roy Kerr may well be today's premier historian of nineteenth-century ballplayers, having penned books about Sam Thompson, Dan Brouthers, and others. Professor Kerr kindly consented to peruse my manuscript in its original draft and responded with a letter generously rich in helpful comments, among which were the following: [2]

> My knowledge of the game after 1900 is spotty, but you managed to include details about most of my favorite hitters from the early 20th Century—Cobb, Speaker (not to mention his defense), Wagner, Eddie Collins. I think you are on to something important....
>
> Everything that you say makes sense and from my perspective seems to derive from the way the game was played in the 19th Century. If you take a look at any photos of George Wright wielding a bat in the 1870's, for example, you will see that same "samurai" pose. Incidentally, I think it would be a good idea to include a photo of some martial artist in that pose, holding the samurai sword.... Many folks who know what a samurai sword is don't really know the stance and hand positions unless they've seen *The Seven Samurai*. Once they see the visual (stance and hand positions), the similarity will become immediately apparent.
>
> Your most challenging assertion, and you acknowledge this, is the idea of adjusting the foot to the specifics of the pitch. I think you are correct here, but of course, this one is the most difficult [assertion] to prove without film footage.
>
> Given my 19th Century interests, I think it would be useful to see Cobb, Speaker, and the others as following and perhaps improving on the batting styles of the earlier period. There are some very simple things that strongly suggest this. When I give talks about the 19th Century, I like to start with some terminology that is hold-over material from that era: e.g. the "pitcher," and more to the point the "strike." Why this term? Because until the beginning of the 1880's, the hitter was not called a hitter, but a "striker." Why? Because that is what he was doing: striking, and not "swinging" in the modern sense.... [From the early 1880's on,] they were referred to as "batsmen." In all of my research, I've only found one reference to the term "hitters" before

1900....

On bat length: you'd be interested to know that I have two specific references to Buck Ewing using a 42" bat: no way that could be swung in the modern sense.

[Dan] Brouthers and strike outs: in 1889, in 589 plate appearances, he struck out just 6 times. His personal advice was never try to kill the ball, but rather, find the sweet spot and strike hard. He hit a home run in 1894 that may have been the longest in the 19th Century—about 465 feet—that never rose more than fifty feet off the ground. He was a line-drive hitter like Hank Aaron, and is remembered more for the home runs than his .342 batting average.

[Sam] Thompson and [Roger] Connor were more of the swing-from-the-ankles types; but Billy Hamilton, Buck Ewing and Brouthers could easily fit into your categories, as could most players from the 19th Century. In a way, I see Cobb, Speaker and company as the culmination of that style of hitting that started back in the 1870's or before, and after their time, as you document, a different style of hitting emerged.

Now the secret's out about my inclusion of a samurai photograph: it was Professor Kerr's idea (and an excellent one, at that). My delving somewhat into the Eighties and Nineties, though not a direct recommendation, also owes its origin to Dr. Kerr's comments and, shortly thereafter, a reading of his books. In fact, I came to be a bit enamored of the balance and self-control of Nineties Style (as I have called it), while at the same time I was growing a little horrified at how aggressive and inelegant, in comparison, Ty Cobb's approach was turning out to be as I unlocked more of its secrets.

Included among Roy Kerr's advice, too, was a suggestion to consult Peter Morris's *Game of Inches*, an encyclopedic work bursting with details about baseball from its infancy. Published in 2006 and revised in 2010, this source has the paradoxical ability to reach far into the past, for Morris has profited from contemporary methods of data collection. Digital searches are not the be-all-and-end-all that the popular imagination makes of them, for they can only key on specific words and phrases: they cannot pursue vague associations that leave no verbal footprint. Nevertheless, especially with so many old documents having now come online, they can trawl for information about a given player in century-old newspaper stories that the researcher of just a few years ago would never find. They can also, sometimes, access the pages of out-of-print books, not to mention double-check the researcher's efficiency at mining easily available resources.

Morris, Roy Kerr, and many other diligent students of the game publishing today are members of the Society of American Baseball Research (SABR), an organization that takes full advantage of technology while also—and perhaps more famously (or infamously)—introducing new statistical measures retroactively. I hasten to add that SABR's members do not share a uniform faith in numbers as capable of representing accurately every aspect of baseball achievement. Both Morris and Kerr, as true historians, respect the complexity—the "nerves" and the "will power"—of the game's human participants. I, too, am a "voluntarist" rather than a "determinist"; and, in fact, crunching numbers—or shredding them, in Brian Kenny's parlance—does little to assist the investigation launched in my book, since we have been asking not *what* was done, but *how*. The ability to sift through enormous volumes of eye-witness and first-hand accounts from the past, however, holds promise for an undertaking like mine.

Nevertheless, it seems that my particular endeavor cannot be much enhanced by state-of-the-art data collection. As of this moment, I have retrieved surprisingly little useful information from century-old narrative or descriptive accounts. As noted often throughout this book, writers from two or three generations in the past often dismiss as matters of uninterest or common knowledge the very details most critical to our present inquiries. The style of the typical sports reporter in 1905, as well, is so larded with ostentatious hyperbole and ventures into an insipid vein of cartoonish humor ("Casey went on the warpath against Boston's defenseless pilgrims with his tomahawk cut from the highest peaks of the Adirondacks") that the dominant impression can often be a big blur. The single exception to the relative void of extended commentary from yesteryear is F.C. Lane's incomparable *Batting*. Originally published in 1925, lately re-issued through SABR and made available electronically (and thus best cited, I determined, by chapter title), the work synthesizes Lane's vast stock of interviews with great hitters of his era. His collection is a gold mine. At several points in my own text, I took care to infuse some of these nuggets during the revision process. I am proud and relieved to say that most such statements directly from the mouths of players were strongly corroborative of my previous conclusions.

And indeed, I wish to emphasize now in closing that Lane's interviews, and a few other rare and precious discoveries, resoundingly support my hypotheses, guesses, and "feels right" intuition: my hunches and low-tech experiments somehow led me in the right direction. There is more than one way to apply a stick effectively to an incoming object—but there are not infinite ways, or even a hundred or, probably, a dozen. A person with two arms and two legs can learn something about these with a lot of persistence: yesteryear's batsmen were not aliens from another planet with appendages different from ours. The body has its own rigorous logic if the mind will but pay attention to the arguments that reach it from nerve and muscle.

For instance, I had deduced a lower-body position for Wee Willie on the order of today's standard "bunt" set-up. Given his extreme choking on the bat, he would have to be able to reach out in front of the plate through all quadrants of the zone; and to do this, he would further have to be able to swivel his active hands forward on limber knees. My deduction was correct, according to Peter Morris: "Willie Keeler made use of a crouch to chop and cut the ball."[3]

My reconstruction of Honus Wagner's swing was largely based on reverse engineering from still photographs. Here is Christy Mathewson's assessment of

Hans:

> He takes a long bat, stands well back from the plate, and steps into the ball, poling it. He is what is known in baseball as a free swinger.... In the history of baseball, there have not been more than fifteen or twenty free swingers altogether, and they are the real natural hitters of the game, the men with eyes nice enough and accurate enough to take a long wallop at the ball.[4]

Our method had led to the conclusion that the Flying Dutchman did all of these things: i.e., employed a massive stick, stood deep in the box (as in far from the plate's inside corner), strode into the pitch, and unleashed an attack upon the ball that might leave him in odd contortions and often parted his top hand early from the handle. "Free swinger" seems a pretty good two-word description.

I had suggested that Napoleon Lajoie, another righty unusually tall for his day, might have embodied a similar approach, if on a more modest scale. Here's what an unnamed writer for the *Kansas City Star* (August 11, 1911) makes of Nap's batsmanship:

> The secret of Lajoie's successful hitting lies in the fact that he adopts the "follow-on" style used by golfers. He doesn't swing his bat from his side, but meets the ball squarely when it reaches a point in front of his chest and then puts his strength into a sort of punch which carries the bat well beyond his left side. All first class batsmen do this, for it enables them to keep their eyes on the ball and to put strength into their bats when they hit the leather.[5]

The photographic record of the Emperor's bat in motion is virtually non-existent—very lean pickings, even from a field as generally barren as this one. To supplement the gap with verbal descriptions may introduce problems of a sort that the commentary above illustrates only too clearly. Such accounts, while leaving unstated what we most want to know, may use terms that now make us scratch our heads. What exactly is the golfer's "follow-on" that Lajoie models but many lesser hitters do not? The intended distinction must surely be between a stroke enlisting much or most of the body and one taken almost exclusively with the hands. If the reporter means to say that Nap used his lower body, then a reference to golf seems an unpromising bridge of analogy; yet the scribe focuses our attention on the upper and not the lower body, urging us to picture a swing that carries high over the front shoulder or, at any rate, well around that shoulder (as opposed to dying more or less where the hands drop after their quick punch). Like so may generations of baseball coaches, this Kansas City chronicler has chosen to highlight an incidental effect of the swing in question rather than the cause that authored the effect; for the potent "follow-on" could only be initiated by a prior, rather vigorous movement in the lower body, particularly since we know that the bat wasn't loaded high above Lajoie's head like a golf club. Even a non-golfer like me realizes that a long step into the tee isn't recommended!

We have, therefore, another big right-hitting righty whose bat probably finishes around his lead shoulder as often as above it—and whose strong top hand, furthermore, likely slips off the handle on certain outside pitches. A somewhat tamer version of Wagner? Perhaps not: I noted earlier that SABR authors Jones and Constantelos attributed to "Larry" a propensity to chase pitches well out of the zone (see ch. 8, n. 8). Yet "free swinger" would seem a poor description of Lajoie if we pay attention to the contrast that F.C. Lane arranges between him and Honus.[6] Nap was more upright, elegant, and regular in his approach, claims Lane. Maybe this is part of the answer to the "golfer" enigma: maybe the Frenchman simply started more erect. The explicit contrast itself, at any rate, implies that the two batting champs invited comparison. One does not distinguish between a pair of objects that could not sanely be considered as other than distinct. You differentiate between a red apple and a yellow apple, not between an apple and an orange.

As a matter of fact, Lane rather often quotes Wagner's own words when they forge a comparison between himself and Lajoie. This nugget is informative in more ways than Honus could have realized: "Arm and wrist batters are those who make good. I have always hit with my arms and so does Lajoie."[7] The "arm" hitter must surely be understood in the idiom of the time as driving toward the outside corner and "getting the arms extended" (as we say today) in order to poke the ball to the opposite field. We have surmised that both of these superior batsmen used such a strategy... yet what a surprise, to find that Wagner does not consider himself a "leg" hitter (which is the other polarity of his contrast here)! In an area where evidence is usually sketchy to non-existent, we can linger in no doubt that Honus Wagner had a very active lower body. To himself and to his contemporaries, though, the Dutchman's stroke was essentially a less aesthetic version of the Frenchman's, with emphasis on the arms or the "follow-on."

Now, we also noted that Hans would not have restricted himself to a single, monolithic, one-size-fits-all-situations approach in his footwork or his grip upon the bat; neither would any other great hitter of his generation. The man himself once remarked, "My idea of a real batter is a man who can choke up on the bat when he feels like it or slug from the handle when it is necessary."[8] So our conclusions based on analysis of photographic records supplemented by reasonable inference are again validated in words from the proverbial horse's mouth.

The citation just above was in fact retrieved by Morris from Lane's *Batting*. Lane appears to have questioned surviving players of the Deadball Era very astutely; and, as I have said, his republished book is a gold mine in an otherwise sandy waste. Yet Wagner's reluctance to endorse a single grip of the bat well illustrates how even *Batting* offers limited help in reconstructing something like an essential DBE swing; and, indeed, we concluded from the photographic record that there probably was no such *essential* stroke. From Johnny Mize to Ted Williams, few great hitters have been reluctant to make categorical claims about the proper practice of their trade... but our batsmen of yesteryear manifest just such a reticence. It certainly seems that Davy Jones was right about his peers: they were a very diverse bunch of characters!

Another passage in Lane's book that Morris finds worthy of emphasis and comment reflects upon the style of nineteenth-century star Jack Bentley: "As the pitcher released the ball, Bentley would step back, raise himself slowly on one foot, much the same as a shot putter would do, and lunge forward. When he met the ball he was literally standing on one leg."[9] I, too, find this account of particular interest. It somewhat verifies our speculation about the era's affinity for a complete transfer of weight that would leave the batsman standing on his forward leg—though in singling out Bentley's method, the entire passage also implies that extravagant transfers were viewed derisively. Bentley appears to have fashioned quite a spectacular descent; it sounds more than a little like Mel Ott's. I assume, with some trepidation, that the reference to the shot-putter equates to a bent forward knee. I have found in experiments that some such "spring device" is quite capable of coming down quickly to intersect the ball's perceived flight: a stiff lift of the leg that works into a bend, then straightening out in a kick without instantly touching the ground. The athlete could then glide into the point of touchdown, with a last-second shift in the foot's placement possible. Yet the whole arrangement is also very energy-intensive and not amenable to keeping the eyes steady. It seems like a big sacrifice to make just to say that you step where you see the pitch coming.

Perhaps I'm reading too much into that brief description—but my inferences are not inconsistent with the shot-putter analogy, and one has to be especially creative in reconstructing footwork. Morris is rather disappointing here, confining his commentary on "leg kicks" to a few paragraphs.[10] Other than reproducing Lane's remark about Bentley, he has little more to offer than the mandatory evocation of Mel Ott and a couple of comments about the obscure batsmen Dan O'Leary and "Doggy" Miller. The resulting discussion makes the forward leg lift sound like an extreme oddity rather than standard operating procedure. What Morris may have been confronting, of course, is a few exaggerated renditions of the usual lower-body load that found a burlesque kind of immortality in the local press. One obstacle that he surely would have encountered outside of print is the frustrating absence of this crucial stage in the swing among photographic records. The taste of the times seems to have prized portraits that featured the set-up as the hitter awaited the delivery and the finish as the hitter prepared to bolt from the box. The photographer's preference for these postures is entirely understandable. In an age when the shutter speeds of most cameras were none too rapid, a shot of bat and body in motion would court ruinous blurs.

Yet we would never be able to get a Cobb or a Speaker (or Babe Ruth, for that matter) from his set-up to his finish if we used a familiar rotational coil and subsequent release of the hips to do it: such is the conclusion reached by my method, and I must stand by it. Certain positions have certain consequences as stored energy is unleashed: there's no way around that fact.

If I may wind up this discussion—and this book—with a return to the fountainhead, I would offer a description from the eve of the Nineties that perfectly frames a portrait of contact at the Mac Point, where the ball is struck just as the barrel reaches maximum acceleration. All evidence converges upon that point's being where a linearly, mildly descending bat intersects the ball's center just before the rear elbow locks. Anatomy and physics are on my side; and the photographic evidence, from spread hands to high finishes, suggests that the most prized contact of the Deadball Era was of just this kind. Finally, Morris's sources confirm my argument. Here is one, at least, that celebrates the stroke of right-handed striker Charlie Ganzel (who turns out to have been surprisingly mediocre—but not in this sportswriter's opinion):

> Gently swinging his bat perpendicularly, he watches the ball like a hawk. When he sees one that suits him, quick as a flash he meets it squarely with a firm but gentle rap and it darts out in a line over the heads of the infield, but usually plows the ground before the outfield can reach it. It is seldom he hits for more than a base, but almost always puts the ball out of everybody's reach. He comes nearer to "placing the ball," if such a thing is possible, than any other player in the country, his favorite spot being between left and center. With men on base it is a most satisfactory thing to see him come to the plate because it is almost a certainty he will hit the ball.[11]

For "perpendicular," read "cutting straight down into the pitch" (though that's a bit overdone: we said *mildly down*). For "quick as a flash," read "relying heavily on hand action." For "firm but gentle rap"… well, I'm not quite sure what to make of that conundrum, but it implies not much of a follow-through, *à la* Keeler. Then we have the low line drive instead of the gargantuan pop-up. I'm sure Professor Kerr is right. This is the origin of the Carey, Clarke, and Speaker swing, and first cousin to Cobb's: a punch of the top hand whose enlistment of the lower body would grow increasingly aggressive over the coming decades.

As for the place hitting, "if such a thing is possible"… that Charlie has a "favorite spot" already disqualifies him by Tris Speaker's generous definition of "placing" as "resistance to one's natural tendency." Let us not knit-pick, however. In this life, you must take the good stuff along with the "idiotic slush" (as another of Morris's unnamed scribes denominates the place-hitting craze).[12]

With this chapter, I have sought to bolster my book's arguments using commentary that would have appeared redundant elsewhere or perhaps too general for the context of any specific chapter—but which validates the general conclusions reached by my photographic analyses and physical experiments. Perhaps I especially wanted to emphasize the necessity and the reliability of the latter: physical experimentation. I have read many descriptions of Cobb's swing or Joe Jackson's sweet sroke that make good copy, have a certain logic, and sometimes even partake of poetry; yet they physically do not work as promised, when tested under authentic conditions. I have also, alas, been forced to worship at the altar of current hitting doctrine, both as a boy and later as a father, only to find—once again—that the rituals brought no actual salvation. The very latest revision of the gospel hadn't any more truth than the previous one. Things have to work physically, materially. An orderliness at the theoretical level isn't sufficient if living, breathing results do not verify original assumptions. I believe this is so of all science and history. If academics sometimes prefer an elegant explanation to the "messy details" that contradict it, as Karl Popper recognized, we must merely remind ourselves that true science may need to be protected from professional scientists.

The same protection must be extended to our sports, which are not really such a trivial matter in comparison to pursuits of the Ivory Tower; for sport is often where our young people learn to project mental and spiritual determination into an act that can be seen either to succeed or to fail. Maybe scientists, for that matter, would do their critical tasks more conscientiously if they diverted themselves in physical endeavors that required playing by strict rules. At any rate, my occasional handling of the historical record in this study as a somewhat secondary resource was never intended to shed contempt in the direction of history as a discipline. On the contrary, I have striven to insist that discipline can exist in historical study only when founded upon a regard for messy detail over elegant synthesis. Show me what works, first and last; then let us try to decipher how very dated testimonies might have been describing or explaining the living, breathing phenomenon.

Notes

Chapter One

1 From Johnny Pesky, *Few and Chosen* (Chicago: Triumph, 2013), p. 28 and continued on p. 31.

2 Cf. Power's comments on p. 303 of Danny Peary, *We Played the Game* (New York: Black Dog and Leventhal, 2002): "I never got into an argument with a sportswriter in Kansas City, but those guys had it in for me. They called me a showboat because I caught everything one-handed and had that pendulum swing." Just a few pages earlier in the same volume, Joe DiMaestri describes Power's fielding style and concludes, "A lot of guys claimed Vic was the best they ever saw" (300).

Chapter Two

1 Walt Hriniak, *A Hitting Clinic the Walt Hriniak Way* (New York: Harper and Row, 1988), 12.

2 Tris Speaker, *Baseball Magazine* (March 1917); quoted in many sources.

3 The following definition is offered at www.baseball-reference.com: "The Deadball Era (also sometimes Dead Ball Era) was a period in the early 20th Century characterized by low scoring and an emphasis on pitching and defense. While its boundaries are not concrete, it is generally recognized to have stretched from the founding of the American League in 1901 to the elimination of the spitball in 1920.

"The Deadball Era marked the end of the sport's rapid evolution in the 19th Century and the beginning of relative stability in rules and structure of the Major League game that took shape in the early 20th.

"Ironically, given the era's name, the ball remained unchanged from the late 19th century until 1911, when it was made livelier in an attempt to increase scoring."

4 As with so many baseball stories, this one gets better with age. I heard Mickey add insomnia to the tale during an interview that he gave late in his life. The version he offers in *The Mick* (New York: Doubleday, 1986), 93, doesn't mention sleeping difficulties; but it does represent Ted Williams in a very dogmatic—almost dictatorial—light that is probably not pure fiction.

5 I do not use the word "remarks" with poetic license, for I can only locate this Williams pronouncement in the video version of *The Science of Hitting* produced in 1974 (directed by Martin Pitts), not in the text of the book version.

6 The album, titled *Stan-the-Man's Hit Record*, was produced through Radio Corporation of America in 1963 for Stan-the-Man, Inc. Joe Garagiola was the emcee. The cover announces that the product in "available through your Phillips 66 dealer."

7 In his *The Way It Is* (New York: Simon and Schuster, 1972), 47-48, Flood actually records the remark as a little less sanitized for popular consumption. The cleaned-up version has been repeated a thousand times in other contexts.

Chapter Three

1 Walt Hriniak, *A Hitting Clinic the Walt Hriniak* Way (New York: Harper and Row, 1988), 56.

2 Mitchell Conrad Stinson, *Edd Roush: A Biography of the Cincinnati Reds Star* (Jefferson, NC: McFarland, 2010), reminds us that "southpaw gloves [were] almost impossible to locate in rural environs" (p, 23).

3 Walt Hriniak, *A Hitting Clinic the Walt Hriniak* Way (*op. cit.*), 56.

4 Rare Sportsfilms, Inc., has released a video titled *Summer of 1958* wherein Kirkland's swing may be observed for a few seconds

5 Charley Lau (revised by Tony LaRussa and Charles Salzberg), The Art of Hitting .300 (New York: Penguin, 1986), 75.
6 Mike Ryan's name springs to mind. Ryan is a successful young hitting instructor based in the Chicago area who has published numerous videos.

Chapter Four
1 Charley Lau, *The Art of Hitting .300 (op. cit.)*, 114.
2 I am reluctant to drop names explicitly lest I seem to be picking fights… but these comments come from Coach O'Leary's sight at www.chrisoleary.com. I truly don't disagree with the coach about several of his pet peeves; for instance, backspin isn't easy to impart consistently to the pitch in game conditions. Yet I would argue that the low backspin liner is a worthy mark to shoot for, that one can multiple frequency of production by careful practice, and that the *attempt* at this swing yields topspin line drives that are better struck. Also, as should become much clearer in later chapters, the ability to generate such liners depends to no small degree on the bat itself—and the Deadball Era saw bats being used that were fundamentally different from ours.
3 Charley Lau, *The Art of Hitting .300 (op. cit.* cit.), 112.
4 *Ibid.*, 113.

Chapter Five
1 Ty Cobb, *My Twenty Years in Baseball* (Mineola, NY: Dover, 2002), 73.
2 From the section on Edd Roush in Lawrence Ritter, *The Glory of Their Times* (New York: HarperCollins, 1992), 228. The collection of Ritter's interviews was first published in 1966 by Macmillan, but is now most readily accessed as an e-book.
3 The cards enclosed in tobacco products are a goldmine of information and can readily be found in reprint. I possess such a set of Old Judge cards printed (originally) in New York by Goodwin and Co. The year was 1887. I shall refer later to these grainy but invaluable photos.
4 From Bob Gibson and Reggie Jackson, *Sixty Feet, Six Inches* (New York: Doubleday, 2009), 66.
5 From Hank Aaron, *I Had a Hammer* (New York: HarperCollins, 1991), 49. Aaron further reveals that he hit a home run with Griggs looking on the first time his batted with his wrists uncrossed. He was in Memphis at the time, playing for the Indianapolis Clowns.
6 See p. 287 of Eric Enders article for *Deadball Stars of the National League*, ed. Tom Simon (Dulles, VA: Brassey's Inc., 2004), 287-290.
7 See Williams' *Science of Hitting (op. cit.*, 58).
8 The "stretched rubber band" analogy has virtually passed into baseball cliché. I first heard it when tuned into a television interview given by Rudy Jaramillo, at that time (around 2000) the hitting coach of the Texas Rangers.
9 Ruth's full remark was as follows: "I copied Jackson's style because I thought he was the greatest hitter I had ever seen, the greatest natural hitter I ever saw. He's the guy who made me a hitter." The quotation is available at www.baseball-almanac.com and, of course, has been cited by dozens of researchers.
10 This description appears near the end of the first chapter in David Fleitz, *Shoeless* (Jefferson, NC: McFarland, 2001). My copy is an e-book. Fleitz also characterizes Joe as, at least on occasion, an uppercut hitter. This is a further indication (if not a dead giveaway) that Jackson's hitting style was rotational.

Chapter Six
1 Bob Gibson and Reggie Jackson, *op. cit.*, 49-50.
2 Perry Husband's *Downright Filthy Pitching* appears to have been published first as an e-book in 2004 and then extended to a print copy in 2005. Both are distributed by CreateSpace Independent Publishing Platform through Amazon.com.
3 Cf. Charley Lau, *The Art of Hitting .300* (*op. cit.* cit.), 117: "When you hit, you've got to extend your arms completely. You've got to hit *through* the ball. This is an Absolute." The phrase, "hit through the ball," has already been discussed, albeit somewhat facetiously. To be more serious, you can readily satisfy yourself that Charley's point of full extension, with elbows locked, happens just as the top hand begins to release the bat. Hitters with a strong top-hand follow-through that holds its grip throughout do not, in fact, ever lock their elbows in the fashion that Lau's model, George Brett is pictured as doing in artificially frozen shots. The rollover of wrists in such hitters would mutate into a top hand release if they tried to straighten their elbows fully. (Hence the one-handed finish of batters fooled by a change-up who normally keep both hands on, but suddenly have to throw themselves at the pitch.)
4 Cal Ripken, Jr., has immersed himself in coaching young people since his retirement from the Major Leagues. Videos like that posted at https://www.youtube.com/watch?v=rGrQgcenEMQ are available which feature him (along with his brother Billy) describing the ideal grip. His instructional book, *Coaching Youth Baseball the Ripken Way* (Champaign, IL: 2006), covers the same ground.
    Williams' *Science of Hitting* (*op. cit.*, 33-34) anticipates most of the same points. Though Ted stresses a tight grip, he does so in the context of the fingers and urges that the bat's handle be kept out of the palm. In fact, his teaching sounds very like the crash clinic that Mickey Mantle claimed he received at the All Star Game (see above: ch. 2, n. 6)!

Chapter Seven
1 Ralph Kiner, *Baseball Forever* (Chicago: Triumph, 2004), 41.
2 This one I unearthed at www.baseball-almanac.com, after searching (of course) "Rod Carew."
3 Palmer collapsed in obvious pain after his one-handed follow-through on a "swing [that] didn't appear out of the ordinary," according to an AP account, "Rangers Lose Palmer for Rest of Season," released on June 4, 1995.

Chapter Eight
1 Paul Waner, *The Sporting News* (April 27, 1955).
2 Lawrence Ritter, *The Glory of Their Times* (*op cit.*), 40.
3 Johnny Mize, *How to Hit* (New York: Holt, 1953), 26.
4 From the chapter in F.C. Lane's *Batting* titled, "The Secret of Heavy Hitting"; originally published in 1925 and republished in 2001 by the Society for American Baseball Research. My copy is an e-book, so I shall offer chapter titles in references.
5 Cobb's *Busting 'Em* was published in 1914 as a series of articles. McFarland has recently (2003) published a print addition. My copy is an e-book, but I can identify this citation as appearing within the first few pages.
6 The Old Judge cards for 1887, mentioned above in ch. 5 n. 3, feature perhaps two dozen hitters who display these qualities in their pose before the camera. Seven whom I have not yet named are Michael Joseph Griffin, Billy Hamilton, Paul Hines, King Kelly, Harry Stovey, Sam Thompson, and John Montgomery Ward.
7 See David Fleitz, *Napoleon Lajoie, King of Ballplayers* (Jefferson, NC: McFarland,

2011), 13, for the first remark. Rusie's is cited on p. 34.

8 From p. 657 of an article for SABR's *Deadball Stars of the American League* (ed. David Jones) by David Jones and Steve Constantelos (Dulles, VA: Potomac, 2006), 657-661.

9 This is a carelessly impressionistic claim for someone to make who hasn't pored over the records month by month; and even in those circumstances, players may often have been suffering from injuries or battling with preoccupations that they kept hidden from the public. Yet there is a suspicious lacuna in Lajoie's career—1907 and 1908—when he was relatively injury-free and had reached his physical peak, yet performed far below his norm. Fleitz (*op. cit.*, 155) observes that averages were down throughout the game in '08 as pitchers enjoyed a surge of dominance. While this appears very broadly true, one would have expected an apex player like Lajoie to be less impacted by the trend. Today's coach would say that his swing had a lot of holes in it.

Chapter Nine

1 This interview with Coot Veal appears in Danny Peary's *We Played the Game* (*op. cit.*), 237-238.

2 Interestingly, there also lingered in the Fifties a species of slugger who held his club high above the rear shoulder (anticipating today's style, except that the bats were usually very heavy) and simply dropped barrel on pitch, often letting the wood go immediately in a one-handed finish. Ralph Kiner writes that Hank Greenberg instructed him in this method (see *op. cit.*, 142). Other practitioners included Del Ennis, Ted Kluziewski, Roy Sievers, Vic Wertz, and Gus Zerniel. Roger Maris belonged to this species more than to the Mantle class. Another parallel with the slugging style of our recent Nineties is how many of this group ended up having severe back strain from the swing.

3 Bob Cluck, *Play Better Baseball* (Chicago: Contemporary Books, 1998), 167.

Chapter Ten

1 Ty Cobb, *My Life in Baseball* (Lincoln, NE: U of Nebraska P. 1993), 148. This work is the putative autobiography, by the way, which was ghostwritten by Al Stump. Charles Leerhsen has alerted us to the sensationalist hack's widespread reputation for highly seasoning his transcriptions, and I attribute the sanguinary tone of this particular passage to Stump. Nothing unequivocally penned by Cobb himself has such an air of latent sadism. Yet the general remarks about how to play the game probably did originate with the dying superstar, whose corrections to the text were trashed by Stump once his informant passed away.

2 From the chapter in F.C. Lane's *Batting* titled, "Choosing a Bat" (*op. cit.*).

3 See Ty Cobb, *My Twenty Years in Baseball* (*op. cit.*), 15.

4 The photo of Flick in *Deadball Stars of the American League* (*op. cit.*), appearing on p. 650, shows a hand spread of perhaps an inch. The practice may not have been widely remarked except in Cobb simply because Cobb's spread was so much broader. The photos of Carey and Paskert appear on p. 179 and p. 214 of the same series' first volume, *Deadball Stars of the National League* (*op. cit.*).

5 In the previously cited Old Judge set of cards distributed in 1887, all four players mentioned show a clear spread of the hands. Others like Dan Brouthers and Buck Ewing are pictured as choking up quite noticeably, though without the spread of hands.

6 The brief entry about Waner (111-117) in Fred McMane, *The 3,000 Hit Club* (Sports Publishing, Inc.: 2000), is replete with anecdotes about Paul's alcohol problems.

7 Ty Cobb remarks in *Busting 'Em* (*op. cit.*), "You would be surprised at the number of men playing ball in the Big League who would not get a very high mark if they were to

undergo an eye test, and who should be wearing glasses." See the beginning of the chapter titled. "Making a Big League Hitter."
8 Cf. Rick Huhn, *The Sizzler: George Sisler, Baseball's Forgotten Great* (Columbia, MO: U of Missouri P, 2004), 157 ff.
9 Cf. Mark Millikin, *Jimmie Foxx, The Pride of Sudlersville* (Lanham, MD: Scarecrow, 1998), 225.
10 Cf. Martin Appel and Burt Goldblatt, *Baseball's Best: The Hall of Fame Gallery* (New York: McGraw-Hill, 1977), 194.
11 Charles Leerhsen, *Ty Cobb: A Terrible Beauty* (New York: Simon and Schuster, 2015), 9.
12 Ty Cobb, *My Twenty Years in Baseball* (*op. cit.*), 147.
13 For another photographic example, see the large photo on p. 27 of Ron Smith, *The Sporting News Chronicle of Baseball* (New York: The Sporting News, 1993). An older Cobb in an Athletics uniform may well be swinging just for the cameraman, who has taken a frontal shot; yet the mid-swing image (which later equipment could handle without blurs) doesn't appear staged, but rather snatched from an active movement. The hands are sufficiently visible, even though the bat's knob is coming almost directly at the camera, to verify the presence of separation between them.
14 From p. 153 in Jan Finkel's article for *Deadball Stars of the National League* (*op. cit.*), 153-156.
15 Ty Cobb, *My Life in Baseball* (*op. cit.*), 148.
16 The same reverse move could also be associated with "stretching the rubber band" as the front foot drops (see previous chapter); but I think coaches are wrong to assume that such "bottom hand back" movement can be nothing more than this, and that it therefore wouldn't exist in a swing if front foot and hands were dropping upon the pitch at about the same instant. Our batsmen of yesteryear would beg to differ.

Chapter Eleven
1 From Ty Cobb, *My Life in Baseball* (*op. cit.*), 147.
2 I located this remark at www.baseball-almanac.com among the "quotes" about Willie Keeler; the site attributes Wagner's utterance to the *50th Anniversary Hall of Fame Yearbook*.
3 See the chapter in F.C. Lane's *Batting* (*op. cit.*) titled, "Position at the Plate." An 1880's star named Dave Orr also appears from the photographic record to have face the field almost fully—and, by the way, to have spread his hands at least as much as Cobb did.
4 I am not ignoring Perry Husband's chart stressing the highly variable points of effective contact; but Coach Husband is operating on the (very safe) assumption that hitters have strides, and with this select group we find strikers who simply bend at the waist and joints to get their barrel in front of the ball.
5 Ty Cobb, *My Twenty Years in Baseball* (*op. cit.*), 151. Although this is the "Stumpian Cobb" speaking again, the utterance is probably authentic. It sounds to me like countless didactic remarks that old hitters make without realizing that they themselves didn't obey their golden rule; for Cobb's roll of the hands, bringing them farther in, is a move that even dubious ancient footage cannot conceal. See also *My Life in Baseball*, (*op. cit.*), 73: "… get all the length possible from your shoulders to the tip of your bat. Let the bat out of your hand as far as possible." These words are indubitably Cobb's, yet they cannot describe even remotely what he did to handle a pitch on the fists, and they remain foggy even in the most ideal circumstances. Hitting is hard… but writing is hard, too.
6 *Ibid.*, 147.

7 Cf. p. 339 of the article by Paul Sallee and Eric Sallee in *Deadball Stars of the National League* (*op. cit.*), 339-341.
8 Roy Kerr, *Big Dan Brouthers: Baseball's First Great Slugger* (Jefferson, NC: McFarland, 2013), features an unusual Appendix B, "Dan Brouthers' Longest Hits," that chronicles some impressive drives. Though tape measures were not deployed in any case, sportswriters of the day make it vividly clear that Dan's blasts occasionally would have rivaled Ruth's.
9 Ted Williams asserts that "Ty Cobb said that he used a 40-ounce bat, but was down to a 35-ounce near the end of his career." By comparison, Ruth's bats were "40 to 50 ounces" (*Science of Hitting* [*op. cit.*, 47]). Charlie Gehringer, pressured by an avuncular Cobb to use his bat, recalled that it measured 34 inches.
10 The full quotation is produced at the beginning of the next chapter; see ch. 12 n. 1.
11 The relevant quotation from F.C. Lane's book is reproduced in the next chapter; see ch. 12 n. 10.

Chapter Twelve
1 From Ted Williams' *Science of Hitting* (*op. cit.*, 47).
2 Bob Cluck, *Play Better Baseball* (*op. cit.*), 166.
3 Williams' *Science of Hitting* (*op. cit.*, 35).
4 The passage about over-striding (*My Life in Baseball*, [*op. cit.*], 147) was discussed in the previous chapter. What was not said there that should be added, however, is that Cobb almost certainly used various degrees of stride: this is implicit in his overall hitting doctrine of versatility and adjustment. The few video clips upon whose basis we might want to assess his stride, then, must be considered with a grain of salt.
5 From Lane's chapter titled, "How They Stand in the Box," in *Batting* (*op. cit.*).
6 From the ninth chapter, "Making a Big League Hitter," in Ty Cobb, *Busting 'Em* (*op. cit.*).
7 In addition to the abundant charges of free-swinging leveled at Lajoie such as are documented in ch. 8, n. 8, Ty Cobb's observation that Larry "had acquired a definite stance at the bat" (actually a comparison with Sam Crawford) is very interesting. Lajoie was not simply flailing: he had set procedure that he followed, and its execution resembled wild swinging to onlookers. See Cobb, *My Twenty Years in Baseball*, (*op. cit.*), 104.
8 From Lane's chapter titled, "How They Stand in the Box," in *Batting* (*op. cit.*).
9 Rogers Hornsby, *My War With Baseball* (New York: Coward-McCann, 1962), 91.
10 See ch. 10, n. 15.
11 From Lane's chapter titled, "How They Stand in the Box," in *Batting* (*op. cit.*).
12 *Ibid.*
13 From Lane's chapter titled, "How They Grip the Bat," in *Batting* (*op. cit.*).
14 See Williams, *The Science of Hitting* (*op. cit.*), 64; and Bob Cluck, *Play Better Baseball* (*op. cit.*), 167.
15 To be sure, Jackson's career was abbreviated; but he logged thirty or more two-baggers only eight times in thirteen seasons, whereas Speaker managed to do so sixteen times in twenty-two seasons. The ratios are not far off, but enough so that we cannot see Joe as an elite doubles-hitter for his era.

Chapter Thirteen
1 From p. 786 of John McMurray's article in *Deadball Stars of the National League* (*op. cit.*), 786-787.
2 Willie Mays, *My Secrets of Playing Baseball* (first published Viking [New York] in

1967; republished by Barnes and Noble in 1970), 70.
3   From Charles Alexander, *Spoke: A Biography of Tris Speaker* (Dallas: Southern Methodist UP, 2009), 121. Alexander is citing John B. Sheridan of *The Sporting News*.
4   Ty Cobb, *My Twenty Years in Baseball*, (*op. cit.*), 104; previously cited in n. 7 of ch. 12.
5   From the chapter in Lane's *Batting* (*op. cit.*) titled, "How They Stand in the Box."
6   Rare Sportsfilms, Inc., produced the DVD where I saw this footage: *1913-1938: "The Sports Album"* (2012).
7   *Ibid.*
8   Mitchell Conrad Stinson, *Edd Roush: A Biography of the Cincinnati Reds Star* (*op. cit.*), provides a close-up shot of the grip on p. 98. Slightly earlier (p. 94), Stinson offers a revealing photo of Edd's follow-through. The bat was so heavy in this case that a high over-the-shoulder finish would not have been possible. Joe Jackson produced similar finishes with his massive "Betsies," though his back foot was dug in and his load shoulder-high.
9   Cited in Alexander, *Spoke* (*op. cit.*), 111.
10 Charley Lau, *The Art of Hitting .300* (*op. cit.*), 72.

Chapter Fourteen
1   Ichiro Suzuki, *Ichiro on Ichiro: Conversations with Narumi Komatsu* (Seattle: Sasquatch, 2004), 24.
2   Appel and Goldblatt (*op. cit.*).
3   I asserted earlier that the compact linear/downward cut is actually quite close to the level and stays in the hitting zone a long time, which I believe to be utterly true. The contrast I seek is this: the linear hitter strives to make ideal contact at a single point and stands to make productive contact if a bit early or late, whereas a more rotational hitter sweeps out an entire area where he anticipates the ball's passing but, in being so imprecise, often gets very weak contact.
4   Ty Cobb, *My Life in Baseball*, (*op. cit.*), 104. Writes Cobb of Crawford, "He was what we call a groove hitter. If a pitcher ever let his delivery slip so as to put a ball in Crawford's groove he would kill it. I noticed also that the moment he came to bat the outfield would shift toward right field. Sam was a dead right field hitter."
5   In F.C. Lane's chapter titled, "Batting Slumps and How to Cure Them" (*op. cit.*), Cobb offers the following advice: "In a slump, raise your elbows. You'll be more likely to swing the bat parallel with the ground, more likely to meet the ball fair. You may be unconsciously cutting up at the ball because your swing isn't right." Obviously, the elbows alone are not supposed to be raised—the hands are meant to go with them to cure the "upswing." Cobb perhaps makes the point more plainly elsewhere, but I have highlighted this passage because it illustrates his awareness of keeping the bat's entry point level, or even slightly declined.
6   Significantly, holding the hands out from the body makes Coach Joe Brockhoff's list of "Seven Deadly Misconceptions in Hitting." Such a posture is indeed ruinous to the contemporary rotational stroke.
7   See Stinson, *Edd Roush* (*op. cit.*), 84.
8   See Peter Morris, *A Game of Inches: the Story Behind the Innovations That Shaped Baseball* (Chicago: Ivan R. Dee, 2010), 282.
9   Collins's bats appear to be notoriously rare. A Collins model for sale on the Internet (by an unnamed source) measured 35 inches long and 38.5 ounces heavy, values that seemed sufficiently probable from photos of a batting Collins that I have reproduced them here. Cobb's praise of Eddie appears early in the first chapter of *Busting 'Em* (*op.*

cit.); e.g., "to-day he is probably the most dangerous [hitter] in baseball… I consider him to be far more valuable to a team than Jackson or even Baker. He is a wonderfully scientific hitter…." That "science" for Ty means using a stroke quite similar to his own is suggested a few paragraphs earlier, where he writes, "He [Collins] is not physically robust, yet he gets his whole body into his swing in such a way that the drives go from his bat like rifleshot."

10 A Speaker bat was auctioned off in Spring of 2015 at www.loveofthegameauctions.com. The precise specs given on the web page were 35.75 inches long and 42.2 ounces heavy.

11 See Bobby Richardson, *The Bobby Richardson Story* (Westwood, NJ: Fleming H. Revell, 1965), 110.

Chapter Fifteen
1 From Dusty Baker, *You Can Teach Hitting* (Carmel, IN: Bittinger, 1993), 193.
2 Mickey Mantle, *My Favorite Summer 1956* (New York: Doubleday, 1991), 68.
3 I know Mr. Altman would not object to my sharing a part of this letter (written almost a decade ago now) that pertains to the present discussion, since I informed him at the time that I was seeking material for a book—not this book, by the way; for, alas, there are far too few George Altmans in the world, and I never came close to collecting all the responses I needed.
4 I garnered this information several years ago from a post by Jesus Cabrera at www.BaseballLibrary.com, a site that appears to have gone defunct.
5 Gibson explains that he apologized to Snider later and insisted that he hadn't intended to break anything. Duke understood. See Gibson and Jackson, *Sixty Feet, Six Inches* (*op. cit.*), 101.

Chapter Sixteen
1 Cobb quoted by F.C. Lane in chapter of *Batting* (*op. cit.*) titled, "The Perfect Hitter."
2 Dusty Baker, *You Can Teach Hitting* (*op. cit.*), 191. See also Jason Kendall, *Throwback* (New York: St. Martin's, 2014), p. 152: "Most contact hitters let the ball travel deep in the zone, so they tend to hit the ball up the middle or the other way; that makes them harder to fool."
3 Baker (*ibid.*, 36 ff. and elsewhere) recommends what hitting coaches have for years called "squishing the bug": i.e., pivoting sharply on the ball of the back foot. This produces much rotation in the swing and makes Joe Brockhoff's list of the "Seven Deadly Misconceptions in Hitting." I have to go with Coach Joe on this one.
4 Williams, *The Science of Hitting* (*op. cit.*), 57.
5 Kiner insists in *Baseball Forever* (*op. cit.*, 207) that the quip originated with teammate Fritz Ostermueller.
6 Frank Robinson, by the way, was the exemplar *par excellence* of the Holmes style—a fact readily overlooked, since he didn't rely on off-field hits exclusively for his extra-base successes (like Holmes). In fact, Frank is almost always described as a dead-pull hitter who stood right on top of the plate. Yet his stride was away from the plate; and from what I have been able to review of his play, I would say that he was very willing to send high pitches, both inside and outside, to the opposite field. This strategy may even be in the vicinity of Cobb's: our Deadball/Negro League connections keep piling up.
7 E.g., Cobb, *My Life in Baseball*, (*op. cit.*), 151.
8 Christy Mathewson, *Pinching in a Pinch: Baseball From the Inside* (Lincoln, NE :U of Nebraska P, 1994), 5.
9 Williams, *The Science of Hitting* (*op. cit.*), 57.

10 Dusty Baker, *You Can Teach Hitting* (*op. cit.*), 192.
11 From the chapter in Lane's *Batting* (*op. cit.*) titled, "How They Stand in the Box."
12 Ty Cobb, *My Life in Baseball*, (*op. cit.*), 146. Cobb often speaks of shifting in the box, so that much is indubitably true. A couple of points in this quotation, however, deserve another "Stump alert." Cobb speaks nowhere else of "choking up a bit more" when loading up to swing; and indeed, this passage could be the origin of the legend that he didn't keep his hands spread in beginning an actual stroke. Yet spread hands are in fact uniquely helpful in oppo-hitting, since the displaced top hand holds the barrel back more securely! Notice, as well, that the verb "punch" is used rather than "push." Stump, another Damon Runyon in his daydreams, makes precisely this sort of colorful substitution in his liberal translating.
13 Rogers Hornsby, *My War With Baseball* (*op. cit.*), 85.

Chapter Seventeen
1 Buck O'Neil, *I Was Right On Time* (New York: Fireside, 1997), 92-93.
2 From the chapter titled, "Pulling the Ball, " in Lane's *Batting* (*op. cit.*).
3 Quoted on p. 649 of Angelo Louisa's article in *Deadball Stars of the American League* (*op. cit.*), 649-651.
4 Peter Morris, *A Game of Inches* (*op. cit* .), 290.
5 *Ibid.*, 391-392.
6 Cf. Ruth's remarks to F.C. Lane in chapter titled, "The Secret of Heavy Hitting," of *Batting* (*op. cit.*): "I am not a little guy. Hitting hard is strength and weight as much as anything else. I am tall and heavy and strong in the arms and in the shoulders."
7 Ty Cobb, *My Twenty Years in Baseball* (*op. cit.*), 104.
8 In Lawrence Ritter's classic collection of interviews, *The Glory of Their Times* (first published by Macmillan in 1966), the fourth chapter, devoted to Sam Crawford, projects an intelligent and thoughtful man who, however, is still struggling to "move on" from Ty Cobb. He avoids mentioning Cobb for a great while, then brings him up with a remark about how people always want to hear about him, then slightly disparages his accomplishments (with sound reasons offered), then races to underscore what a superstar Cobb was. The interview, though merely a print transcript, has several uncomfortably defensive and self-conscious moments. I have heard an earlier radio interview (and there are bound to be several) where Crawford is more aggressive, claiming of Cobb that "nobody liked him."
9 See the top photo on p. 47 of Richard Bak, *Lou Gehrig: An American Classic* (Dallas: Taylor, 1995).
10 John Altamura, in an online article titled, "The 20 Biggest Bats in MLB History" (at www.bleacherreport.com), credits Gehrig with swinging a yard-long bat weighing in at 41.5 ounces; and as for Harper's practice lumber, it equals Lou's in length but is substantially heavier at 47 ounces. One or two Mr. Altamura's values conflict with what I have found in refereed sources; but Harper is, by any measure, very Gehrig-like in his load and swing.

Chapter Eighteen
1 Ty Cobb, *My Twenty Years in Baseball* (*op. cit.*), 70.
2 From Frank Frisch, *Frank Frisch: The Fordham Flash* (Garden City, NY: Doubleday, 1962), 15.
3 Ty Cobb, *My Twenty Years in Baseball* (*op. cit.*), 66.
4 From Danny Peary's collection of interviews, *We Played the Game* (New York: Black Dog and Leventhal, 1994), 46.

5 In a letter written just a few months before his death, Mr. Kell kindly confirmed some of my queries about his betting technique. He acknowledged that he would sometimes spread his hands with two strikes (as a photo I had seen of him suggested), and that he routinely choked up a little. The game lost one of its great gentlemen when George passed away.
6 These statistics come courtesy of www.BaseballReference.com. "Sacrifice hits" (i.e., sacrifice bunts) alone are offered, presumably because the bunt hit was not recorded as such in the past. This indeed proves the point from another direction: i.e., a drag bunt for a hit was so common that it was not distinguished from any other kind of single.

Chapter Nineteen
1 Ty Cobb, *My Twenty Years in Baseball* (*op. cit.*), 72.
2 From Lane's chapter titled, "The Theory of Place Hitting," in *Batting* (*op. cit.*).
3 From Peter Morris, *A Game of Inches* (*op. cit*.), 43.
4 *Ibid.*, 43.
5 Those who dismiss Maris as a mediocre player who had one great year should a) recall that he was the American League MVP for the season preceding 1961, and b) do enough research to recognize that Roger's left hand was permanently damaged during the 1964 season because Yankee medical and managerial staff lied to him in order to keep him on the field. In support of the latter, an excellent place to start is chapter 32 of Tom Clavin and Danny Peary, *Roger Maris, Baseball's Reluctant Hero* (New York: Touchstone, 2010)—appropriately titled, "The Betrayal."
6 From Lane's chapter titled, "The Theory of Place Hitting," in *Batting* (*op. cit.*).
7 Cf. Peter Morris, *A Game of Inches* (*op. cit*.), 20.
8 From Lane's chapter titled, "The Theory of Place Hitting," in *Batting* (*op. cit.*).
9 Incredibly, Lane's chapter titled in *Batting*, "Hitting With the Feet," devotes not a single word to describe all the various stance-shifting and foot-shuffling that we know went on during this era. Instead, the discussion is exclusively about speed out of the batter's box and on the base paths.
10 From Lane's chapter titled, "The Theory of Place Hitting," in *Batting* (*op. cit.*).
11 Cf. Cobb's remarks in ch. 10, "Tragedies of the Diamond," of *Busting 'Em* (*op. cit.*): "… a youngster is liable to hurt himself for the season by overworking before the winter stiffness and staleness is out of his muscles. This is particularly true of young pitchers, who are invariably so eager to show that some of them endeavor to curve a ball on the first day."
12 From Lane's chapter titled, "The Theory of Place Hitting," in *Batting* (*op. cit.*).
13 See Cobb, *My Twenty Years in Baseball* (*op. cit.*), 101.

Chapter Twenty
1 N.A. Dorfman, *The Mental Keys to Hitting* (Lanham, MD: Diamond, 2001), 56.
2 From F.C. Lane's chapter titled, "Taking Advice," in *Batting* (*op. cit.*).
3 Willie Mays, *My Life In and Out of Baseball* (New York: E.P. Dutton, 1966), 55-57, tells the poignant story of a boy he names Lewis who was tragically "overcoached." I cannot resist citing a little of this passage, if only to remind adults of the serious responsibility they undertake in coaching: "On account of two men who were both good baseball men, and who meant nothing but the best for Lewis himself, he was coached out of what should have been a good and easy confidence-building Pony League season as a 14-year-old. He knew now that his high school coach had real doubts as to how he might perform as a sophomore. And what might have been a baseball career for a boy just went down the drain" (57).

Chapter Twenty-One
1 Charley Lau, *The Art of Hitting .300* (*op. cit.*), 67.
2 Quoted in Robert Peterson, *Only the Ball Was White: A History of Legendary Black Players and All-Black Professional Teams* (New York and Oxford: Oxford UP, 1970), 111.
3 I must say that I was particularly shocked at the handling of Cobb in the prestigious Ken Burns documentary, *Baseball* (1994). The complex incident that involved thrashing a rude spectator "with no hands," for instance, receives an utterly one-sided, uncritical presentation; and historian Dan Okrent is aired in an august academic setting sniffing that Cobb was "an embarrassment to the game," which would have been better off without him. Such treatment seeps into biographies of other ballplayers, as well, and becomes "common knowledge." John Skipper's *Charlie Gehringer* (Jefferson, NC: McFarland, 1993), diminishes Cobb's role in creating a Hall of Fame hitter to a matter of loaning Gehringer a bat (chapter 3), and the work later refers to Charlie's mentor as "his nasty manager Ty Cobb" (chapter 12)
4 Charles Leerhsen, *Ty Cobb: A Terrible Beauty* (*op. cit.*), devotes much of his "Epilogue" (especially 400-402) to analyzing the various ways, over a span of three decades, that Stump professionally exploited his association with Ty Cobb.
5 See Leon Wagner's chapter in Part Two of the interviews and personal commentary assembled by Jackie Robinson in *Baseball Has Done It* (Philadelphia: Lippincott, 1964), 191.
6 See especially Leerhsen (*ibid.*), 21 and 304-306.
7 This reaction registered by Cobb upon seeing a young Willie Mays play has been logged by many sources, though it does not appear in Leerhsen. Even the Burns documentary *Baseball* mentions it.
8 Cf. Wagner's comment in *Baseball Has Done It* (*op. cit.*), 189: "There's Billy Moran, he's from Georgia—I love him like a brother. He speaks with a Southern accent, but he knows there's a lot of tension down South, and he talks to me with understanding."
9 Charles Alexander, *Spoke* (*op. cit.*), 212-214, offers a very full discussion of Speaker's supposed membership in the Klan, an allegation which reduces entirely to the recollections of eighty-nine-year-old Fred Lieb. Speaker has also been accused of sharing in the Masonic Order's anti-Catholic sentiments; and yet (as Alexander observes), he was best man at Catholic Ray Chapman's wedding, and he himself would later marry a Catholic woman.
10 Charley Lau, *The Art of Hitting .300* (*op. cit.*), 198-199.
11 I might have mentioned Evan Gattis in this context, whose results are somewhat Leon-Wagneresque with regard to power (and whose spread is easier to spot because he doesn't wear gloves).
12 Reddick's company produced the "Mike Trout Hitting Secrets" video in 2014. The contrastive sequences of practice and game performance do something of which I disapprove, which is juxtapose two swings without providing the necessary context of type of pitch, velocity, location, etc.; but the overall thesis that hitters don't always play as they practice seems very plausible to me.
13 I lately viewed two video analyses of Babe Ruth's swing on YouTube, both highly complimentary. One was apparently created by a coach named Bill Mooney; the other was not associated with a name but appeared on HittingPerformLab.com. I was delighted to hear the former reject the "squishing the bug" paideia, by the way, and the latter deplore the "stay back" dictum. Maybe the old school really is primed for a comeback!
14 Charley Lau, *The Art of Hitting .300* (*op. cit.*), 102-103.

15 First aired on April of 2015, the documentary was titled *Big Dreams*.

Chapter Twenty-Two
1 From Lawrence Ritter's interview with Jones in *The Glory of Their Times* (*op cit.*), 26.
2 Wheat tells F.C. Lane: "Naturally I was a right-handed hitter. But I forced myself to learn left-handed batting. Even now I can hit a ball harder right-handed, but the percentage in favor of the left-handed batter is too great to be ignored…" (from "The Pros and Cons of Left Hand Batting" in *Batting* [*op. cit.*]). Lane and his informants never use the term "switch-hitter," interestingly; but someone who bats both ways would typically have less motive to spread his hands with the strong hand on top because, just as Max reveals here, the stronger hand tends to monopolize the job of supplying power when it's closer to the barrel.
3 From F.C. Lane's chapter titled, "Pulling the Ball," in *Batting* (*op. cit.*).
4 David Fleitz, *Napoleon Lajoie, King of Ballplayers* (*op. cit.*), 107, reproduces an ad for Wright and Ditson's patented "Lajoie bat" which graphically shows how the bottom hand can grip either above or below the second knob; but the second position has no advantage over the conventional single-knob bat, so the stick's real virtue must have been that choked-up hands would not slide down. Apparently, this asset was not generally appreciated.
5 In a newsreel featured on the Rare Sportsfilms, Inc., DVD *1913-1938: "The Sports Album"* (*op. cit.*), none other than Jimmie Foxx explains how swinging less hard and letting a heavy bat carry its impetus into contact is an effective strategy. Hank Greenberg was known to make similar remarks. As I argued earlier in the book, this theory seems to have substance, according to my experiments, if the swing is indeed sloping.

Chapter Twenty-Three
1 Karl Popper, *The Open Universe: An Argument for Indeterminism* (New York: Routledge, 1992), 44.
2 The contents of this personal e-mail have been partially reproduced with Professor Kerr's kind permission.
3 Peter Morris, *A Game of Inches* (*op. cit* .), 63.
4 Christy Mathewson, *Pinching in a Pinch* (*op. cit.*), 7.
5 Cited in Morris, *A Game of Inches* (*op. cit* .), 46-47.
6 See F.C. Lane's chapter titled, "Position at the Plate," in *Batting* (*op. cit.*).
7 *Ibid.*, from the chapter titled, "How They Grip the Bat."
8 Cited in Morris, *A Game of Inches* (*op. cit* .), 47.
9 Cited in Morris, *ibid.*, 49.
10 *Ibid.*, 49.
11 Cited in Morris, *A Game of Inches* (*op. cit* .), 49, from a column of unknown authorship in *The Detroit Free Press*; April 28, 1887.
12 Cited in Morris, *A Game of Inches* (*ibid.*), 45, from a column of unknown authorship in *The Perry* [Iowa] *Chief*; September 6, 1889.

CONTACT THE AUTHOR

Thanks for making it through to the end: I know that the sledding was tough sometimes! Contact me at semperluxmundi@yahoo.com with comments, or follow me on Twitter at @GringoViejo41.

Made in the USA
Coppell, TX
26 December 2019